SPLENDID

LOW-CARBING

A Complete Guide for Low-Carb Living

by

Jennifer Eloff

Author of Best-selling Cookbooks

"Splendid Desserts"

And

"More Splendid Desserts"

W9-DGU-111

Eureka Publishing
Calgary

I

Copyright © Jennifer Eloff, 2001

Canadian Cataloguing in Publication Data

Eloff, Jennifer, 1957

Splendid Low-Carbing – A Complete Guide for Low-Carb Living
First Printing ~ August 2001
2nd Edition ~ June 2002

Includes Index.

ISBN 0-7795-0004-0
1. Low-carb diet recipes. 2. Sugarless recipes.
3. Desserts, cooking and baking low-carb recipes.
4. Title 5. Complete Guide for Low-Carb Living.

Photography: Ian and Daniel Eloff
Front and Back Cover Design: Ian and Jonathan Eloff

Pictured on front cover:
Hawaiian Pizza and Chocolate After Dinner Mint Log
Pictured on back cover:
Chocolate Strawberry Torte, Chocolate-Dipped Strawberries,
Loaf Pan Bran Bread, Fruit Pizza, Hamburger Buns,
Chocolate Eclairs and Burgers

Portrait of Jennifer from "Born Again" by Jonathon Earl Bowser

Eureka Publishing
www.sweety.com
P.O. Box 2305
Station "M"
Calgary, Alberta
T2P 2M6

Printed in Canada by **Blitzprint** using the latest "Print On Demand" technology.

CONTENTS

ACKNOWLEDGMENTS

Most importantly, this book is dedicated with love and humble thankfulness to God our Father in heaven, Jesus, God's Son and my Savior, and the Holy Spirit, without whom this project would not have been possible. Some 12 years ago, I did not even have the confidence to change anyone else's recipes, let alone come up with inspired recipes for special diets. However, today, I have two national best-selling cookbooks to my name, another cookbook still to be published and my latest, *Splendid Low-Carbing*, a complete guide for low-carb living. My endurance, inspiration, guidance and talent so obviously comes from God, therefore, may all the glory belong to God! If you too, would like to experience the life changing power of having a personal relationship with Jesus, then please visit my web site, **www.sweety.com** for more.

Many thanks go to my husband, Ian, and sons, Daniel and Jonathan, for their patience during the development of this book. Their valuable taste-testing skills helped me decide whether or not to include recipes. Thanks also go to Ian for his financial help, for believing in me, and especially for putting up with practically nothing but "low-carb talk" for a year-and-a-half, while I lived and breathed this project. Thanks Ian and Daniel for the wonderful food photography and helping me put the final book together. Thanks to Daniel for helping build the web site and assisting with anything that went wrong with the computer, when his dad was not available. Thanks go to Jonathan, my youngest son, for spending many hours designing the beautiful book covers. Many thanks go to my talented and sweet mother-in-law, Kay Eloff, who put together a beautiful, handwritten recipe book for me, of her favorite recipes, several of which Ian fondly remembers from his childhood, and which now also appear in this cookbook.

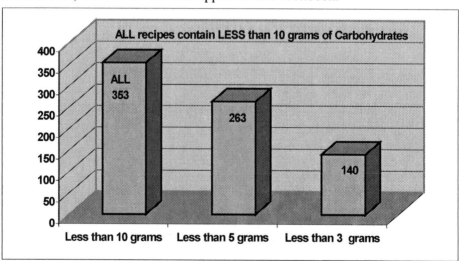

For further reduction of carbs, try substituting liquid or powdered Sucralose for SPLENDA® Granular in recipes; *see notes on page 19.*

FOREWORD

In 1899 sugar consumption was less than 10 lbs per person per annum, and the incidence of diabetes, heart disease and stroke was very low. By 1999 sugar consumption was greater than 170 lbs per person per annum, and the incidence of these diseases is now very high. To be sure, *sugar* is only the most obvious highly refined carbohydrate that we have introduced into our lives in recent human history, but by no means the only one. Bleached white flour, with almost all of the wheat's goodness removed, ground to the consistency of "Talcum powder," is just as potent a carbohydrate. Often in fast foods and processed foods, these two products are combined with plenty of fat added as well, making very unhealthy, fattening foods. So what is it about us humans, that makes us deny the facts, even when they stare us directly in the face? Haven't we looked around us and noticed how overweight we have become? We hear that this is because the "Baby Boomers are aging". Well, yes, we are, but why then are so many children overweight? And how about our Native populations who struggle with obesity and diabetes today in epidemic proportions? With carbohydrate-rich "fast foods" now their new staple diet, little wonder! How about those northern tribes who lived in the frozen tundra, eating only protein and blubber all winter long? They did not develop diabetes and grow wildly obese.

The answer is simple, we are hooked on carbohydrates … and that's not a difficult thing to have happen! Ever hear of heavy drinkers who constantly admit to alcohol being a problem in their lives? They will far rather cover up its harmful effects and highlight its positive effects … and the same holds true for drug users and for others hooked on addictive, but damaging behaviors.

So, just how easy or cost-effective is it to feed all Americans and Canadians on mostly protein versus mostly carbohydrates? The answer is: "It is not practical or cost-effective at all," and most importantly, it's not nearly as profitable! The foods lower down on the food chain are easier to produce, cost less to produce, transport easier, process easier, package easier, market easier and are much more profitable for industry. For them, pasta and cereal make way more profits than eggs and steak. A lot of government decisions are made based on these general principles and not based on our health. If all of America switched away from carbohydrates to animal protein, we would be paying very high prices for steak, chicken, pork, lobster, shrimp, etc., and then what would all those politicians eat? It's almost in our best interest to keep the low-carb diet a secret! It seems the ruling elite has done so for some time now. So, you think I'm overstating things?

People act, for the most part, like a herd. In South Africa where we grew up in our youth, steak, lobster, shrimp, etc. were kept for the colonial European rulers, while bread and grains were subsidized and fed to the local ethnic folks who worked in their industries. They could not afford to feed the entire populace on fancy foods. The result was that, contrary to popular, but incorrect images of ethnic Africans, they grew to be wildly obese and developed all sorts of illnesses, not common to their populace, before we arrived on the scene and changed their diets. I know this, because my dad spent his life living among them as a traveling African doctor. Sadly, the colonial rulers themselves mixed liberal amounts of refined sugar and flour in with their rich diets, swilling it all down with huge amounts of alcohol, and also inhaling copious quantities of tobacco smoke. So, ironically, many died just as early as their enslaved ethnic populace!

Okay, so what do we feed cattle when fattening them up (quickly) for sale and slaughter? Protein and fat? No, carbohydrate-laden grains! So what do we feed people suffering from impaired carbohydrate metabolism? - too many carbohydrates, including sugar and white flour, in their "balanced diet," and drugs to counter the effects of these! So now two very profitable industries profit *even more!* If we go along with the herd, we will eventually suffer the same fate as the herd. It's good that we regard ourselves as enlightened and support each other with facts and truth. Live apart from the herd - free and happy and healthy!

Now, to practical matters, Jennifer is a best-selling cookbook author. Through the years, she has developed several great cookbooks for people on special diets, such as people with diabetes and for those on sugarless diets. The problem is, I get to test all of her recipes … and I do mean ALL! Sometimes I would come home and be faced with 3 cheesecakes, a pile of muffins and a pie, and that was supper! Now, I do take my job very seriously, and often have to "scoff a lot," just to make very sure whether it will "pass" or "fail." Needless to say, the roughly 1 year it usually took to develop an entire book, resulted in me putting on weight. At the end of her 3rd book, I weighed 217 lbs. Considering I started at 195 lbs., that means I gained 22 lbs. by being her devoted "Chief Tester" during that time.

At the end of each development cycle, we usually go into diet mode, so that we do not suffer under the cumulative effect the next time around. Having tried the low-fat diet, the milk-shake diets, Weight Watchers, Jenny Craig, and even the "Don't deny yourself anything – and still lose weight" diet, we looked around for something different. Then we discovered the Low-Carb diets. Jennifer bought the books, studied up on these diets and we decided we would try it. It works … but just one problem. By about the 50th egg, even with a side order of steak and shrimp, I was about ready to quit. It's effective, but after the initial thrill is over, it's BORING! I missed so many of our old comfort foods – but we were told (by the Puritans), they mean "the kiss of death" on this diet. I issued a challenge to Jennifer, "You are a cookbook author. See if you can make this diet something we could live by for years at a stretch. Make it a practical lifestyle." *Jennifer took up the challenge*, and again I was her "Chief Tester," however, instead of gaining some 20 lbs. as in the past, instead I am now down to 187 lbs. and driving down to my marriage weight of 179 lbs., which I have not seen for nearly 22 years!

God Bless, and do enjoy these tasty, low-carb recipes … we sure have!

INTRODUCTION

My husband and I needed to lose weight! You see, I'd just written my 3rd Diabetic low-fat Splenda cookbook, which I have not published yet, and after eating all those low-fat desserts, we were both quite overweight! Anyhow, about 2 years ago, I kept getting e-mails asking me whether I had low-carbohydrate recipes made with SPLENDA® Granular. This was the first time I had heard about low-carbohydrate diets, and I thought these people must feel incredibly deprived – poor things!

Ironically, my husband and I were addicted to carbohydrate-rich foods, so when I inquired what it was all about, I recoiled in horror, so to speak, and the following was my reaction: "What do you mean you don't have bread and white flour cakes anymore? What do you mean you don't have sugar anymore? (Although I could understand this one a little more, as there is a good substitute in SPLENDA® Granular). You eat all that fat, red meat and eggs? Don't you know that's bad for your health?" However, once these dear folks pointed out how well they were feeling, how much weight they had lost, how their cholesterol and triglycerides had fallen, and that, in fact, fat is perfectly okay on the low-carbohydrate way of eating, my horror turned to sheer curiosity.

I rushed to the nearest bookstore to buy my first low-carbohydrate diet book – Dr. Atkins New Diet Revolution! I followed the reading of that wonderful, informative book, with Protein Power (Drs. Michael and Mary Eades, M.D.'s), The Carbohydrate Addict's LifeSpan Program (CALP) (Drs. Richard and Rachel Heller, Ph.D.'s), Go-Diet (Drs. Jack Goldberg, Ph.D. and Karen O'Mara, D.O.) and The Zone (Dr. Barry Sears, Ph.D.). I also read Dr. Bernstein's Diabetes Solution by Richard K. Bernstein, M.D. (He, incidentally, controls his Diabetes 1 condition through the low-carb diet he devised.) and know of several others like Somersizing, Sugar Busters (not very low-carb) and the Paleolithic Diet, etc. which all have their merits. The myriad of low-carb diets can be confusing, however, there is a book by Dana Carpender, "How I Gave Up My Low-Fat Diet and Lost 40 Pounds," which details several of the low-carb diets and after reading her book, you can decide which approach to take. Be sure to keep an eye open for her latest book, "500 Low-Carb Recipes," published by Fair Winds Press. My advice to you is, try one of the diets, and if it does not suit, try one of the others. Everyone is different, and most all the low-carb diets will work, as long as you remain compliant with the rules. Some people have even mixed and matched, say Atkins and CALP, or have lost weight on Atkins and maintained on CALP or the Zone.

It is also a good idea to buy a book with Food Counts and especially carbohydrate counts. There are several available, however, I use one that is called, "The Complete Book of Food Counts," by Corinne T. Netzer.

My horror, which had turned to curiosity, now blossomed into admiration for these people, who had the resolve and courage to follow this rather controversial way of eating. After reading the books, I understood for the first time that my husband and I too had been struggling with hyperinsulinism, and hence our middle-aged spread. Hyperinsulinism simply means in layman's terms that the body is producing too much insulin in response to eating carbohydrates. This hormone is also responsible for storing fat. Too much insulin therefore equates into extra fat being stored in the body, and this hormone, produced by the pancreas, favors storing fat in the abdomen.

Next, I tried Atkins induction. I took probably 5 or 6 days to finally kick into ketosis, and from that point I counted my 2-week induction stint. I lost 6 pounds and was sold on the diet! I had never lost that much in such a short time in all my life. It was exhilarating, but even better than that, I had incredible energy, and I felt on top of the world. However, even although I enjoyed the sudden liberation to eat eggs and bacon, nuts, seeds, fancy vegetables and salads with creamy sauces, red meat, cheese and real whipping cream, I sorely missed bread! I would pick up low-carb cookbooks and feverishly leaf through them looking for a bread recipe that looked like real bread. Each time I felt bitterly disappointed. As well, many of the cookbooks, did not have enough sweet treats and desserts.

Instead of going through with the diet, I stopped at a 10-pound loss and decided to postpone my dream of reaching my goal weight. I switched my creative focus to writing a low-carb cookbook, which would address some of the comfort foods my husband and I missed so much. I knew I would have to find replacements for these missed foods which tasted like the real thing, in order for us to remain committed to our new way of eating. I figured others probably missed old comfort foods too, such as bread, hamburgers, pizza, tortillas, pancakes, crepes, cinnamon buns, muffins, loaves, sugarless jams, sauces, cakes, trifle, fruit pizza, chocolate, fudge, toffee and truffles, etc. Besides the above, typically, apples, bananas, carrots, potatoes and perhaps one or two other food items are not part of a low-carb diet, however, since I don't like feeling deprived, I found ways to use these old favorites in some of my recipes, yet still keeping the recipes low-carb. I was also interested in keeping the fat moderate and not too high. Some low-carb recipes in other books or floating on the internet are so high in fat, that frankly, it still has the ability to shock me, probably because of my years of indoctrination on low-fat diets.

Now that I have accomplished the above task of making some of our old comfort foods low-carb and still tasting similar and delicious, people unfamiliar with the diet might ask, "Where's the diet and where's the customary deprivation?" It is true that the long-term lifetime low-carb diet is a very liberal diet in every sense of the word (adequate protein, dairy foods such as cream, yogurt and buttermilk, a huge variety of vegetables, some fruit and grains), and now this is even more true with these breakthrough recipes! I wanted a complete guide to low-carb eating which I could reference daily for our own use as well. Therefore, it is an honest cookbook, in that, if I didn't like a recipe and would not care to make it again, it did not go in the book. It took a year-and-a-half to complete. At first "low-carb" was a dirty word in our household. My son, Jonathan, who used to love my desserts, did not take well to my initial low-carb efforts. Instead of giving up, I took up the challenge to make things that even my sons would approve of. With God's help it finally happened, and now there are many favorites that Jonathan has in the cookbook, such as Fruit Pizza, Frozen Yogurts, Sponge Cake, Chocolate Eclairs and Cinnamon-Swirl Egg Bread. My oldest son has never really been a dessert person, however, even he has his favorites, such as the Creamy Delight Orange Mousse, Apple-Cinnamon Lattice Loaf and Pizzas (his favorite food!).

Although I am happy to present the baking and desserts sections of my cookbook, I do want to put in a word of caution. We all need to know our own limitations. It is entirely possible to start eating high-carb by eating too many legal treats and low-carb breads! If you are so addicted to carbohydrates that this begins to happen, then you may want to make them an occasional treat. Most of us, however, will be able to enjoy these foods in moderation, particularly in the pre-maintenance and maintenance stages of low-carb dieting.

Everyone is different! My husband is able to eat the low-carb breads, for instance, and still lose weight. I cannot, unless I follow the CALP plan. For me, just knowing all those delicious recipes are in my low-carb cookbook, and that I can make them anytime I really want to, is an enormous psychological comfort. The last thing one wants, is to feel deprived or bored, as those emotions can derail one in the long run.

My husband is a walking, talking testimony to the effectiveness of low-carbohydrate eating. Ian, who is 45 years old and 5'10," went from an unhealthy 217 pounds to a healthy, lean and muscular 187 pounds, while I developed my recipes. He is now not far from his goal weight of 179 pounds, his weight when we were married in 1979. His blood work is excellent and his blood pressure is perfectly normal, plus his blood sugar levels are stable, and any mood swings are a thing of the past.

Pearls of Wisdom re Low-Carbing: These are not by any means all the pearls of wisdom, just ones I picked out, as they happen to be interesting to me.

1. Don't rely only on the bathroom scale to track your progress. People lose inches sometimes, without it showing up on the scale as weight lost. Therefore, take your measurements up front, and occasionally measure again.

2. The Hellers had an interesting point about weighing. Weigh each day, but don't panic over slight fluctuations. Calculate your average weight per week,

and in this way compare one week's average weight with the next to get actual weight lost.

3.   If you begin to eat too many carbohydrates, your glycogen stores in the muscles and liver will quickly begin to be replenished, and remember glycogen stores water.   Therefore, it is not uncommon to see a 2-pound or more water weight gain with an indiscretion.   The easiest way to lose that weight is to go onto induction-style eating (Atkins) for a couple of days, and drink lots of water, until the glycogen stores are depleted and the water is once again released.

4. Keep a food diary. If you are counting carbs, it is a good idea to jot down whatever you're eating. Also at some time, if you discover you're not losing, it may be a good time to check how many calories you are consuming. An easy way to calculate calories required, is to take goal weight x 10 for couch potatoes, goal weight x 12 for moderately active people or goal weight x 15 for extremely active people. Check out www.fitday.com to keep track of food intake and carbs.

5. Plan meals ahead if possible.   Begin a week ahead and do the grocery shopping.   Then each day plan accordingly, first thing in the morning or the evening before. It's like the old adage, "If you fail to plan, you plan to fail."

6.   Join a Bulletin Board on the internet for a daily support network of low-carbing friends. You will pick up much wisdom there.

7. Exercise lowers insulin, increases the metabolism and maximizes weight loss.

8. Do not nibble between meals. I learned this point the hard way! The whole point of the low-carb woe is to do an end run on insulin output and by nibbling all day long, your insulin levels will be higher.   It can mean the difference between maintaining and losing weight for some people.

9. Balanced meals will have less insulin impact as will keeping the meal to one hour, as per the Hellers' advice.

10. Drink tons of water, at least 2 quarts (2 L or 8 cups) per day, or preferably more, if you want to lose tons of weight and have healthy liver and kidney function.

11.   Take your supplements. Most of the low-carb doctors go into detail with regard to supplements, and I have "Dr. Atkins' Vita-Nutrient Solutions Book" which is very complete. Check with your doctor regarding supplements.

12.   Low-carb eating turns many people into gourmet cooks! It is necessary to cook to keep meals interesting and varied. Be prepared to eat more vegetables than you have ever eaten in your entire life!

13. The average American and Canadian eats 300 grams of carbohydrate per day. Most people on low-carb diets who have made it to maintenance will be able to maintain anywhere from 30 to 90 grams of carbohydrate per day, whereas younger, active folk with less damaged metabolisms, will be able to have up to 150 grams. However, at 150 grams, fat intake should be lowered accordingly.

14. If, on maintenance, one resumes eating as in the past on high-carb diets, the weight will come back very quickly. This is true of any diet, though. Whatever you do to lose the weight, that is the way you will maintain it, with only a slight liberation of the weight loss diet. There is a much higher chance of keeping the weight off through low-carbing (which keeps insulin lower) than on the high carb/low-fat diet (which keeps insulin levels higher), because there is an enzyme in the body that needs insulin in promoting fat storage. This enzyme is hyperactive after dieting, and that's why you see people put on weight so quickly after losing weight. It is the body's survival mechanism and it is very efficient.

15. Keep legal treats to a bare minimum, while in the losing weight phase and try to eat them right after your main meal, rather than between meals as snacks.

16. Cut Ketostixs in half to get real value for your money!

17. Before going on the diet, consult a doctor about it, and have your blood work done. Later, you can compare notes after having been on the woe for a while.

18. Ladies, buy a new negligee, as this diet is reported to make one frisky!

No one diet suits everyone and, thankfully, if hyperinsulinism is your problem, there are several hybrids of the popular low-carb diet to choose from. It is for this reason, I have not singled out any one low-carb diet. If you're bored with your program, switch to another. Also, I discovered, you cannot please all of the people all of the time. I first started out using soy flour, but then to my chagrin, I discovered many people don't care for it, so I bent over backwards to substitute whey protein powder in my recipes, wherever possible. However, I'm sure if one were to make a recipe that contained just water, some well-meaning people would be asking, "Does it contain chlorine?" or "Is it distilled water, reverse osmosis water or lake water or spring water?" or some will simply exclaim, "I don't like water!" Hopefully, you can see some humor in this comment! The best I can hope for is that my book will be helpful, and it is up to each person to decide which recipes they would like to include in their chosen way of eating.

On our website, **www.sweety.com** you will find up-to-date tips, photos of recipes in this cookbook and follow-up cookbooks and links to other low-carbohydrate sites. In time, these will become even more comprehensive.

HELPFUL HINTS

1. Usable Carbs or Net Carbs = carbohydrates per serving minus the fiber. The reason for this is that the value for the carbohydrates calculated is actually the carbohydrates plus the fiber. Most Fiber is indigestible or poorly absorbed. The carbohydrate values shown in all the recipes and their variations are actually the usable carbs, so the math has already been done for you. All recipes are below 10 grams carbohydrate; most are below 5 grams and many are below 3 grams.

2. *Nutritional Analysis* - I used the Food Smart Program designed for Windows and which was published in cooperation with the Canadian Diabetes Association.

3. *Serving Sizes or Yield* - Optional ingredients were not included in the nutritional analysis. If a recipe calls for one ingredient OR another one, the analysis is based on the first ingredient. If the carbs differ significantly when using the second ingredient, you will usually find the analysis in the variations or helpful hints below the recipe. Sometimes dessert serving sizes are slightly smaller than standard sizes, for example, 10 servings for a pie (since many cheesecakes are also made in a pie dish and they make 12 standard servings) and 18 servings for a loaf versus 16.

4. *Shelf Life* - of goodies made with SPLENDA® Granular is short, especially in hot weather. It's best to refrigerate baked goods, including breads, after a day. Remove desserts one hour before serving. Most baked goods will freeze well for one month. Refrigerate sealed jams or chutneys one year or freeze for longer.

5. *People with Celiac Disease* - Many of the recipes will be suitable for people with Celiac Disease. Simply replace soy or spelt flour with finely ground rice flour, wherever these flours are used in small quantities.

6. *Oven Temperature* - Unfortunately, one cannot rely on an oven thermometer or the indicator light for accuracy. I recommend an auxiliary thermometer placed inside the oven as a backup. Everyone's oven is different, however, I have endeavored wherever possible to provide indicators, in addition to the baking times. As a rule, it is always wise to monitor your baking. Remember, don't open the oven door during the first 10 minutes of baking, as drafts can interfere with the rising process. Use your oven light during this period, if necessary.

7. *Equipment* - Useful equipment to have in the kitchen would be: a plastic mixing bowl set, electronic scale, mechanical scale, instant-read thermometer, small rolling pin, big rolling pin, egg separator, double boiler, several spatulas, small and large whisks, sharp bread knife, food processor and/or electric mixer, blender, ice cream maker, coffee/nut grinder, manual pasta maker, sieve, canning jars, lids and rings, tongs, bread machine, loaf, muffin and cake pans, cookie sheets, Bundt pan, pie dishes, springform pan, square, and rectangular glass baking dishes, electric frying pan, wok, crock-pot, pressure cooker, deep-fat fryer, vegetable steamer, regular nonstick frying pans and saucepans. Some of these are essential and others are optional extras, however, it is up to you to decide which ones you will need (Think birthday presents, mother's day, etc.)

8. Crusts - were the bad guys in the old low-fat days and are still the bad guys today on the low-carb diet. In the old days, crusts added extra fat; nowadays it is the extra carbohydrates they add, which concerns us. For many of the desserts, it is possible to omit the crust, if desired, or simply sprinkle a pie dish with a light dusting of ground or finely chopped, toasted nuts. Typically, my crusts add no more than 2 or 3 grams of carbohydrate per serving.

9. Thickening Agent - This agent is primarily used to thicken sauces, instant blender puddings, frostings and toppings. Sprinkle over sauces gradually and stir in. I tried using vegetable gums on their own, however, the end result was always too gummy. Use this agent in very small quantities to prevent that gummy feel. Keep in mind, Thickening Agent, soy flour, cocoa, vegetable gums and gelatin will serve to cut sweetness somewhat. Use in small quantities and add extra sweetener, where necessary.   Vegetable gums, while listed as containing carbohydrate, are composed mostly of indigestible fiber.

10. Bake Mixes - You will notice that Bake Mixes, which you can make yourself, are the secret to many of my recipes. They are not a cup-for-cup substitution for white flour, however, see Ultimate Bake Mix, page 108 for that purpose. You will soon figure out the simple techniques I employed in the recipes. Soon you will be able to modify some of your own favorite recipes. In breads, the Bake Mixes impart a wonderful rich, nutty flavor. Whole spelt flour or whole wheat flour may be substituted for spelt flour. The reason I used spelt flour (also see #15) was not only for the gluten content and the fact that it is biologically unrelated to wheat, but also for its higher protein content and its taste. I cannot stand an obvious "soy" taste, and if I had only used soy flour, taste would have gone out the window, in my opinion.   That said, there is an alternative - Whey Bake Mix (soy-free) - which is wonderful in baking. It has about the same number of carbs as the Bake Mix which uses soy flour, the only difference occurring in breads where the extra soy flour in the recipes is replaced with spelt flour.   This accounts for about 0.7 grams carbohydrate extra per serving. Also some breads made with Whey Bake Mix don't rise quite as high (but almost), however, they have a different flavor, and are quite crusty, which you may prefer. If you do a lot of baking, whip up a double batch of the Bake Mix of your choice for convenience.   Store in an airtight container at room temperature. Ultimate Bake Mix may be substituted for any of these bake mixes.

11. Ultimate Bake Mix - This is a cup-for-cup all-purpose and cake flour substitution for convenience and to make life on this WOL even more livable.

See page 108 for more details. It may be used to bring down the carbohydrates in my books, *Splendid Desserts* and *More Splendid Desserts* by 50 to 65% (for example, in Glazed Lemon Loaf, *More Splendid Desserts*, the carbs are reduced by 12 grams per slice, a 64% reduction!) This bake mix tastes like the real thing and usually works in muffin, loaf and cake recipes without a problem (adjust liquid by adding gradually until the right consistency is achieved). I cannot guarantee the results in cookies. I do know this bake mix will not work in the "koeksister" recipe in *More Splendid Desserts*. However, do remember, if you indulge in too many slices of a cake made with this bake mix, you will see a water weight gain, as your glycogen stores are replaced. Go back to strict low-carbing for a day or two and it should come off. It is best to eat a slice of this cake after a balanced meal, in which case you should see no after-effects on the scale. Do not snack on it at various times of the day, as the carbs add up quickly, and the extra insulin will make your appetite soar. Would you in the old low-fat days have indulged in high-fat, calorific cakes every other day? Of course, not! View cakes made with the Ultimate Bake Mix similarly on our diet.

12. Breads - Vital wheat gluten can vary from 75 to 80% gluten. I used Bob's Red Mill Vital Wheat Gluten (see #18, vital wheat gluten), available in Canada and America (also at www.CarbSmart.com). It is 80% protein (a super gluten). My breads work best (rise higher) with this percentage gluten unless otherwise indicated. The dough typically should look fairly moist as it is mixing and kneading. Baking can sometimes be a bit of an art form. Besides the minor differences in products coming from different companies, bread machines differ, temperatures can make a difference and other factors such as altitude could have an influence on your baking. My bread machine is over 7 years old (Hitachi Model HB-B201) and makes a large, wide loaf. When dough is elastic and needs to be rolled out, allow to rest under towel 10 minutes at a time between rolling.

If you keep all the other parameters the same in the Bran Bread Machine Bread, you can play with the variables, $^1/_2$ cup (125 mL) wheat bran and $^1/_3$ cup (75 mL) soy flour, by substituting other ingredients. For instance, you could use oat bran instead of wheat bran and spelt flour, whole wheat flour, triticale flour, rye flour, oat flour, amaranth flour, quinoa flour or any other flour instead of soy flour. The carbs will not be significantly affected. If you use spelt flour instead of soy flour, the carbs go up by 0.7 grams per serving. However, if you also replace the wheat bran with flour of any kind, the carbs will go up 2 to 3 grams per serving.

Whey breads are milder tasting and form a nice crust. They also toast very well. The soy breads are more moist in texture and rise to the top in the bread machine.

13. Quick Sweet Treats - Sometimes the craving to have something sweet after a meal can be overwhelming. Most of these suggestions are for ongoing weight loss stages and close to or on maintenance and not for strict induction as described by Dr. Atkins. What can one make in a hurry? Small amounts of fruit (like fruit cocktail) are good on SPLENDA®-sweetened plain yogurt. Frozen, thin banana slices are good to keep in the freezer. One slice will be one gram carbohydrate. Or slice an apple into 20 thin slices. Place in cereal bowl with 1 tbsp (15 mL) lemon juice, 1 tbsp (15 mL) water and 2 tbsp (25 mL) SPLENDA® Granular. Microwave 2 minutes, or until soft. One slice will be one gram carbohydrate. Refrigerate leftovers. I enjoy some frozen blueberries, with 1 tbsp (15 mL) whipping cream and SPLENDA® Granular to taste. Frozen strawberries may be defrosted briefly in microwave oven, sliced, sweetened with SPLENDA® Granular and topped with a dollop of Crème Fraiche, page 172, whipped cream or plain yogurt. A strawberry milk shake, page 16 is quick to whip up. Sweeten yogurt and sprinkle with "Granola," page 109 or chopped nuts or sweeten cottage cheese or ricotta cheese and add vanilla or cinnamon extract. Keep low-carb chocolate in the refrigerator or freezer for just such occasions. Another idea is to whip up an instant pudding, or instant ice cream as detailed in this book.

14. The Versatility of Cheese - Spread grated Cheddar or Monterey Jack cheese to cover surface in nonstick 6-inch (15 cm) pan. Melt until turning brown or until it flips easily (takes a while); flip, cook briefly and fold over. Use as a taco. (From CarbSmart Newsletter). If it becomes too brittle to handle, nuke it 25 seconds in microwave oven. Melt 0.5 oz (15 g) grated cheese in microwave oven 40 seconds (ovens do vary) on high power. Allow to cool; remove. Use as a cracker, spreading 1 tsp (5 mL) Splenda jam or cream cheese on it.

15. Spelt Flour - For some folks, this may be the first time you've heard of this complex carbohydrate flour, which is lately being re-discovered. All-purpose, whole wheat flour or whole grain spelt flour may be substituted for unbleached spelt flour, if desired. Many people have wheat allergies or find that wheat is a trigger for carbohydrate cravings. Spelt was grown in Europe more than 9000 years ago according to modern research. Spelt flour was used in Old Testament Bible times (Exodus 9:31-32 and Ezekiel 4:9) and is biologically unrelated to wheat flour. It does contain some gluten, however, it is a different quality to wheat gluten. It is loaded with vitamins and minerals, contains a complex carbohydrate and has a higher protein content than wheat flour. It tastes better than most other grains and is suitable for both cooking and baking. It is, however, no lower in carbohydrates than all-purpose flour. *Note:* Where small amounts of spelt flour are used in a recipe as an alternative to soy flour, use vital wheat gluten (75 to 80% protein) instead, if desired.

16. Soy Flour and other soy products - This relatively low-carbohydrate and inexpensive flour is very useful to the low-carb dieter! Just as with any other product which is very popular (even SPLENDA® Granular), there are those who do not like it. Personally, I believe "most things in moderation" is a good motto. One does not see too many overweight Asian people, besides Asian women have a tremendously easier time of menopause than we Western women do. Soy flour has been touted as a wonder food to help ease menopause, build bones and even prevent breast cancer, but then I've heard completely opposing views. For now, the overall consensus is the apparent benefits (many studies done) of soy products far outweigh any negatives. On the most negative site on the web regarding soy flour, the apparent safe level for soy flour per day that they recommend is approximately 3 tbsp (45 mL). That would probably amount to a couple of slices of one of my breads, which contain some soy flour. However, if you have a thyroid problem, the consensus is that it is best to avoid soy products. Wherever possible, I have provided alternatives.

There may be some confusion about the different soy products used in this book. I've used low-fat soy flour in my recipes (as opposed to full-fat soy flour), because I preferred the taste, and because it is even more concentrated in protein. Soy powder has a finer texture and may be substituted in crusts and cheesecakes where small amounts of soy flour are used. It tends to have a milder flavor than soy flour and produces a slightly less dense texture in the final product. However, soy flour is better suited to mixing with nut flours and other flours. Look for organic low-fat soy flour, which has a rich, mild flavor. Not all soy flours are made equal. Shop around to find a mild-flavored soy flour. It may take some time to get used to soy flour, however, I cannot detect an obvious soy taste in any of my recipes, as I use it judiciously and in small quantities. There are one or two recipes which use soy protein isolate. This product has virtually zero carbs. It may not be substituted for soy flour or soy powder. Look for these products at upscale health food stores and in larger grocery chains, as well as on the internet.

Be careful with cookie recipes, especially ones where most of the moisture comes from butter. Soy flour can make cookies dry and powdery tasting. To correct this problem, try replacing some of the butter with whipping cream. Wherever dough needs to be kneaded on a lightly floured surface, use soy protein isolate, if desired, so that 0 grams of carbohydrates are added.

According to the U.S. Soy foods Directory on the internet, soy flour should be stirred before measuring, as it can become packed in its container. They also recommend refrigerating soy flours and whole grain flours, however, I've not found this to be necessary in our dry climate.

17. *Whey Protein Powder* - This is the popular alternative to soy flour, which I employed in my recipes, however, it is quite expensive. My husband was not wild about the idea at first, but you can get a club card and discounts at most health food stores Some health food stores have natural whey protein powder available in bulk bins. I used natural whey protein powder without any sweeteners added. The two brands I used were Supreme Supplements Whey Protein (Canadian, Phone: (888) 834-7760) and Ultimate Nutrition Inc., ProStar Whey (American, Fax: (860) 793-5006, www.ultimatenutrition.com).

18. *Vital Wheat Gluten* - This product is wheat flour with the starch removed and is usually 75 to 80% gluten (natural protein in the wheat endosperm). I used Bob's Red Mill Gluten (Natural Foods Inc., Milwaukie, Oregon, also available at **www.CarbSmart.com**) which is 80% gluten. 75% Gluten will not work as well in my bread recipes as they will not rise as high, and therefore the yield will be less and the carbohydrates higher. Some recipes call for 75% gluten. Gluten flour, on the other hand, is half vital wheat gluten and cannot be substituted for vital wheat gluten. My program says $^1/_4$ cup (50 mL) or 38 grams (1.3 oz) vital wheat gluten has 6.0 g carbs, whereas gluten flour has 16.2 grams carbs.

19. *SPLENDA*® *Granular* - Most of you will be familiar with this low-calorie sweetener. We've been using it in Canada for almost a decade before FDA approval in the States and, after developing 4 Splenda Cookbooks (one yet to be published), I'm very familiar with its nuances in cooking and baking. Most everything is possible with this product, once you have mastered it, except for a few things. Keep in mind SPLENDA® Granular weighs about $^1/_8$ as much as sugar, and this does affect volume and texture in some baking recipes. Caramelizing, or producing the same effects as brown sugar are not possible to my knowledge. It was initially thought that double-layered cakes were a problem (and they can be tricky), as well as making chocolate or meringues, however, you will see these are quite possible. Some adjustment of ingredients in recipes where sugar provides texture and volume will be necessary.

Sucralose, created from sugar, has no carbohydrates or calories. The sugar molecule was altered in such a way that the body no longer recognizes it. Maltodextrin, a carbohydrate derived from corn, is a filler used to help the product measure cup-for-cup like sugar. The carb content in 1 cup (250 mL) sugar is 199.8 grams and only 24 grams in 1 cup (250 mL) SPLENDA® Granular. Sucralose is inert and remains stable at the high baking temperatures.

Some people have raised the concern that maltodextrin features higher on the glycemic index scale than sugar! However, it all depends on the quantity you ingest per serving of a dessert. If one were to eat a pound of maltodextrin, one would be in trouble, however, the way Splenda is formulated from sucralose and maltodextrin, this results in very little weight being imparted by maltodextrin. In fact, 1 cup (250 mL) SPLENDA® Granular weighs 26 grams (almost nothing!) and 1 cup of sugar weighs 226 grams. Therefore, one serving of dessert sweetened with, say, 1 cup (250 mL) SPLENDA® Granular has very little maltodextrin in it, and it will have very little impact on glycemic reactions, however, the opposite is true for a sugar-sweetened dessert, which is quite high in carbohydrates and calories too.

My family has probably been the biggest consumer of SPLENDA® Granular on this planet! A decade later, we're not showing any apparent adverse effects.

20. *Flax Seed* - This is another wonder food which everyone is talking about and which I use in several of my recipes. It is the world's richest source of Omega-3, an essential fatty acid. It is also rich in Omega-6, another essential fatty acid. Flax seeds are nature's "Tomoxifen" (anti-cancer drug) latest studies reveal. Also called linseed, it is a good source of fiber.

21. *Eggs* - Unless otherwise specified, large eggs were used.

22. *Yogurt, Buttermilk and Kefir* - Happily, the Go-Diet authors, Jack Goldberg and Karen O'Mara changed my outlook with regard to these products. The live cultures such as lactobacillus are hugely beneficial to your health in many ways (see pages 21 and 48 of their book), not the least of which is helping combat yeast overgrowth, promoting colon health and boosting the immune system. According to laboratory studies, 1 cup (250 mL) plain yogurt contains only about 4 grams of carbohydrate, since these live bacteria have changed the lactose into lactic acid, and this is not taken into account in the nutritional analysis. Daily consumption of yogurt is therefore highly recommended. I used this information to calculate the carbohydrate values in applicable recipes.

23. *Almonds* - are a most versatile nut! To grind nuts, a coffee/nut grinder will produce a finer product than a blender would. Commercially available ground almonds are very convenient. However, if you're grinding blanched almonds from scratch, then keep this in mind: 1 tbsp (15 mL) blanched almonds produces about 1.3 tbsp (20 mL) ground almonds. Therefore, if you need $^2/_3$ cup (150 mL) ground almonds, divide that by 1.3 to arrive at approximately $^1/_2$ cup (125 mL) blanched almonds, ground. When working in reverse order, multiply by 1.3. This rule does not apply to most other nuts. Refrigerate or freeze ground almonds and other nuts, if not using frequently, to keep fresh longer. At our health food store, I discovered a mechanical Grain Mill, Model 555, from Back to Basics Product Inc., Draper, Utah 84020, USA ($121 Canadian). It seemed to indicate that it would make nut flours as well.

24. *Skim Milk Powder* - blended finely in blender may replace whole milk powder in recipes. Fine skim milk powder is found in some health food stores

25. *Lower Fat Alternatives* - To lower fat content, half-and-half cream may be substituted in many cases, where whipping cream has been used. You can get the same result and the same carbohydrate content by mixing half whipping cream and half 2% or 1% milk in a jug. This may work out cheaper than especially buying half-and-half cream. Lower fat alternatives may often be substituted.

26. *Healthy Butter* - Do use this recipe, if you find you like it. It saves money and it is so useful to have in the refrigerator, as it spreads like soft margarine and tastes like butter. It is higher in monounsaturated fats and lower in saturated fats.

BEVERAGES

HOT CHOCOLATE DRINK MIX
My favorite comfort drink for wintry days.

$2^1/_4$ cups SPLENDA® Granular (550 mL)
$1^1/_3$ cups whole milk powder (325 mL)
$^2/_3$ cup cocoa (150 mL)

> *Yield:* 4 cups (1 L)
> 1 tbsp (15 mL) per serving
> 18.3 calories
> 0.9 g protein
> 0.8 g fat
> *2.0 g carbs*

In large bowl, combine SPLENDA® Granular, whole milk powder and cocoa. Stir thoroughly with wooden spoon. Place in closed plastic container and store at room temperature. The shelf life is very long.

To make cup of Hot Chocolate: Place 1 tbsp (15 mL) Hot Chocolate Drink Mix in cup and using tiny whisk, stir in 1 tbsp (15 mL) whipping cream. Whisk in cold water almost to top. Microwave on high power 1 minute 10 seconds. Whisk vigorously again and enjoy. A much richer cup of hot chocolate can be made with 2 tbsp (25 mL) Hot Chocolate Drink Mix, however, I have grown to like the former. Whisk in extra hot chocolate drink mix, if desired. It dissolves quite well in hot liquid.

Helpful Hint: A tiny whisk is ideal for making this hot chocolate drink. Calculate the carbs, depending on the amount of Hot Chocolate Drink Mix you choose to use, plus the carbs in the cream. I found my rich cocoa powder in a health food store. It's quite a bit richer in flavor, I think, than the kind bought in regular stores in a can.

Finely blended skim milk powder may be used instead of whole milk powder. Some health food stores now carry skim milk powder in the fine powder form, instead of the coarse, granular form.

STRAWBERRY MILK SHAKE

This is a rich, thick milk shake, but oh so good! Add more sweetener to taste, if desired.

1 cup whipping cream (250 mL)
$^3/_4$ cup ice cold water (175 mL)
1 cup frozen strawberries, (250 mL)
  (unsweetened)
$^2/_3$ cup plain yogurt (150 mL)
$^1/_2$ cup SPLENDA® Granular (125 mL)

> *Yield:* 7 servings
> ½ cup (125 mL) per serving
> 141.8 calories
> 1.9 g protein
> 12.8 g fat
> *4.5 g carbs*

In blender, combine whipping cream, water, strawberries, yogurt and SPLENDA® Granular; blend until smooth. Serve immediately.

EGGNOG

A traditional, rich festive drink, normally too high in carbohydrates.

2 cups half-and-half cream (500 mL)
1 carton egg substitute, defrosted (227 mL)
$^1/_2$ cup SPLENDA® Granular (125 mL)
$1^1/_4$ cups water (300 mL)
1 tbsp rum extract (15 mL)
1 tsp vanilla extract (5 mL)
nutmeg sprinkle, for garnish

> *Yield:* $4^1/_2$ cups (1.125 L)
> $^1/_2$ cup (125 mL) per serving
> 122.9 calories
> 4.5 g protein
> 9.3 g fat
> *4.7 g carbs*

Place half-and-half cream, egg substitute and SPLENDA® Granular in heavy saucepan. Over medium heat, cook until very hot and mixture coats metal spoon. Remove from heat. Place saucepan in sink of ice water.

Stir over ice water 3 minutes. Stir in water, rum and vanilla extracts. Pour into glass jug and refrigerate. Chill at least 12 hours. Serve in small party wine glasses. Sprinkle each serving with nutmeg, if desired.

Helpful Hint: The sweetness may be adjusted and real rum may be added to taste (omit rum extract). Just remember to add the extra carbs.

RHUBARB PUNCH

This unusual punch was served successfully at a wedding reception.

4 cups fresh or frozen rhubarb, (1 L)
  chopped
2 cups SPLENDA® Granular (500 mL)
2 cups water, divided (500 mL)
$^1/_2$ can (6 oz) frozen unsweetened pineapple
  juice concentrate (178 mL)
10 cups ice cold water (2.5 L)
4 cups carbonated lemon-flavored water,
  chilled (1.25 L)

Yield: 40 servings
$^1/_2$ cup (125 mL) per serving
15.6 calories
0.1 g protein
0.0 g fat
3.7 g carbs

In large saucepan, combine rhubarb, SPLENDA® Granular and 1 cup (250 mL) water. Bring to boil; reduce heat and simmer 10 minutes or until rhubarb is soft. Cool slightly. In blender, blend rhubarb and 1 cup (250 mL) water until smooth.

In large punch bowl, combine rhubarb, frozen unsweetened pineapple concentrate and 10 cups (2.5 L) ice cold water. Slowly stir in carbonated water. Serve immediately.

Helpful Hints: For a sweeter punch, use diet Sprite for about the same net carbohydrates per serving instead of carbonated lemon-flavored water, or use 12.5 oz (355 mL) frozen, unsweetened pineapple juice concentrate. (***5.0 g Carbs***) If the rhubarb is out of your garden, then sieve the cooked, blended rhubarb to catch any fibers. Leftover punch may be stored in airtight juice containers.

ICED LEMON TEA

A refreshing summer beverage.

1 cup water (250 mL)
2 tea bags
3 cups cold water (750 mL)
$^1/_2$ cup SPLENDA® Granular (125 mL)
$^1/_4$ cup lemon juice, (50 mL)
  from concentrate

Yield: 5 servings
$^3/_4$ cup (175 mL) each
12.7 calories
0.0 g protein
0.0 g fat
3.5 g carbs

In medium saucepan, bring 1 cup (250 mL) water to boiling. Turn off heat. Add 2 tea bags; leave in 5 minutes. Remove tea bags. To large juice container add tea, cold water, SPLENDA® Granular and lemon juice. Pour into glass over lemon ice cubes below, and garnish with lemon slice on edge of glass, if desired.

Variations: **Lemon Tea Sparkler:** Just before serving add $^1/_2$ cup (125 mL) SPLENDA® Granular and 2 tbsp (25 mL) lemon juice to Iced Lemon Tea above; stir. Gently stir in 3 cups (750 mL) carbonated lemon-flavored mineral water. Serve. *Yield:* 9 servings, $^3/_4$ cup (175 mL) each. (*3.5 g Carbs*)

Lemonade: Combine $^1/_2$ cup (125 mL) lemon juice, 1 cup (250 mL) SPLENDA® Granular and 9 cups (2.25 L) cold water in juice container. Stir and refrigerate. *Yield:* 9 servings, 1 cup (250 mL) per serving. (*3.8 g Carbs*)

Lemon Ice Cubes: Combine $3^2/_3$ cups (900 mL) cold water, $^1/_3$ cup (75 mL) lemon juice, $^1/_2$ cup (125 mL) SPLENDA® Granular and 1 drop yellow food coloring. Fill 2 ice trays. Freeze. *Yield:* 32 ice cubes. (*0.6 g Carbs*)

Helpful Hint: If you decide to use fresh lemon juice instead, add 2 tsp (10 mL) lemon juice from concentrate as well.

DIET GINGER BEER

The inspiration for this recipe came from my husband, Ian.

2 lemons
20 cups (5 qts) water (5 L)
$^3/_4$ cup lemon juice (175 mL)
2 oz ginger root, peeled, chopped (60 g)
2 tsp ground ginger (10 mL)
4 cups SPLENDA® Granular, OR (1 L)
  to taste
carbonated water

Yield: 5 quarts (5 L)
$^1/_2$ cup (125 mL) per serving
11.4 calories
0.0 g protein
0.0 g fat
3.0 g carbs

Remove peel carefully from lemons, and also using sharp knife remove and discard as much white pith as possible. Slice lemons thinly and remove seeds. In large kettle, combine lemon slices, peel, water, lemon juice, ginger root and ground ginger.

Bring to full rolling boil over high heat. Stir occasionally. Reduce heat to medium, put lid on and simmer 20 minutes. Let cool. Refrigerate overnight, and strain through colander. Stir in SPLENDA® Granular. Store in juice containers in refrigerator. Use $^1/_2$ cup (125 mL) ginger syrup and add carbonated water to taste.

For further reduction of carbs, try substituting liquid or powdered Sucralose for SPLENDA® Granular in recipes, which, though not available in retail stores, are available (in bulk) through inquiry from www.Splenda.com :

SPLENDA® Granular	Carbs
1 tsp (5 mL)	0.5 g
1 tbsp (15 mL)	1.5 g
$^1/_8$ cup (25 mL)	3.0 g
$^1/_4$ cup (50 mL)	6.0 g
$^1/_3$ cup (75 mL)	8.0 g
$^1/_2$ cup (125 mL)	12.0 g
$^2/_3$ cup (150 mL)	16.0 g
$^3/_4$ cup (175 mL)	18.0 g
1 cup (250 mL)	24.0 g

How to use this table: In the above dessert, replacing 4 cups (1 L) SPLENDA® Granular with sucralose eliminates 24.0 g x 4 = 96 g carbs. Divide this number by the number of servings: 96 / 40 = 2.4 g carbs. Therefore, the number of carb grams per serving, for this particular recipe, will then be 3.0 g – 2.4 g = 0.6 g.

APPETIZERS

CURRIED WALNUTS

These are unusual, and people often want to know how they were made.

1 tsp curry powder (5 mL)
$^1/_2$ tsp salt (2 mL)
2 cups walnut halves (500 mL)
1 tbsp butter (15 mL)

> *Yield:* 8 servings
> $^1/_4$ cup (50 mL) per serving
> 206.2 calories
> 4.3 g protein
> 20.0 g fat
> *4.2 g carbs*

In small bowl, combine curry powder and salt. Set aside. In medium saucepan in water, boil walnuts 3 minutes; drain. Lightly grease baking sheet; spread walnuts out on it. Bake in 350°F (180°C) oven 15 minutes, or until just beginning to turn brown. Remove from oven and immediately stir in 1 tbsp (15 mL) butter until walnuts are coated. Sprinkle with curry mixture and stir. Store in bowl uncovered.

SPICED ALMOND CLUSTERS

These are so popular!

$1^1/_2$ cups slivered almonds, (375 mL)
  (blanched)
1 egg white
$^1/_3$ cup SPLENDA® Granular (75 mL)
2 tsp cinnamon (10 mL)

> *Yield:* 6 servings
> $^1/_4$ cup (50 mL) per serving
> 234.4 calories
> 8.4 g protein
> 20.1 g fat
> *4.6 g carbs*

In medium bowl, toss almonds with egg white. In small bowl, combine SPLENDA® Granular and cinnamon. Stir cinnamon mixture into almonds. Spread out on lightly greased baking sheet and bake in 300°F (160°F) oven 20 to 25 minutes. Break up into clusters.

SPICY CHEDDAR BITES

The name says it all for these savory cracker-like cookies.

$^1/_4$ cup butter, softened (50 mL)
1 cup grated old Cheddar cheese (250 mL)
3 tbsp spelt, OR (45 mL)
  all-purpose flour
2 tbsp soy flour, OR (25 mL)
  spelt flour
$^1/_8$ tsp salt (0.5 mL)
$^1/_8$ tsp hot chili powder (0.5 mL)

> **Yield:** 38 servings
> 1 serving
> 21.1 calories
> 0.7 g protein
> 1.9 g fat
> **0.5 g carbs**

In medium bowl, beat butter. Stir in cheese, spelt or all-purpose flour, soy or spelt flour, salt and hot chili powder. Shape and roll dough into log about 8-inches (20 cm) long and $1^1/_4$-inches (3 cm) in diameter. Wrap in wax paper, and refrigerate 1 to 2 hours, or freeze 15 minutes.

Cut into thin slices. Place on 2 well-greased cookie sheets. Bake 10 to 12 minutes, or until golden in 350°F (180°C) oven. Allow to cool slightly, before removing with a flat, firm spatula.

HAM ROLL-UPS

These are excellent! Siced chicken or turkey breast may be used instead.

4 oz cream cheese, softened (125 g)
1 tbsp chopped chives, OR (15 mL)
  green onion
$^1/_4$ tsp garlic powder (1 mL)
5 thin slices ham (24 g each)
5 thin slices Swiss Cheese (24 g each)

> **Yield:** 5 servings
> 6 pinwheels each
> 112.1 calories
> 10.6 g protein
> 7.2 g fat
> **0.9 g carbs**

In food processor with sharp blade or blender, process cream cheese, chives or green onion and garlic powder until smooth.

On large plate, assemble ham roll-ups. Place ham slice down and pat dry with paper towel. Place slice of Swiss cheese on top and spread 2 tsp (10 mL) cream cheese mixture over surface. From long side, roll up, using extra cream cheese mixture, if necessary, as "glue." Slice into 6 pinwheels. Repeat.

Variation: **Mexican Roll-Ups:** Add 2 oz (60 g) canned chopped green chilies, drained. Use toothpicks and serve with Salsa for dipping. (*1.0 g Carbs*)

MEXICAN DIP

The best! Everyone raves about this dip when I serve it.

4 oz light cream cheese, softened (125 g)
$1^1/_4$ cups grated Cheddar cheese (300 mL)
$^1/_3$ cup sour cream (75 mL)
$^1/_4$ cup medium-hot Salsa (50 mL)
1 garlic clove, crushed
3 tbsp finely chopped chives (45 mL)

Yield: 2 cups (500 mL)
1 tsp (5 mL) per serving
8 calories
0.4 g protein
0.7 g fat
0.2 g carbs

In food processor with sharp blade or in blender, process cream cheese, until smooth. Add cheddar cheese, sour cream, half of Salsa and garlic; process. In small bowl, combine processed cheese mixture, remaining Salsa and chives. Cover with plastic wrap and refrigerate until ready to serve. Serve cold or microwave on high power 30 seconds. Serve with assorted vegetables and/or low-carb crackers (and Tortilla chips for those not following a low-carbohydrate diet).

Helpful Hint: Finely chopped green onions may be used instead of chives.

SIERRA COCKTAIL MIX

Mixed nuts, seeds and raisins are a good snack anytime.

1 cup salted peanuts (250 mL)
1 cup unsalted sunflower seeds (250 mL)
$^3/_4$ cup salted roasted almonds (175 mL)
$^1/_2$ cup unsalted pumpkin seeds (125 mL)
$^1/_2$ cup salted roasted cashews (125 mL)
2 tbsp seedless raisins (25 mL)

Yield: 4 cups (1 L)
$^1/_4$ cup (50 mL) per serving
191.0 calories
6.8 g protein
16.0 g fat
5.3 g carbs

In large bowl, combine peanuts, sunflower seeds, roasted almonds, pumpkin seeds, cashews and raisins.

GARDEN VEGETABLE SHRIMP SPREAD
This is lovely for a party where several appetizers will be served.

Seafood Sauce:
$^1/_2$ cup 14% sour cream (125 mL)
3 tbsp Ranch-style salad dressing (45 mL)
1 tbsp Splenda ketchup, page 89 (15 mL)
Filling:
12 oz. light cream cheese, softened (375 g)
1 cup 14% sour cream (250 mL)
$1^1/_4$ cups frozen salad shrimp, (300 mL)
  thawed
Seafood Sauce above
2 cups mixed shredded Mozzarella (500 mL)
  and Cheddar cheese
$^3/_4$ cup diced green pepper (175 mL)
$^3/_4$ cup seeded, diced tomato (175 mL)
1 green onion, finely chopped

Yield: 12 servings
1 serving
215.3 calories
11.1 g protein
4.7 g fat
4.2 g carbs

Seafood Sauce: In small bowl, stir together sour cream, Ranch-style salad dressing and Splenda Ketchup, page 89.

Filling: In food processor or blender with sharp blade, process cream cheese and sour cream. Spread evenly in 9-inch (23 cm) glass pie dish. Top with shrimp, Seafood Sauce, mixed Mozzarella and Cheddar cheeses, green pepper, tomato and green onion. Cover and chill until ready to serve alongside low-carb crackers or cucumber slices.

Variation: Shrimp Salad: Combine Seafood Sauce with 2 cups (500 mL) frozen cooked salad shrimp, thawed. Serves 2. (*5.8 g Carbs*)

Helpful Hint: In place of Splenda Ketchup, page 89, use regular ketchup or 1 tbsp (15 mL) tomato paste, 1 tsp (5 mL) SPLENDA® Granular and $^1/_2$ tsp (2 mL) vinegar.

INDONESIAN COCKTAIL MEATBALLS
These are always a hit!

1 lb minced lamb or beef (0.454 kg)
$^1/_4$ cup oat bran (50 mL)
1 tsp salt (5 mL)
$^1/_2$ tsp black pepper (2 mL)
1 garlic clove
Indonesian Sauce:
$^1/_3$ cup water (75 mL)
$^1/_4$ cup SPLENDA® Granular (50 mL)
2 tbsp soy sauce (25 mL)
2 tbsp lemon juice (25 mL)
2 tbsp peanut butter (25 mL)
1 tbsp olive oil (15 mL)
1 tbsp grated ginger root (15 mL)
2 cloves garlic, crushed
4 drops Tabasco Sauce

> ***Yield:*** 40 meatballs
> 4 per serving
> 141.2 calories
> 9.8 g protein
> 9.9 g fat
> ***3.3 g carbs***

In medium bowl, combine minced lamb or beef, oat bran, salt, black pepper and garlic clove. Form into 1-inch (2.5 cm) balls. In electric frying pan or large frying pan, fry meatballs on one side 5 minutes, flip and fry 3 to 5 minutes more, or until browned and cooked through. Brush with small amount of Indonesian Sauce, before serving on toothpicks or cocktail skewers alongside remaining Indonesian Sauce for dipping.

Indonesian Sauce: In medium saucepan, combine water, SPLENDA® Granular, soy sauce, lemon juice, peanut butter, olive oil, ginger root, garlic and Tabasco sauce. Bring to boil, stirring constantly. Add extra water, if the sauce is too thick.

Variation: **Hamburgers:** Double recipe, adding one beaten egg, $^1/_3$ cup (75 mL) oat bran and omitting Indonesian Sauce.
Yield: 18 hamburgers, 1 hamburger per serving. (***1.2 g Carbs***)

BACON CHEESE SPREAD
Your friends will beg you for this recipe!

8 oz light cream cheese, softened (250 g)
$^1/_2$ cup mayonnaise (125 mL)
$1^1/_2$ cups Cheddar cheese (375 mL)
2 tbsp chopped chives, OR (25 mL)
  green onions
1 tsp dried parsley (5 mL)
$^1/_4$ tsp garlic powder (1 mL)
8 crisply cooked bacon slices

> *Yield:* 12 servings
> 1 serving
> 176.4 calories
> 7.5 g protein
> 15.7 g fat
> *1.1 g carbs*

In food processor with sharp blade or in blender, process cream cheese and mayonnaise until smooth. In medium bowl, combine cream cheese mixture, Cheddar cheese, chives or green onions, parsley and garlic powder until well combined. Spread evenly in 9-inch (23 cm) glass pie dish.

Place bacon on bacon rack and cover with two paper towels. Microwave on high power 7 to 8 minutes. Cut into small pieces with pair of kitchen scissors. Garnish top of cheese spread with bacon pieces. Bake in 350°F (180°C) oven 15 minutes and serve with low-carb crackers.

GUACAMOLE DIP
This is an excellent Guacamole dip.

1 avocado, peeled, pitted and mashed
$^1/_4$ cup sour cream (50 mL)
$^1/_4$ cup mayonnaise (50 mL)
2 tbsp finely chopped onion (25 mL)
$^1/_2$ tomato, seeded and finely chopped
1 garlic clove, crushed
1 tsp lemon juice (5 mL)
$^1/_2$ tsp black pepper (2 mL)
$^1/_8$ tsp salt (0.5 mL)
2 drops hot pepper sauce
4 slices crisp, cooked bacon, chopped

> *Yield:* $1^2/_3$ cups (400 mL)
> 1 tsp (5 mL) per serving
> 13.0 calories
> 0.4 g protein
> 1.2 g fat
> *0.2 g carbs*

In medium bowl, combine avocado, sour cream, mayonnaise, onion, tomato, garlic, lemon juice, black pepper, salt and hot pepper sauce. Stir in bacon. Serve with fresh vegetables or low-carb crackers.

Helpful Hint: Use a pair of kitchen scissors to snip bacon into small pieces.

SOUPS AND SALADS

GERMAN SAUSAGE MINESTRONE SOUP
A hearty, delicious soup!

2 tbsp olive oil (25 mL)
5 Oktoberfest pork sausages
$^1/_2$ cup chopped onion (125 mL)
1 clove garlic, crushed
3 cups water (750 mL)
2 cups coarsely chopped cabbage (500 mL)
$1^1/_2$ cups canned tomato tidbits (375 mL)
1 tbsp instant chicken stock mix (15 mL)
1 tbsp SPLENDA® Granular (15 mL)
1 tsp dried parsley (5 mL)
$^1/_2$ tsp black pepper (2 mL)
$^1/_2$ tsp dried basil (2 mL)

Yield: 8 servings
1 serving
210.3 calories
7.2 g protein
17.6 g fat
5.0 g carbs

In frying pan in hot oil, brown and cook sausage. Set aside. Pour off excess fat. Brown and cook onion and garlic until tender. In large kettle, combine sausage, onion and garlic, water, cabbage, tomato tidbits, instant chicken stock mix, SPLENDA® Granular, parsley, black pepper and basil. Bring to boil over medium heat and simmer 20 minutes. Grind extra black pepper over each serving of soup, to taste, if desired.

Helpful Hint: As liquid diminishes after several servings, add extra water. Heat soup and stir before serving.

MULLIGATAWNY SOUP

This delicious, popular east Indian soup may be served on a chilly, winter evening as a starter to a light meal.

2 tbsp Healthy Butter, page 96 (25 mL)
$^1/_2$ cup chopped onion (125 mL)
1 green pepper, finely chopped
1 apple, finely chopped
1 tbsp Thickening Agent, (15 mL)
  page 109
2 tsp medium curry powder (10 mL)
$^1/_4$ tsp salt (1 mL)
8 cups water (2 L)
1 can tomato sauce (680 mL)
3 chicken bouillon cubes, crumbled
1 tbsp SPLENDA® Granular (15 mL)
2 tsp lemon juice (10 mL)
12 oz cooked chicken, cubed (0.340 kg)

Yield: 12 servings
1 cup (250 mL) each
95.3 calories
9.7 g protein
2.9 g fat
7.1 g carbs

In deep, heavy saucepan, melt Healthy Butter, page 96. Add onion, green pepper and apple. Saute 5 minutes. Stir in Thickening Agent, page 109, curry powder and salt. Gradually stir in water. Stir in tomato sauce, chicken bouillon cubes, SPLENDA® Granular and lemon juice. Bring to boil and stir occasionally. Simmer at medium-low heat 30 minutes. Stir occasionally to prevent vegetables from sticking to bottom of saucepan. Add chicken. Simmer 10 minutes longer.

Helpful Hints: A food processor makes short work of chopping vegetables and apple finely. For children, stir some cooked macaroni into their portion, if desired.

CREAM OF CAULIFLOWER SOUP
Excellent! Try the variations that appeal to you.

2 cups raw cauliflower, cooked (500 mL)
$^3/_4$ cup water from cooking (175 mL)
1 tbsp instant chicken stock mix (15 mL)
1 tsp Thickening Agent, page 109 (5 mL)
$^1/_4$ tsp white pepper (1 mL)
$1^1/_4$ cups water (300 mL)
$^1/_2$ cup whipping cream (125 mL)
1 tbsp butter (15 mL)
ground black pepper, to taste (optional)

> **Yield:** 4 servings
> 1 serving
> 55.0 calories
> 1.8 g protein
> 3.9 g fat
> **3.1 g carbs**

In blender, combine cauliflower and $^3/_4$ cup (175 mL) water. Blend until smooth. Set aside.

In medium saucepan, combine chicken stock mix, Thickening Agent, page 109 and white pepper. Combine $1^1/_4$ cups (300 mL) water and whipping cream. Gradually stir this mixture into dry ingredients. Add butter and bring to boil. Remove from heat and stir in cauliflower mixture. Return to low heat until soup is heated through. Serve with freshly ground black pepper and a little grated Cheddar cheese, if desired.

Variations: (Use white pepper to taste when other spices are indicated)
Broccoli (*2.8 g Carbs*); **Asparagus**, use $^1/_2$ tsp (2 mL) finely shredded lemon peel and $^1/_8$ tsp (0.5 mL) nutmeg, if desired (*3.6 g Carbs*); **Onion**, use $1^1/_2$ cups (375 mL) and 1 clove garlic, crushed (*5.9 g Carbs*); **Pea**, use 1 cup (250 mL) and 2 tsp (10 mL) snipped mint or $^1/_4$ tsp (1 mL) dried sage, if desired (*6.7 g Carbs*); **Celery**, use $^1/_4$ tsp (1 mL) dried basil (*2.8 g Carbs*); **Zucchini**, use $^1/_8$ tsp (0.5 mL) ground nutmeg (*2.7 g Carbs*); **Spinach**, use 10 oz (300 g) frozen and $^1/_8$ tsp (0.5 mL) dried tarragon, crushed (*3.4 g Carbs*); ***Mushroom**, use 4 cups (1 L) and 1 tbsp (15 mL) dried parsley (*3.8 g Carbs*); **Green Beans** (*5.7 g Carbs*); **Carrot**, use 1 cup (250 mL), 1 tsp (5 mL) dried parsley, $^1/_4$ tsp (1 mL) dried basil and $^1/_8$ tsp (0.5 mL) white pepper (*6.9 g Carbs*); **Potato**, use $1^1/_2$ medium potatoes, mashed (*8.4 g Carbs*), **Curried Cauliflower**, as above and use $^1/_2$ tsp (2 mL) curry powder. (*3.1 g Carbs*)

Helpful Hint: For less spicy soup, reduce white pepper to $^1/_8$ tsp (0.5 mL). Cook (saute in butter, boil or steam) all vegetables before blending. *For mushroom soup, blend 3 cups (750 mL) cooked mushrooms and stir 1 cup (250 mL) chopped mushrooms into soup.

SHRIMP CURRY SOUP
This is a lovely main course soup.

2 tbsp butter (25 mL)
4 large green onions, chopped
2 cloves garlic, minced
1 cup tomato sauce (250 mL)
$1^1/_2$ tsp curry powder (7 mL)
1 tsp ground ginger (5 mL)
1 tsp Thickening Agent, page 109 (5 mL)
$^1/_2$ tsp salt (2 mL)
$^1/_8$ tsp ground cumin (0.5 mL)
$^1/_8$ tsp cayenne pepper (0.5 mL)
$1^1/_2$ cups coconut milk (375 mL)
4 cups raw shrimp (1 L)
1 cucumber, peeled and cubed

Yield: 6 servings
1 serving
300.6 calories
25.9 g protein
18.2 g fat
8.6 g carbs

In electric frying pan, melt butter and add green onions and garlic. Fry until soft, stirring in tomato sauce, curry powder, ginger, Thickening Agent, page 109, salt, cumin and cayenne pepper. Reduce heat and simmer 10 minutes. Stir in coconut milk slowly and bring close to boil. Reduce heat and add shrimp and cucumber; simmer 10 minutes, while stirring occasionally. Serve immediately.

FRENCH ONION SOUP
A classic.

2 tbsp butter (25 mL)
2 cups thinly sliced onions (500 mL)
4 cups beef broth (1 L)
2 tsp Worcestershire sauce (10 mL)
$^1/_8$ tsp white pepper (0.5 mL)
6 slices low-carb toast,
  (optional)
Cheddar cheese, (optional)

Yield: 6 servings
1 serving
69.7 calories
3.0 g protein
4.3 g fat
4.4 g carbs

In large saucepan, melt butter. Add onions and cook until soft and translucent, approximately 8 minutes. Add beef broth, Worcestershire sauce and white pepper. Bring to boiling. Reduce heat and simmer 10 minutes.

If desired, toast low-carb bread, sprinkle with cheese and broil until melted. To serve, float one slice toast atop soup in individual soup bowls.

CROCK-POT TOMATO SOUP

Everyone raves about my tomato soup!

$2^1/_2$ cups V8 Tomato Juice (625 mL)
$2^1/_2$ cups boiling water (625 mL)
8 oz canned tomato sauce (250 mL)
1 small onion, thinly sliced
1 bay leaf
3 tbsp SPLENDA® Granular (45 mL)
1 tbsp instant beef stock mix (15 mL)
$^1/_4$ tsp dried basil (1 mL)
$^1/_8$ tsp black pepper (0.5 mL)

Yield: 6 cups (1.5 L)
1 cup (250 mL) per serving
30.8 calories
1.2 g protein
0.1 g fat
6.3 g carbs

In crock-pot, combine V8 Tomato Juice, boiling water, tomato sauce, onion, bay leaf, SPLENDA® Granular, instant beef stock mix, basil and black pepper. Stir, cover and cook on low setting 4 hours. Strain before serving.

Helpful Hint: If it is too spicy for your liking, add an extra cup (250 mL) water.

GREEK SALAD

An old favorite adapted for a low-carb menu.

2 large tomatoes, chopped
1 seedless cucumber, pared and cubed
1 cup Feta cheese, crumbled (250 mL)
$^1/_2$ cup canned, pitted, large black olives,
  coarsely chopped (125 mL)
Greek Dressing:
$^1/_4$ cup olive oil (50 mL)
2 tbsp red wine vinegar OR (25 mL)
  lemon juice
2 tsp dried oregano (10 mL)
$^1/_4$ tsp coarsely ground black pepper (1 mL)
$^1/_8$ tsp salt (0.5 mL)

Yield: 6 servings
1 serving
223.6 calories
7.0 g protein
19.8 g fat
4.5 g carbs

In large bowl, combine tomatoes, cucumber, Feta cheese and olives.

Greek Dressing: In small bowl, combine olive oil, red wine vinegar or lemon juice, oregano, black pepper and salt. Pour over vegetables and toss.

CHICKEN WITH SPICY AVOCADO DRESSING

Below is an alternate dressing that is also nice.

2 cups cubed cooked chicken (500 mL)
$^1/_4$ cucumber, chopped
1 hard boiled egg, chopped
2 slices cooked, crisp bacon, crumbled
Spicy Avocado Dressing:
1 avocado, mashed
$^1/_2$ cup sour cream (125 mL)
3 tbsp lemon juice (45 mL)
1 tbsp finely chopped onion (15 mL)
1 clove garlic, crushed
$^1/_2$ tsp salt (2 mL)
$^1/_8$ tsp black pepper (0.5 mL)

Yield: 4 servings
1 serving
273.5 calories
28.4 g protein
15.5 g fat
3.5 g carbs

In medium bowl, combine chicken, cucumber, egg and bacon. In small bowl, combine avocado, sour cream, lemon juice, onion, garlic, salt and black pepper. Pour dressing over chicken mixture and stir to combine. Serve in pretty wine glasses lined with lettuce leaves, if desired, as an hors d'oeuvre.

Variation: **Creamy Dressing:** In small bowl, combine $^1/_2$ cup (125 mL) sour cream, 2 tbsp (25 mL) Ranch dressing, 1 tbsp (15 mL) SPLENDA® Granular and $1^1/_2$ tsp (7 mL) prepared mustard. (***1.9 g Carbs***)

Helpful Hints: If desired, serve chicken salad in creamy dressing in an avocado half. This makes a lovely hors d'oeuvre as well.

BROCCOLI SALAD

I love the addition of sunflower seeds.

3 cups broccoli florets, chopped (750 mL)
$^1/_2$ cup salted sunflower seeds (125 mL)
$^1/_4$ cup chopped red onion (50 mL)
$^1/_4$ cup grated Cheddar cheese, (50 mL)
  (optional)
Mayonnaise Dressing:
$^1/_2$ cup mayonnaise (125 mL)
$^1/_4$ cup sour cream (50 mL)
1 tbsp SPLENDA® Granular (15 mL)
1 tbsp lemon juice (15 mL)

Yield: 6 servings
1 serving
227.7 calories
4.0 g protein
21.6 g fat
4.4 g carbs

Lightly steam broccoli florets about 3 minutes. Transfer broccoli to medium bowl and refrigerate, while preparing dressing.

Mayonnaise Dressing: In small bowl, combine mayonnaise, sour cream, SPLENDA® Granular and lemon juice.

Assembly: In large casserole dish, combine broccoli, sunflower seeds, red onion and Cheddar cheese, if using. Stir in Dressing. Serve.

Helpful Hints: To further reduce the carbs, omit sunflower seeds and red onion, if desired.

This salad makes a wonderful addition to a summer picnic.

CHEF'S SALAD

This is an ideal low-carb salad and if it is to be a meal, double the serving.

1 head Romaine lettuce
6 oz cooked chicken, cubed (180 g)
6 oz Swiss cheese, cubed (180 g)
6 oz cooked, canned ham, cubed (180 g)
2 medium tomatoes, coarsely chopped
2 hard-boiled eggs, sliced
3 large, pitted olives, thinly sliced

Yield: 8 servings
1 serving
159.7 calories
16.2 g protein
9.1 g fat
2.3 g carbs

Shred lettuce. Rinse and remove water in lettuce spinner. In large salad bowl, place lettuce and arrange chicken, Swiss cheese, ham, tomatoes, hard-boiled eggs and olives on top. Serve with dressing of your choice such as Thousand Island Dressing, page 100.

FRESH GARDEN SALAD

Healthy, fresh produce makes this a delicious salad anytime.

1 head Romaine, Leaf, OR
  Iceberg lettuce
2 tomatoes, chopped
1 cucumber, sliced
1 medium carrot, shaved into thin slices
3 tbsp chopped chives (45 mL)
sunflower seeds, (optional)

Yield: 8 servings
1 serving
20.7 calories
1.1 g protein
0.2 g fat
2.9 g carbs

Tear Romaine, Leaf or Iceberg lettuce into bite size pieces. Place in lettuce spinner and rinse thoroughly, before spinning to get rid of excess moisture. In large salad bowl, toss lettuce, tomatoes, cucumber, carrot and chives to combine. Serve with dressing of choice and sprinkle with a few sunflower seeds, if desired, for added crunchy texture.

AVOCADO WALNUT SALAD

This is my husband's favorite salad.

Herbal Vinaigrette Dressing:
$^1/_4$ cup olive oil (50 mL)
3 tbsp white wine vinegar (45 mL)
1 tbsp SPLENDA® Granular (15 mL)
1 tsp dried parsley (5 mL)
1 tsp dried oregano (5 mL)
$^1/_2$ tsp garlic powder (2 mL)
$^1/_2$ tsp seasoned salt (2 mL)
$^1/_2$ tsp salt (2 mL)
$^1/_4$ tsp black pepper (1 mL)

Avocado Walnut Salad:
8 cups washed Iceberg lettuce pieces (2 L)
$^1/_2$ cup coarsely grated red cabbage (125 mL)
$^1/_3$ cup grated carrot (75 mL)
2 avocados, peeled, pitted and chopped
$^1/_3$ cup walnut pieces (75 mL)

Yield: 8 servings
1 serving
185.2 calories
3.0 g protein
17.5 g fat
5.2 g carbs

Herbal Vinaigrette Dressing: In small bowl, combine olive oil, white wine vinegar, SPLENDA® Granular, parsley, oregano, garlic powder, seasoned salt, salt and black pepper. Set aside.

Avocado Walnut Salad: In large bowl, combine lettuce, cabbage, carrot and avocados. Toss with Herbal Vinaigrette Dressing. Sprinkle walnut pieces over top for garnish. Serve immediately.

Helpful Hint: Commercially available, prepared garden salad may be used instead, in which case omit red cabbage and carrot. This salad does not keep well, therefore halve the recipe, if serving fewer people.

COLESLAW

A good old standby with a little shredded carrot.

4 cups shredded cabbage (1 L)
$^1/_2$ cup shredded carrot (125 mL)
Dressing:
$^1/_2$ cup mayonnaise (125 mL)
$^1/_3$ cup sour cream (75 mL)
2 tbsp vinegar (25 mL)
2 tsp SPLENDA® Granular (10 mL)
$^1/_2$ tsp dry mustard (2 mL)

> **Yield:** 8 servings
> 1 serving
> 129.5 calories
> 1.1 g protein
> 12.6 g fat
> **2.8 g carbs**

In medium bowl, combine cabbage and carrot. In small bowl, combine mayonnaise, sour cream, vinegar, SPLENDA® Granular and dry mustard. Stir into vegetables. Refrigerate until ready to serve.

Helpful Hint: For convenience, buy pre-packaged coleslaw.

FAUX POTATO SALAD

Excellent copycat! Some people will actually prefer this to regular potato salad.

5 cups chopped cauliflower (1.25 L)
  (approximately one small cauliflower)
8 slices bacon
$^3/_4$ cup mayonnaise (175 mL)
$^1/_4$ cup sour cream (50 mL)
2 tsp white vinegar (10 mL)
2 tsp SPLENDA® Granular (10 mL)
$^1/_2$ tsp onion salt (2 mL)

> **Yield:** 10 servings
> 1 serving
> 169.8 calories
> 5.3 g protein
> 15.7 g fat
> **1.5 g carbs**

In large pot in boiling water, cook cauliflower until tender, about 8 minutes. Drain and set aside to cool to room temperature.

Place bacon on bacon rack and cover with two paper towels. Microwave on high power 7 to 9 minutes. Cut into small pieces with pair of kitchen scissors.

In large bowl, combine mayonnaise, sour cream, vinegar, SPLENDA® Granular and onion salt. Add cauliflower and bacon pieces; stir to combine. Place in casserole dish, cover and refrigerate until cold.

SESAME ASPARAGUS SALAD
Simple, yet an eye-catching presentation.

1 lb fresh asparagus stalks (0.454 kg)
5 cups water (1.25 L)
4 tsp soy sauce (20 mL)
2 tsp sesame seed, OR olive oil (10 mL)
1 tbsp sesame seeds (15 mL)

Yield: 6 servings
1 serving
30.5 calories
1.6 g protein
1.8 g fat
2.0 g carbs

Break off asparagus tough ends by bending stalk back, until it snaps. In large saucepan, bring water to boil. Drop asparagus stalks in rapidly boiling water and parboil 5 minutes. Drain immediately and rinse in cold water. Pat dry using paper towels.

In small bowl, combine soy sauce and sesame seed or olive oil. In casserole dish, toss soy sauce mixture with asparagus stalks. Sprinkle with sesame seeds. Chill in refrigerator an hour or two before serving.

Helpful Hint: The next day leftover asparagus may be served warm.

LIME GINGER COCKTAIL MOLD
A pretty salad, delicious, even as dessert!

$^3/_4$ cup SPLENDA® Granular (175 mL)
$^2/_3$ cup lime juice (150 mL)
3 envelopes unflavored gelatin
$^1/_4$ tsp ground ginger (1 mL)
2 cups boiling water (500 mL)
4 drops green food coloring
$^1/_2$ cup canned fruit cocktail in juice,
   drained (125 mL)

Yield: 6 servings
1 serving
36.3 calories
3.2 g protein
0.1 g fat
6.3 g carbs

In medium bowl, combine SPLENDA® Granular, lime juice, unflavored gelatin and ground ginger. Stir in boiling water, until softened gelatin dissolves. Stir in green food coloring. Pour into gelatin mold. Refrigerate until softly set. Stir in fruit cocktail and refrigerate until completely set.

Serving suggestion: Unmold on bed of red and green leaf lettuce, garnished with cherry tomatoes and drizzled with Raspberry Vinaigrette, page 96, if desired.

EGGS

QUICHE LORRAINE
My favorite is Swiss Cheese and Onion Quiche below.

Crust:
$^1/_2$ cup ground almonds (125 mL)
$^1/_3$ cup grated Parmesan cheese (75 mL)
2 tbsp soy, OR spelt flour (25 mL)
3 tbsp unsalted butter, melted (45 mL)
1 egg yolk
Filling:
6 bacon slices
3 eggs
$1^1/_2$ cups table cream, 18 % BF (375 mL)
$^1/_2$ tsp salt (2 mL)
$^1/_8$ tsp white pepper (0.5 mL)
1 cup grated Swiss, OR Cheddar Cheese (250 mL)

Yield: 8 servings
1 serving
278.7 calories
14.2 g protein
23.2 g fat
3.7 g carbs

Crust: In medium bowl, combine ground almonds, grated Parmesan cheese, soy or spelt flour, melted butter and egg yolk. Press into 9-inch (23 cm) glass pie dish. Bake at 350°F (180°C) 10 minutes.

Filling: Place bacon slices on microwave bacon rack or on plate with two paper towels; cover with paper towel. Microwave on high 6 or 7 minutes until cooked, but not completely crisp. When cool, chop bacon into small pieces. Spread over prepared piecrust. With wire whisk, beat eggs, table cream, salt and white pepper. Stir in cheese. Pour egg mixture over bacon. Bake 15 minutes at 400°F (200°C). Reduce heat to 325°F (160°C); bake 25 minutes more. Let stand 10 minutes before serving.

Variations: **Swiss Cheese and Onion Quiche:** Omit bacon. Stir-fry one cup (250 mL) chopped onion in 2 tbsp (25 mL) butter, until soft. (*5.2 g Carbs*)

Mushroom Quiche: Saute $^1/_2$ lb (227 g) raw mushrooms, sliced, 2 tbsp (25 mL) chopped chives or green onions. Sprinkle with $^1/_4$ tsp (1 mL) salt. (*4.7 g Carbs*)

Deluxe Quiche Lorraine: Use 2 cups (500 mL) whipping cream and 4 eggs (*3.7 g Carbs*). **OR**, if desired, omit crust. (*2.3 g Carbs*)

BACON AND TOMATO FRITTATA

Frittata's originated in Spain. This is a very quick breakfast with minimal work.

4 slices bacon
1 small tomato, chopped
3 eggs
2 tbsp half-and-half cream (25 mL)
$^1/_8$ tsp salt (0.5 mL)
1 cup grated old Cheddar cheese (250 mL)

> **Yield:** 4 servings
> 1 serving
> 181.5 calories
> 15.0 g protein
> 12.3 g fat
> **1.8 g carbs**

On microwave bacon rack or on plate with two paper towels, place bacon. Cover with paper towel. Microwave 6 minutes on high power, or until crisp. Cut into small pieces. In small bowl, beat eggs, cream, and salt. Pour in 2-quart (2 L) casserole dish with lid. Sprinkle bacon and tomato over top. Sprinkle cheese overall. Microwave on high power 5 minutes or until set.

Helpful Hint: Use savory ground beef or chopped ham, sliced sausage, finely chopped peppers, onions or whatever you have on hand. Serve on a slice of buttered low-carb toast, if desired.

FRENCH OMELET

A staple on the low carb diet.

2 eggs
1 tbsp whipping cream (15 mL)
$^1/_8$ tsp salt (0.5 mL)
2 tsp butter (10 mL)

> **Yield:** 1 omelet
> 1 serving
> 234.2 calories
> 13.0 g protein
> 19.2 g fat
> **1.9 g carbs**

In small bowl, beat eggs, whipping cream and salt together with a fork or wire whisk. In medium skillet, melt butter and tilt pan to spread. Pour in egg mixture. Cook over medium heat. Fill slightly set omelet on one side with cheese and ham, bacon, tomato, savory mince, or whatever your heart desires. When omelet has almost set completely, fold one side over to cover filling and cook few minutes more, until no runny egg remains.

CREAM CHEESE SCRAMBLED EGGS

My favorite "quickie" breakfast.

2 eggs
1 tbsp half-and-half cream (15 mL)
salt sprinkle
pepper sprinkle
2 tsp Healthy Butter, page 96 (10 mL)
2 tbsp light cream cheese (25 mL)

> *Yield:* 2 servings
> 1 serving
> 154.1 calories
> 7.7 g protein
> 13.0 g fat
> *1.4 g carbs*

In small bowl, combine eggs, half-and-half cream, salt and pepper sprinkle. Beat lightly with fork. In medium saucepan, melt butter and add egg mixture. Add light cream cheese cut into small pieces. Allow eggs to begin setting around edges. Lift and fold eggs, so that uncooked portions flow freely underneath. Continue cooking in this manner until eggs are set.

Variations: **Scrambled Eggs Archduchess:** Omit cream cheese. Scramble eggs until they thicken. Add $1/4$ cup (50 mL) canned, sliced mushrooms and $1/2$ cup (125 mL) diced cooked ham (*1.6 g Carbs*).

Shrimp Scramble: Add $1/2$ cup (125 mL) cooked salad shrimp. (*1.3 g Carbs)*

CHEESE AND BACON SOUFFLE

This breakfast keeps one going until lunch time.

Cheese Sauce, page 88, use only
  1 cup (250 mL) Cheddar cheese
3 egg whites
$1/3$ cup crisp, cooked bacon bits (75 mL)

> *Yield:* 4 servings
> 1 serving
> 247.2 calories
> 10.2 g protein
> 20.9 g fat
> *1.7 g carbs*

Prepare Cheese Sauce, page 88 using only 1 cup (250 mL) Cheddar cheese and reserve egg whites. In medium bowl, beat egg whites until stiff. In large bowl, pour Cheese Sauce and fold in stiffly beaten egg whites and bacon bits.

Grease bottom of $1^1/_2$-quart (1.5 L) souffle dish. Pour souffle into dish. Bake in 350°F (180°C) oven 30 to 40 minutes or until golden brown.

HARD-BOILED EGGS

This is my son, Daniel's no-fail method for preparing hard-boiled eggs. It is so hassle-free that once you try this method, you will be sold on it.

6 large eggs
hot water

> *Yield:* 6 servings
> 1 serving
> 74.5 calories
> 6.2 g protein
> 5.0 g fat
> *0.6 g carbs*

In medium saucepan, place eggs and cover with hot water. Almost cover saucepan completely with lid and cook over medium-high heat 20 minutes (set timer). Remove from heat. Pour water off. Pour running cold water over eggs in saucepan. Remove shells, dipping eggs in cold water, whenever too hot to handle. Refrigerate in covered container.

Variation: **Stuffed Eggs:** Cut hard-boiled eggs in half and remove yolks. In medium bowl, mash together with $^1/_4$ cup (50 mL) mayonnaise, 1 tsp (5 mL) prepared mustard, $^1/_2$ tsp (2 mL) hot pepper sauce and $^1/_4$ tsp (1 mL) salt. Fill whites with mixture. Cover eggs and refrigerate until ready to serve.
Yield: 12 servings. (*0.4 g Carbs*).

Vary the filling for Stuffed eggs above by adding 3 tbsp (45 mL) crumbled, crisp-fried bacon or 3 tbsp (45 mL) chopped ham or 2 tbsp (25 mL) chopped green onion or chives.

Helpful Hints: Eggs are a low-carb dieter's best friend, as they are low in carbohydrates, and they tend to digest slowly, warding off hunger for hours. To help you stay on track, keep some in the refrigerator for weak moments, when the snacking urge strikes.

BREAKFAST SQUARES

Enough to feed a crowd. Use any meat instead of sausages, if desired.

1 lb Bratwurst sausages (0.454 kg)
7 extra-large eggs
$^1/_4$ cup half-and-half cream (50 mL)
2 tbsp soy flour, OR spelt flour (25 mL)
$^1/_8$ tsp salt (0.5 mL)
$^1/_8$ tsp white pepper (0.5 mL)
2 cups Cheddar cheese (500 mL)

> *Yield:* 12 servings
> 1 serving
> 214.4 calories
> 12.5 g protein
> 17.1 g fat
> *2.1 g carbs*

Remove sausage meat from skins. Place in large skillet and fry until cooked. Set aside.

In blender, combine eggs, half-and-half cream, soy or spelt flour, salt and white pepper. Blend until smooth. Pour into 9 x 13-inch (23 x 33 cm) glass baking dish. Stir in sausage meat and Cheddar cheese. Bake in 350°F (180°C) oven 20 minutes, or until set.

SCRAMBLED EGG BAKE

Looks as good as it tastes!

1 tbsp butter (15 mL)
2 tbsp chopped green pepper (25 mL)
2 tbsp chopped red pepper (25 mL)
4 slices pepperoni, chopped
6 eggs, beaten
1 tbsp butter (15 mL)
$^1/_2$ tsp Thickening Agent, page 109 (2 mL)
$^2/_3$ cup half-and-half cream (150 mL)
1 cup grated Cheddar or Swiss cheese (250 mL)
$^1/_2$ tsp dried parsley (2 mL)

> *Yield:* 6 servings
> 1 serving
> 225.5 calories
> 11.6 g protein
> 18.7 g fat
> *2.5 g carbs*

In large skillet, melt butter. Add green and red pepper and stir-fry until tender crisp. Stir in pepperoni. Pour eggs overall. Allow eggs to begin setting around edges. Lift and fold eggs, so that uncooked portions flow freely underneath. Continue cooking in this manner until eggs are set. Place in 1 quart (1 L) casserole dish. Set aside.

In small saucepan, melt butter. Stir in Thickening Agent, page 109 and gradually whisk in half-and-half cream. Stir until very hot. Stir in cheese and continue cooking, until sauce is thickened and cheese is melted. Fold cheese sauce into eggs. Sprinkle parsley over top. Bake in 350°F (180°C) oven 15 minutes.

DELUXE OMELET PIZZA
The delicious taste of pizza without the carbs!

Omelet Crust:
4 extra-large eggs, separated
2 tbsp butter (25 mL)
2 tbsp soy, OR spelt flour (25 mL)
$^1/_2$ cup half-and-half cream (125 mL)
$^1/_4$ cup water (50 mL)
$^1/_2$ tsp salt (2 mL)
$^1/_8$ tsp white pepper (0.5 mL)

Pizza Sauce:
$^3/_4$ cup tomato sauce (175 mL)
2 tbsp tomato paste (25 mL)
1 tbsp SPLENDA® Granular (15 mL)
$^1/_2$ tsp basil (2 mL)
$^1/_4$ tsp oregano (1 mL)
2 drops hot pepper sauce

Topping:
7 oz sliced ham (200 g)
2 cups grated Mozzarella cheese (500 mL)
2 tbsp drained, crushed pineapple, (25 mL)
 (optional)

Yield: 24 servings
1 serving
62.4 calories
4.5 g protein
4.2 g fat
1.6 g carbs

In medium bowl, beat egg whites until stiff. In small bowl, beat egg yolks with fork. Set aside. In small saucepan, melt butter. Stir in soy or spelt flour and gradually stir in cream and water. Add salt and white pepper. Bring to boil. Stir some into egg yolks. Return mixture to saucepan and stir over very low heat 1 minute or until thickened. Sieve. In large bowl, pour sauce and fold in egg whites. Spread in greased and lightly floured 15 x 10-inch (38 x 25 cm) jelly roll pan. Bake in 350°F (180°C) oven 10 to 15 minutes. Spread pizza sauce atop, adding sliced ham, Mozzarella cheese and pineapple, if using. Bake another 10 to 15 minutes.

Pizza Sauce: In small bowl, combine tomato sauce, tomato paste, SPLENDA® Granular, basil, oregano, and hot pepper sauce.

Variations: (Use any meat such as salami or pepperoni, beef sausage, hamburger, etc.) **Tuna-Cheese Roll:** *Filling:* Follow directions for omelet crust white sauce, except omit eggs and use 3 tbsp (45 mL) soy or spelt flour and $^1/_8$ tsp (0.5 mL) salt. Stir in 1 cup (250 mL) grated Cheddar cheese. Stir in one can (170 g) chunk-style tuna. *Omelet Roll:* Prepare as for Omelet Crust. Loosen edges of crust after baking. Spread filling over crust. Roll up from one short side, using a thin, firm spatula for assistance. *Yield:* 6 servings. (*3.8 g Carbs*)

STRAWBERRY DESSERT OMELET
This is my top favorite omelet!

Strawberry Filling:
$^3/_4$ cup fresh strawberries (175 mL)
1 tbsp SPLENDA® Granular (15 mL)
Dessert Omelet:
3 extra-large eggs, separated
2 tbsp SPLENDA® Granular (25 mL)
1 tbsp soy, OR spelt flour (15 mL)
$^1/_2$ tsp vanilla extract (2 mL)
$^1/_8$ tsp lemon extract (0.5 mL)
$^1/_8$ tsp salt (0.5 mL)
$1^1/_2$ tbsp butter (22 mL)

Yield: 2 servings
1 serving
224.8 calories
11.1 g protein
16.6 g fat
6.6 g carbs

Strawberry Filling: Slice strawberries thinly. Place in small bowl and sprinkle with SPLENDA® Granular. Set aside.

Dessert Omelet: Beat egg whites until thickening. Add SPLENDA® Granular and beat until stiff peaks form. In medium bowl, using fork, beat egg yolks, soy or spelt flour, vanilla extract, lemon extract and salt. Fold egg yolk mixture into egg whites, using fork in quick whisking motion.

In ovenproof skillet, melt butter. Pour in egg mixture. Cook 1 minute over medium heat. Bake in 350°F (180°C) oven 5 to 10 minutes, or until puffy and brown underneath. Fill one half with strawberries. Fold over. Slice in half and serve with Crème Fraiche, page 172, if desired.

Variation: Quick Strawberry Dessert Omelet: *(This is often one I make when it is just for me.)* In small bowl, whisk 1 egg, 1 tsp (5 mL) soy flour or vital wheat gluten, 1 tsp (5 mL) SPLENDA® Granular and 1 tbsp (15 mL) half-and-half cream with fork. Pour into greased nonstick 6-inch (15 cm) frying pan. Cook until set. Slice 2 strawberries and place on one half of omelet. Fold over and serve with a dollop of Crème Fraiche, page 172. (**3.3 g Carbs**).

Helpful Hints: Frozen unsweetened strawberries may be used instead. Thaw in microwave oven slightly, slice, sprinkle with sweetener and set aside. Drain.

MEAT

BOBOTIE

*Introduced to South Africa by the Cape Malays, this Indonesian curried meat
loaf is to South Africa what Moussaka is to Greece and Lasagne is to Italy.
Traditionally, Bobotie is served with yellow rice (add turmeric), chutney and
banana slices dipped in milk.*

2 rye crisp breads, OR
  2 slices low-carb bread
$^2/_3$ cup half-and-half cream (150 mL)
2 lbs ground lamb, OR (0.9 kg)
  lean ground beef
1 cup diced onion (250 mL)
1 tbsp curry powder (15 mL)
2 tsp salt (10 mL)
$1^1/_2$ tsp ground turmeric (7 mL)
$^1/_2$ tsp black pepper (2 mL)
$^1/_4$ cup slivered almonds, (50 mL)
  (optional)
2 tbsp seedless raisins, (25 mL)
  snipped in half
2 tbsp SPLENDA® Granular (25 mL)
1 tbsp lemon juice (15 mL)
4 eggs
4 bay leaves, (optional)

Yield: 10 servings
1 serving
269.7 calories
20.5 g protein
17.5 g fat
5.7 g carbs

In small bowl, break rye crisp breads or low-carb bread in pieces and soak in
half-and-half cream. Set aside. In large skillet, fry ground lamb or beef and
onion, until meat is browned. Pour off fat. Stir in curry powder, salt, turmeric
and black pepper. Over small bowl, strain crisp bread and cream mixture; set
aside cream. Stir softened crisp bread or low-carb bread, almonds (if using),
raisins, SPLENDA® Granular, lemon juice and 2 eggs into meat mixture until
well combined.

Turn into 2 quart (2 L) casserole dish and press down firmly. Stick bay leaves in
upright position in top of meatloaf. Bake uncovered in 350°F (180°C) oven 20
minutes. In small bowl, beat remaining eggs and leftover cream together; pour
over meatloaf. Cover and bake another 20 minutes. Remove bay leaves.

RACK OF LAMB

My husband's favorite! The marinade has a nice little bite to it.

2.7 lbs lamb racks, about 4 (1.25 kg)
Lamb Marinade:
$^1/_2$ cup SPLENDA® Granular (125 mL)
$^1/_4$ cup lemon juice (50 mL)
2 tbsp mustard (25 mL)
1 tbsp Worcestershire sauce (15 mL)
1 tbsp soy sauce (15 mL)
1 tbsp olive oil (15 mL)
1 tsp dried oregano (5 mL)
$^1/_2$ tsp Tabasco sauce (2 mL)

Yield: 8 servings
1 serving
360.3 calories
42.3 g protein
18.9 g fat
2.6 g carbs

Rinse lamb and place in 9 x 13-inch (23 x 33 cm) glass baking dish. In small bowl, combine SPLENDA® Granular, lemon juice, mustard, Worcestershire sauce, soy sauce, olive oil, oregano and Tabasco sauce. Pour marinade over lamb. Marinate several hours or overnight.

Place lamb racks in shallow roasting pan, fat side up. Pour marinade in small saucepan and bring to boil; simmer 10 minutes. Roast lamb in 475°F (240°C) oven 10 minutes. Brush with marinade, using it all. Roast another 20 minutes or until internal temperature reaches 175°F (79°C). To get that barbecued look, broil under broiler 4 to 5 minutes. Carve between ribs to serve.

Helpful Hint: Marinade yields $^2/_3$ cup (150 mL). (**21 g Total Carbs**)

STUFFED ROLLED ROAST

This roast looks impressive, but is so easy!

2 lb beef eye of round roast (0.9 kg)
4 slices bacon
$1/_2$ cup finely chopped onion (125 mL)
$1/_2$ cup chopped green pepper (125 mL)
$1/_2$ cup finely chopped red pepper (125 mL)
$1/_2$ tsp salt (2 mL)
$1/_4$ tsp garlic powder (1 mL)
$1/_8$ tsp black pepper (0.5 mL)
$1^1/_2$ tsp steak spice, divided (7 mL)

Yield: 8 servings
1 serving
233.3 calories
33.9 g protein
8.7 g fat
2.4 g carbs

To butterfly roast, beginning from one long side of roast, using a sharp knife, cut horizontally through center of meat to within $1/_4$-inch (0.5 mm) of other side. Spread open. Cover roast with plastic wrap. Use mallet to pound as thin as possible. Set aside.

Cook bacon in pan until crisp; chop finely and set aside. In 2 tbsp (25 mL) bacon fat, cook onion until tender. Add green pepper, red pepper, salt, garlic powder and black pepper. Cook until barely tender, 2 minutes. Stir in bacon bits.

Remove plastic from roast. Sprinkle with half steak spice. Spread vegetable-bacon mixture over roast. Roll up from one short side. Tie with string to secure. Sprinkle roast with remaining steak spice.

Place roast in shallow roasting pan. Insert meat thermometer, if not using instant-read kind. Roast in 325°F (160°C) oven 1 hour and 15 minutes or until meat thermometer reads 160°F (71°C). Cover with foil and leave standing 5 minutes before carving.

Helpful Hints: Look for a roast which is flat and broad, rather than tall. Instead of chopping bacon with a knife, it is easier to use kitchen scissors to cut bacon into small pieces.

BACON-WRAPPED MEAT LOAF

This is based on one of my husband's favorite recipes for meat loaf from his childhood.

2 eggs, fork beaten
1 tbsp instant beef stock mix (15 mL)
1 tbsp vinegar (15 mL)
2 tsp SPLENDA® Granular (10 mL)
$^1/_2$ tsp salt (2 mL)
$^1/_2$ tsp black pepper (2 mL)
2 lbs lean ground beef (0.9 kg)
$^1/_2$ cup finely chopped onion (125 mL)
$^1/_3$ cup wheat, OR oat bran (75 mL)
$^1/_4$ cup tomato paste (50 mL)
6 slices raw bacon, thawed

Yield: 10 servings
1 serving
252.9 calories
22.5 g protein
16.1 g fat
2.8 g carbs

In small bowl, combine eggs, beef stock mix, vinegar, SPLENDA® Granular, salt and black pepper. In large bowl, combine ground beef, egg mixture, onion, wheat or oat bran and tomato paste. Place on 15 x 10-inch (38 x 25 cm) jelly roll pan. Form into 14-inch (36 cm) loaf or roll. Wrap bacon around loaf, leaving small spaces in between. Bake in 350°F (180°C) oven 1 hour and 20 minutes.

Variation: **Hamburgers:** Omit tomato paste, vinegar and SPLENDA® Granular. Form meat mixture into 16 hamburgers, 3-inches (8 cm) across. Serve with small piece bacon on top, if desired. (*1.1 g carbs*)

Helpful Hint: Any pinkish-red color that you may see in the meat loaf after it has cooked, is due to the tomato paste, and does not mean it is undercooked.

LASAGNA

My husband loved this after not having had lasagna for quite a while.

Low-Carb Pasta, page 127
2 lb lean ground beef (0.9 kg)
$^1/_2$ cup chopped onion (125 mL)
4 cloves garlic, crushed
$^3/_4$ cup water (175 mL)
$5^1/_2$ fl. oz. tomato paste (156 mL)
2 tsp dried basil (10 mL)
$1^1/_4$ tsp salt (6 mL)
1 tsp dried oregano (5 mL)
$^3/_4$ tsp white pepper (3 mL)
2 cups whole milk ricotta cheese (500 mL)
1 egg, fork beaten
$^1/_2$ cup Parmesan cheese (125 mL)
2 tsp dried parsley (10 mL)
4 oz sliced Mozzarella cheese (125 g)
4 oz sliced Cheddar cheese (125 g)

Yield: 12 servings
1 serving
385.6 calories
34.6 g protein
24.1 g fat
6.6 g carbs

Prepare Low-Carb Pasta, page 127, according to directions for lasagna. Layer enough pasta to cover 9 x 13-inch (3 L) glass baking dish. Set remaining pasta aside.

In large skillet, cook beef, onion and garlic over medium heat until no pink remains. Pour off excess fat. Stir in water, tomato paste, basil, salt, oregano and white pepper. Lower heat and simmer uncovered 10 minutes. In medium bowl, combine ricotta cheese, egg, $^1/_4$ cup (50 mL) Parmesan cheese and dried parsley.

To assemble, spread half cheese filling over pasta, half meat sauce and half Mozzarella and Cheddar cheeses. Repeat, using remaining pasta. Sprinkle with remaining Parmesan cheese. Bake in 375°F (190°C) oven 25 minutes. Let stand 10 minutes before serving.

BAKED BARBECUE POT ROAST

This is a popular pot roast in our family. Keep in mind, the less sauce you pour over your portion, the lower the carbs will be. Also a great sauce for beef stew.

1, 4-lb boneless beef rump roast (1.8 kg)
2 tbsp olive oil (25 mL)
1 large onion, sliced
1 large clove garlic, minced
Barbecue Sauce:
1 cup canned crushed tomatoes (250 mL)
1 cup water (250 mL)
$^2/_3$ cup SPLENDA® Granular (150 mL)
$^1/_2$ cup white vinegar (125 mL)
$^1/_2$, $5^1/_2$ oz can tomato paste (78 mL)
1 tbsp Worcestershire sauce (15 mL)
2 tsp instant beef stock mix (10 mL)
2 tsp salt (10 mL)
1 tsp dry mustard (5 mL)
$^1/_4$ tsp black pepper (1 mL)

Yield: 12 servings
1 serving
258.4 calories
35.6 g protein
9.1 g fat
7.4 g carbs

In 5-quart (5 L) Dutch oven, place beef rump roast. In large skillet, in olive oil, fry onion and garlic until translucent. Arrange on and around roast.

Barbecue Sauce: In medium bowl, combine crushed tomatoes, water, SPLENDA® Granular, vinegar, tomato paste, Worcestershire sauce, instant beef stock mix, salt, dry mustard and black pepper. Pour over and around roast. Bake in 400°F (200 °C) oven 30 minutes, reduce heat to 350°F (180°C) and bake $2^1/_2$ hours, basting roast occasionally with Barbecue Sauce.

Variations: Spicy Pork Chops: Stir $^2/_3$ cup (150 mL) water into Barbecue Sauce. In large roaster, layer 2 lbs (1.8 kg) boneless pork loin center cut chops. Cover and bake in 350°F (180°C) oven 2 hours.
Yield: 10 servings. (**4.5 g Carbs**)

Zesty Short Ribs: Use 3 lbs (1.4 kg) boneless beef short ribs, instead of pork chops. In large roaster, layer short ribs and $1^1/_2$ inches (4 cm) water. Bake in 350°F (180°C) oven 1 hour. Pour water off. Cover with Spicy Barbecue Sauce and bake another hour. *Yield:* 10 servings. (**4.5 g Carbs**)

MOUSSAKA

This is a favorite dish in Greek and Middle Eastern cuisines.

1 pound lean ground beef, OR (0.454 kg)
  lamb
$^1/_2$ cup chopped onion (125 mL)
2 cloves garlic, minced
1, 8 oz can tomato sauce (227 mL)
2 tbsp tomato paste (25 mL)
2 tsp dried parsley (10 mL)
$1^1/_8$ tsp salt (5.5 mL)
1 tsp ground cinnamon (5 mL)
$^1/_2$ tsp dried oregano (2 mL)
1, 2 lb large eggplant , unpeeled (0.9 kg)
$^1/_2$ cup olive oil (125 mL)
White Sauce:
$^2/_3$ cup whipping cream (150 mL)
$^2/_3$ cup water (150 mL)
2 tbsp butter (25 mL)
2 tbsp soy flour (25 mL)
$^1/_4$ tsp salt (1 mL)
$^1/_8$ tsp white pepper (0.5 mL)
$^1/_8$ tsp paprika (0.5 mL)
3 egg yolks, fork beaten

Yield: 12 servings
1 serving
252.6 calories
9.0 g protein
22.7 g fat
3.2 g carbs

In large skillet, add ground beef or lamb, onion and garlic. Brown beef; pour off fat. Add tomato sauce, tomato paste, parsley, salt, cinnamon and oregano. Simmer 15 minutes.

Slice eggplant horizontally in $^1/_4$-inch (0.5 cm) thick slices. Brush with oil on one side and place oiled side down in broiler pan. Broil 6 minutes, turn, brush with oil and broil another 6 minutes. (Set timer each time.)

White Sauce: In small bowl, combine whipping cream and water. Set aside. In heavy saucepan, melt butter over low heat. Add soy flour, salt, white pepper and paprika to melted butter. Over low heat, stir together until smooth. Gradually stir in cream mixture, using a wire whisk. Increase heat, and stir constantly with wire whisk, heating to scalding. Stir some of hot liquid into beaten egg yolks. Pour into saucepan and while stirring bring to boil. Remove from heat.

Layer about half eggplant slices in 9 x 13-inch (3 L) glass dish to cover bottom. Spread beef mixture over eggplant. Top with remaining eggplant and pour White Sauce over Moussaka. Bake in 350°F (180 °C) oven 25 to 30 minutes or until golden brown. Let stand 15 minutes before serving.

MEXICAN LASAGNA

Good enough for company too! Looks like a work of art!

2 lbs lean ground beef (0.9 kg)
$^1/_2$ cup chopped onion (125 mL)
4 garlic cloves, crushed
4 tsp dried parsley (20 mL)
2 tsp dried basil (10 mL)
2 tsp ground cumin (10 mL)
1 tsp salt (5 mL)
1 tsp hot chili powder (5 mL)
$^1/_4$ tsp black pepper (1 mL)
1 cup water (250 mL)
$^1/_2$ cup mild or medium salsa (125 mL)
$^1/_4$ cup tomato paste (50 mL)
8 High-Protein Tortillas, page 124, OR
  Whey Tortillas, page 123
2 cups ricotta cheese (500 mL)
1 cup grated Monterey Jack cheese, or Mozzarella (250 mL)
1 egg, fork beaten
1 cup Cheddar cheese (250 mL)

Yield: 12 servings
1 serving
332.2 calories
30.8 g protein
19.5 g fat
7.3 g carbs

In large skillet, cook ground beef, onion and garlic, adding parsley, basil, cumin, salt, chili powder and black pepper. When beef is browned, pour off fat. Stir in water, mild or medium salsa and tomato paste. Bring to boil; reduce heat and simmer 10 minutes.

Layer 4 Tortillas on bottom of 9 x 13-inch (3 L) glass dish. Cut to size and use extra pieces to cover bottom of glass dish. Spread savory beef over top. Cover with remaining 4 Tortillas. In medium bowl, combine ricotta cheese, Monterey Jack cheese and egg. Spread over top of Tortillas. Garnish with remaining Cheddar cheese, in diagonal rows, leaving spaces in between. Bake in 350°F (180°C) oven 30 minutes. If desired, for company fare, after baking, garnish diagonal spaces alternately with chopped tomato, chopped lettuce and chopped green onions or black olives and a little extra Cheddar cheese.

BURRITOS
Spicy, savory beef.

1 lb lean ground beef (0.454 kg)
$^1/_2$ cup chopped onion (125 mL)
2 garlic cloves, crushed
2 tsp dried parsley (10 mL)
1 tsp dried basil (5 mL)
1 tsp ground cumin (5 mL)
$^3/_4$ tsp salt (3 mL)
$^1/_2$ tsp hot chili powder (2 mL)
$^1/_2$ cup medium Salsa (125 mL)
$^1/_2$ cup water (125 mL)
2 tbsp tomato paste (25 mL)
14 High-Protein Tortillas, page 124
  OR Whey Tortillas, page 123
$1^3/_4$ cups Mozzarella, OR (425 mL)
  Monterey Jack Cheese
7 tbsp sour cream (105 mL)

Yield: 14 servings
1 serving
233.7 calories
19.9 g protein
14.6 g fat
7.4 g carbs

In large skillet, cook ground beef, onion and garlic. Pour off excess fat. Add parsley, basil, cumin, salt, and hot chili powder. Stir in Salsa, water and tomato paste. Bring to boil; reduce heat and simmer 10 minutes.

Divide savory beef evenly between 14 tortillas. Top beef with 1 tbsp (15 mL) grated Mozzarella or Monterey Jack Cheese and $1^1/_2$ tsp (7 mL) sour cream. Seal Tortilla edges with sour cream. Sprinkle with another tbsp (15 mL) cheese. Microwave to heat.

Helpful Hints: For slightly lower carb fare, use Crepes (omit sweetener), page 122. *Yield:* 16 servings. (*4.5 g Carbs*)

For a really delicious, low-carb and satisfying meal, use Cheddar cheese Taco shell, page 11 and fill with Burrito meat, chopped tomato, shredded lettuce and sour cream.

ZUCCHINI PASTA WITH SPAGHETTI MEAT SAUCE

Excellent – very tasty!

5 small zucchini
3 tbsp olive oil (45 mL)
2 cloves garlic, minced
2 lbs lean ground beef (0.9 kg)
1, 14 oz can Italian tomato sauce (398 mL)
1, $5^1/_2$ oz can tomato paste (156 mL)
$^1/_4$ cup water (50 mL)
2 tsp SPLENDA® Granular (10 mL)
$1^1/_2$ tsp salt (7 mL)
1 tsp Italian-style seasoning, OR basil (5 mL)
$^1/_2$ tsp hot chili powder (2 mL)
grated, sharp Cheddar cheese,
  a sprinkle

Yield: 8 servings
1 serving
335.8 calories
23.7 g protein
22.6 g fat
7.3 g carbs

Using vegetable peeler, slice ribbons of zucchini, turning vegetable constantly until it no longer slices easily. Slice remaining pieces thinly with sharp knife. Heat vegetable oil in large skillet or wok. Stir-fry garlic until browning. Add zucchini ribbons and stir-fry until zucchini is tender. Add salt and pepper to taste. Drain zucchini in colander and set aside.

In large, deep frying pan, or electric frying pan, brown ground beef. Pour off excess fat. Stir in tomato sauce, tomato paste, water, SPLENDA® Granular, salt, Italian-style seasoning and hot chili powder. Cook on high 5 minutes, stirring to combine. Reduce heat and simmer 15 minutes. Serve on bed of zucchini pasta with a sprinkle of grated, sharp Cheddar cheese.

Variation: **Meatballs in Spaghetti Sauce:** Double Indonesian Cocktail Meatballs recipe, page 24. To make the Spaghetti Sauce: in blender, combine tomato sauce, tomato paste, $^1/_2$ cup (125 mL) water, SPLENDA® Granular, $^1/_8$ tsp (0.5 mL) salt, Italian-style seasoning or basil and hot chili powder. Add extra water, if sauce is too thick for your liking. Serve over Low-Carb Pasta, page 127, if desired.
Yield: 16 servings, 5 meatballs each, plus Spaghetti Sauce. (*5.4 g Carbs*)

CURRIED PORK LOIN CHOPS

If you close your eyes, this almost tastes like chicken!

6 boneless pork loin chops (about 1 kg)
1$^1/_2$ cups water (375 mL)
2 tbsp instant chicken stock mix (25 mL)
Seasoning salt to taste
Mushroom Sauce, page 93
  (use 2 cups (500 mL)
  canned, sliced mushrooms)
$^1/_4$ cup mayonnaise (50 mL)
2 tsp mild curry powder (10 mL)
2 tsp dried parsley (10 mL)

Yield: 6 servings
1 serving
451.7 calories
37.8 g protein
31.2 g fat
2.5 g carbs

In electric frying pan or large skillet, place pork loin chops. In medium bowl, pour water and stir in instant chicken stock mix. Pour over pork chops, bring to boil, reduce heat, cover and simmer 20 minutes.

In 9 x 13-inch (3 L) glass baking dish, place drained pork loin chops. Sprinkle pork loin chops liberally with seasoning salt. In medium bowl, combine Mushroom Sauce, page 93 with mayonnaise, curry powder and parsley. Spread over pork chops and bake in 350°F (180°C) oven 40 minutes.

Helpful Hint: For extra tender pork, pressure cook in chicken broth 30 minutes, instead of braising in skillet.

HAMBURGER PIZZA

These pizzas have been enjoyed even by people who are not on this woe.

Whey Pizza Crusts, page 105, OR
  Pizza Crusts, page 104
$1^1/_2$ lb lean ground beef (0.680 kg)
$^1/_4$ cup chopped onion (50 mL)
1 tbsp instant beef stock mix (15 mL)
$^1/_4$ tsp Thickening Agent, page 109 (1 mL)
$^1/_3$ cup water (75 mL)
1, $5^1/_2$ oz can tomato paste (78 mL)
$^1/_4$ cup vinegar (50 mL)
2 tsp SPLENDA® Granular (10 mL)
$^1/_2$ tsp basil (2 mL)
$^1/_4$ tsp oregano (1 mL)
$^1/_2$ cup raw mushrooms, sliced thinly (125 mL)
$2^1/_2$ cups Mozzarella cheese (625 mL)
4 slices bacon (optional)

> **Yield:** 24 slices
> 1 slice
> 150.5 calories
> 13.5 g protein
> 8.6 g fat
> **4.1 g carbs**

Prepare Whey Pizza Crusts, page 105 or Pizza Crusts, page 104, roll out and place on 2, 12-inch (30 cm) pizza pans. Cover with clean tea towels and set aside.

In large skillet, cook ground beef and onion. Pour off fat. Stir in instant beef stock mix, Thickening Agent, page 109 and water. Cook until thickened and simmer 5 minutes.

In small bowl, combine tomato paste, vinegar, SPLENDA® Granular, basil and oregano. Spread over two pizza crusts. Spread prepared ground beef and sliced mushrooms over top. Sprinkle with Mozzarella cheese. Cut bacon into small pieces and spread over pizzas, if using. Bake on lower shelf in 375°F (190°C) oven 20 to 25 minutes or until browned. Cover loosely with foil, if cheese starts browning too much.

Variations: **Pepperoni Pizza:** Use 4 oz (125 g) pepperoni and 2 tbsp (25 mL) chopped green pepper. (*4.1 g Carbs*)

Hawaiian Pizza: Use 4 oz (125 g) ham and 3 tbsp (45 mL) pineapple tidbits or crushed pineapple (in juice, drained). (*4.2 g Carbs*)

Salmon Pizza: See page 78. (*3.3 g Carbs*)

Helpful Hint: If you choose Soy Pizza Crusts, page 104, add **2.6 g carbs** per serving.

MEATZA PIZZA PIE

This tasty idea came from fellow low-carbers!

1 lb lean ground beef (0.454 kg)
$^1/_4$ cup finely chopped onion (50 mL)
1 egg
1 clove garlic, crushed
1 tsp salt (5 mL)
$^1/_4$ tsp black pepper (1 mL)
Filling:
$^1/_3$ cup tomato paste (75 mL)
2 tbsp vinegar (25 mL)
1 tsp SPLENDA® Granular (5 mL)
$^1/_4$ tsp dried basil (1 mL)
$^1/_8$ tsp dried oregano (0.5 mL)
$^1/_2$ lb, 3 cooked sausages, sliced (0.227 kg)
1 cup sliced Mozzarella cheese (250 mL)
2 tbsp Parmesan cheese (25 mL)

Yield: 8 servings
1 serving
264.7 calories
18.3 g protein
19.6 g fat
2.7 g carbs

Combine beef, onion, egg, garlic, salt and pepper. Press into 9-inch (23 cm) glass pie dish. Bake in 375°F (190°C) oven 15 minutes. Pour off fat carefully.

In small bowl, combine tomato paste, vinegar, SPLENDA® Granular, basil and oregano. Spread over beef layer. Layer Mozzarella cheese slices over tomato layer. Layer sausages next and sprinkle with Parmesan cheese. Bake 15 to 20 minutes until cheese is melted.

Helpful Hint: Use any meat instead of sausages, if desired.

BARBECUED RASPBERRY SPARERIBS

These are restaurant-style delicious.

4 lbs pork side spareribs (1.8 kg)
Raspberry Glaze:
$^1/_2$ cup Splenda Ketchup, page 89 (125 mL)
$^1/_4$ cup raspberry fruit spread, (50 mL)
  sieved
2 tsp Worcestershire sauce (10 mL)
2 tsp white vinegar (10 mL)
1 tsp prepared mustard (5 mL)
$^1/_2$ tsp Liquid Smoke, optional (2 mL)

Yield: 8 servings
1 serving
379.4 calories
26.6 g protein
27.0 g fat
5.6 g carbs

Cut spareribs into manageable sizes. In large pot of boiling water, boil ribs gently 1 hour. Place ribs in 9 x 13-inch (23 x 33 cm) glass baking dish. Brush both sides with Raspberry Glaze and allow to marinate in refrigerator 1 hour, if possible.

Raspberry Glaze: In medium bowl, combine Splenda Ketchup, page 89, raspberry fruit spread, Worcestershire sauce, vinegar, prepared mustard and Liquid Smoke, if using.

Grill ribs uncovered over medium coals, until well-browned both sides, about 8 minutes per side. Baste with Raspberry Glaze as needed.

Helpful Hints: Pressure cooking the ribs would work as well, plus it would cut down on the odor of boiling the spareribs for so long. Do use the extractor fan when boiling these spareribs.

SAUSAGE IN ZUCCHINI BOATS
An attractive presentation!

6 medium-sized zucchini,
  halved lengthwise
1 lb Bratwurst sausages (0.454 kg)
$^1/_3$ cup chopped onion (75 mL)
1 clove garlic, crushed
3 rye crisp breads, ground
1 egg, fork beaten
$^1/_4$ cup grated Parmesan cheese (50 mL)
$1^1/_2$ cups Cheddar cheese, grated (375 mL)

Yield: 12 servings
1 serving
189.8 calories
10.1 g protein
14.3 g fat
3.3 g carbs

In electric frying pan, in boiling water cook half the zucchini. Remove after 10 minutes to 9 x 13-inch (23 x 33 cm) glass dish. Scoop out zucchini, leaving $^1/_4$-inch (0.5 cm) shell. Mash insides and set aside in colander over medium bowl to drain. Repeat with remaining zucchini.

Pour water out of electric frying pan. Remove sausage meat from skins. In electric frying pan over high heat, cook Bratwurst sausage meat, onion and garlic about 10 minutes. Chop sausage finely as it cooks. Stir in mashed squash, rye crisp breadcrumbs and egg. Scoop into zucchini boats and sprinkle with Parmesan and Cheddar cheeses. Bake in 350°F (180°C) oven 30 minutes.

Helpful Hint: If you do not have an electric frying pan, use the largest frying pan you own.

POULTRY

STIR-FRIED CHICKEN AND VEGETABLES

Excellent! Food for a few days or to feed a crowd.

8 boneless, skinless chicken breasts
1 tsp salt (5 mL)
3 tbsp olive oil (45 mL)
2 tbsp water (25 mL)
3 tbsp olive oil (45 mL)
3 tbsp finely chopped ginger (45 mL)
1 clove elephant garlic, crushed
2 cups sliced mushrooms (500 mL)
1 large onion, thinly sliced
1 green pepper, cut in thin strips
1 red pepper, cut in thin strips
10 fl oz sliced water chestnuts (284 mL)
1 tbsp instant chicken stock mix (15 mL)
2 tsp dried hot chili seeds (10 mL)
3 tbsp soy sauce (45 mL)
$^1/_4$ tsp Thickening agent, page 109 (1 mL)
$^3/_4$ cup slivered almonds, toasted (optional) (175 mL)

Yield: 16 servings
1 serving
195.7 calories
28.0 g protein
6.7 g fat
3.4 g carbs

On meat cutting board, slice chicken breasts in half. Slice chicken crosswise into thin strips. Sprinkle with salt. In large wok, heat 3 tbsp (45 mL) olive oil until hot. Add chicken, stirring to coat with oil. Add water, cover and cook about 5 minutes, stirring occasionally, until chicken turns white. Set aside.

In large electric frying pan, in 3 tbsp (45 mL) hot oil, stir-fry ginger and garlic until browned. Add mushrooms and onion, stir-frying until onions are translucent. Add green pepper, red pepper and water chestnuts. Stir-fry until tender crisp, about 3 minutes. Add chicken to vegetables. Sprinkle with instant chicken stock mix and dried hot chili seeds. In small bowl, to soy sauce, add Thickening Agent, page 109. Stir into chicken-vegetable mixture and cook until sauce thickens slightly. Toss in almonds, if using.

CHICKEN ASPARAGUS CASSEROLE

This casserole is reminiscent of one from my husband, Ian's, childhood.

2 slices rye crisp bread
$^1/_4$ cup grated Parmesan, OR (50 mL)
  Romano cheese
$^1/_4$ cup Mozzarella cheese (50 mL)
5 cups diced cooked chicken (1.25 L)
7 oz raw asparagus spears, (210 g)
  ends removed
1 large onion, chopped, sauteed
6 slices cooked bacon, crumbled
1 tbsp dried parsley (15 mL)
2 tsp instant chicken stock mix (10 mL)
2 cups water (500 mL)
4 eggs, fork beaten
$^1/_2$ tsp salt (2 mL)

Yield: 8 servings
1 serving
272.1 calories
27.9 g protein
14.6 g fat
4.7 g carbs

In blender, blend rye crisp bread and Parmesan or Romano cheese. In small bowl, combine Parmesan cheese mixture and Mozzarella cheese. Cut asparagus diagonally into $1^1/_2$-inch (4 cm) lengths.

In large 3 quart (3 L) casserole dish with lid, alternate layers of chicken, asparagus, onion, bacon, parsley and Parmesan cheese mixture. Set aside last amount of Parmesan cheese mixture. In medium bowl, stir instant chicken stock mix into water, adding eggs and salt. Pour over chicken casserole. Sprinkle with remaining Parmesan cheese mixture.

Cover and bake in 350°F (180°C) oven 1 hour, removing lid in last 20 minutes.

CRUSTY CHICKEN ROLLS

These look impressive.

$^1/_2$ cup ground almonds (125 mL)
$^1/_2$ cup Parmesan cheese (125 mL)
3 tbsp soy flour (45 mL)
2 eggs, fork beaten
1 tbsp water (15 mL)
10 boneless chicken breasts (1.0 kg)
salt sprinkle
8, 0.8 oz thin slices ham (24 g)
8, 0.8 oz thin slices Swiss cheese (24 g)

> **Yield:** 10 servings
> 1 serving
> 282.6 calories
> 36.4 g protein
> 13.5 g fat
> **2.0 g carbs**

In small bowl, combine ground almonds, Parmesan cheese and soy flour to form "breading." Spread out on dinner plate. In another small bowl, combine eggs and water. Fold chicken breasts open on sheet of plastic wrap, cover with another sheet of plastic wrap, and pound thin with mallet. Sprinkle with salt. Place one slice ham and one slice Swiss cheese down center of each chicken breast. Tuck any side pieces toward center, and roll up beginning from narrow end.

Dip chicken roll in egg wash and spoon "breading" over. Place chicken rolls in a 9 x 13-inch (3 L) glass baking dish, seam side down. When all ten chicken rolls are prepared, pour remaining egg wash over top of each. Sprinkle again with remaining "breading." Bake in 375°F (190°C) oven 45 minutes or until tops are crusty and browned.

Helpful Hint: Spooning the "breading" over the chicken rolls is preferable to rolling them in the mixture, because this prevents clumping.

SAUSAGE APPLE STUFFING

Delicious stuffing may be used to stuff poultry, or used as stovetop stuffing.

1 lb pork sausage meat, (0.454 kg)
  (seasoned)
1 apple, peeled, cored and chopped
$^1/_2$ cup chopped onion (125 mL)
$^1/_4$ cup grated Parmesan cheese (50 mL)
1 egg
$^1/_4$ tsp salt, or to taste (1 mL)
$^1/_4$ tsp black pepper (1 mL)

Yield: 8 servings
1 serving
262.4 calories
15.7 g protein
19.9 g fat
4.5 g carbs

In medium skillet, cook pork sausage meat until cooked through and no longer pink. Set aside. In drippings, cook apple and onion until tender, about 10 minutes, stirring occasionally. Cook over medium heat until onion is soft and translucent. Remove from heat.

Add pork sausage meat, Parmesan cheese, egg, salt and pepper; stir until well combined. If using as stovetop stuffing, return to low heat and stir until egg is cooked.

TANDOORI CHICKEN OR TURKEY

This curried chicken you will often find in Indian restaurants.

8 chicken or turkey breasts without skin
2 cups sour cream (500 mL)
2 garlic cloves, crushed
1 tbsp medium curry powder (15 mL)
2 tsp ground ginger (10 mL)
$1^1/_2$ tsp ground cumin (7 mL)
$1^1/_2$ tsp ground coriander seed (7 mL)
1 tsp salt (5 mL)
$^1/_2$ tsp ground turmeric (2 mL)

Yield: 8 servings
1 serving
224.3 calories
32.2 g protein
8.6 g fat
3.1 g carbs

With sharp knife, make shallow slits in top and underside of chicken. In medium bowl, combine sour cream, garlic, curry powder, ginger, cumin, coriander seed, salt and turmeric. Stir to combine well. In 9 x 13-inch (23 x 33 cm) glass baking dish, marinate chicken in curried mixture overnight. Wrap each chicken breast in foil. Bake in 350°F (180°C) oven 45 minutes, or until tender and no longer pink.

Remove chicken from foil; drain. Broil 6-inches (15 cm) from heat about 2 minutes (set timer to prevent burning) or until golden.

SPICY CHICKEN AND VEGETABLES

The heat can be reduced by using mild chili powder, however, my family liked it very well this way. My son, Daniel, always says, the hotter, the better.

$^1/_4$ cup butter (50 mL)
4 large chicken breasts, halved
1 cup onion, chopped (250 mL)
$1^1/_4$ cups raw mushrooms (300 mL)
1 clove garlic, crushed
1 cup water (250 mL)
1 cup diced, canned tomatoes (250 mL)
1 chicken bouillon cube, crumbled
$1^1/_2$ tsp paprika (7 mL)
$1^1/_4$ tsp salt (6 mL)
1 tsp ginger (5 mL)
$^1/_4$ tsp hot chili powder (1 mL)
$^1/_2$ cup whipping cream (125 mL)
$1^1/_2$ tsp Thickening Agent, page 109 (7 mL)

Yield: 6 servings
1 serving
252.6 calories
20.1 g protein
16.0 g fat
6.9 g carbs

In large electric frying pan or Dutch oven, melt half butter and brown chicken well. Set aside. Melt remaining butter in electric frying pan. Add onion and saute until translucent; add mushrooms and garlic; saute 2 minutes. Add chicken, water, tomatoes, chicken bouillon cube, paprika, salt, ginger and hot chili powder. Cover and simmer 40 minutes, or until chicken is tender. Remove chicken.

In small bowl, combine $^1/_4$ cup (50 mL) whipping cream and Thickening Agent, page 109 with wire whisk; stir in remaining cream. Stir into sauce until it boils and thickens. Add chicken again briefly to heat and serve with sauce.

BUTTERMILK CHICKEN

While this tasty chicken is baking, prepare extra vegetables.

2 tbsp Healthy Butter, page 96 (25 mL)
$^1/_2$ cup chopped onion (125 mL)
2 cups sliced mushrooms (500 mL)
$^1/_2$ tsp salt (2 mL)
1 cup buttermilk (250 mL)
$^1/_4$ cup whipping cream (50 mL)
2 tsp paprika (10 mL)
2 tsp dried parsley (10 mL)
1 tsp garlic powder (5 mL)
1 tsp dried oregano (5 mL)
$^1/_2$ tsp black pepper (2 mL)
4 large chicken breasts, halved
$^1/_2$ tsp salt (2 mL)
$^1/_2$ tsp Thickening Agent, page 109 (2 mL)

Yield: 6 servings
1 serving
187.3 calories
20.8 g protein
9.0 g fat
3.6 g carbs

In large skillet, melt Healthy Butter, page 96. Add onion; saute until translucent. Add mushrooms and salt; saute 2 minutes. In medium bowl, combine buttermilk, whipping cream, paprika, parsley, garlic powder, oregano and black pepper. Pour into 9 x 13-inch (23 x 33 cm) glass baking dish. Stir in vegetables. Sprinkle chicken with salt and add. Turn chicken several times to coat well with buttermilk mixture. Bake in 325°F (160°C) oven 45 minutes, turning chicken twice.

Remove chicken and keep warm. Transfer buttermilk sauce to medium saucepan. In small bowl, stir Thickening Agent, page 109 into 1 tbsp (15 mL) buttermilk sauce. Stir into remaining sauce. Bring to boil. Pour over chicken and serve.

OKTOBERFEST CHICKEN CACCIATORE

Great served over spaghetti squash or on its own (subtract 5 g carbs). Any pork sausage may be substituted.

2 medium spaghetti squash
2 tbsp Healthy butter, page 96 (25 mL)
$^1/_2$ tsp salt (2 mL)
2 tbsp olive oil. (25 mL)
1 lb chicken breasts, (0.454 kg)
  cut into $^1/_2$-inch strips
$^1/_2$ cup chopped onion (125 mL)
2 garlic cloves, crushed
$^1/_2$ green pepper, chopped
2 cooked Oktoberfest sausages, chopped
1, 14-oz can sliced mushrooms (284 mL)
$^3/_4$ cup canned crushed tomatoes (175 mL)
$^1/_2$ cup water (125 mL)
3 tbsp tomato paste (45 mL)
2 tbsp red wine vinegar (25 mL)
$^1/_2$ tsp salt (2 mL)
$^1/_4$ tsp black pepper (1 mL)

Yield: 8 servings
1 serving
216.8 calories
19.9 g protein
10.2 g fat
8.8 g carbs

Pierce shell of spaghetti squash several times. Place on baking sheet in 350°F (180°C) oven 45 minutes, turn and bake another 15 minutes or until shell yields to pressure. Let cool enough to handle. Cut squash in half. Remove seeds. Remove spaghetti strands with fork. Toss squash with Healthy Butter, page 96 and $^1/_2$ tsp (2 mL) salt. Keep warm.

In electric frying pan or large nonstick skillet, heat olive oil; add chicken, onion and garlic. Cook over medium-high heat, stirring occasionally until onion is tender and translucent and chicken is cooked. Add green pepper; cook 1 minute. Add chopped Oktoberfest sausage, mushrooms, tomatoes, water, tomato paste, red wine vinegar, $^1/_2$ tsp (2 mL) salt and black pepper. Reduce heat to low; simmer 10 minutes or more, until sauce thickens. Serve over $^1/_2$ cup (125 mL) spaghetti squash.

CHICKEN WING DRUMETTES

Delicious! These are a great addition to a finger food party.

$^1/_2$ cup olive oil (125 mL)
$^1/_2$ cup soy sauce (125 mL)
$^1/_2$ cup SPLENDA® Granular (125 mL)
2 tbsp finely chopped ginger (25 mL)
3 cloves garlic, crushed
$^1/_4$ tsp hot chili powder (1 mL)
3 lbs chicken wing drumettes (1.4 kg)

Yield: 10 servings
1 serving
407.1 calories
25.3 g protein
32.6 g fat
1.9 g carbs

In medium bowl, combine olive oil, soy sauce, SPLENDA® Granular, ginger, garlic and hot chili powder. In 9 x 13-inch (23 x 33 cm) glass baking dish, pour marinade over chicken, turning to coat. Cover baking dish with foil and marinate chicken overnight in sauce.

Place on greased cookie sheets. Brush with marinade. Bake in 350°F (180°C) oven 25 minutes. Baste chicken with marinade again. Bake another 20 minutes. Place under grill 10 minutes to brown, if necessary. Watch carefully.

Helpful Hints: This marinade would also be excellent for pork spareribs or Chicken Shish Kebabs.

Use 1 tbsp (15 mL) ground ginger and $^3/_4$ tsp (3 mL) garlic powder, instead of fresh ginger and garlic, if desired.

CHICKEN OR TURKEY ENCHILADAS

Looks as good as it tastes! For convenience, use commercial Salsa and Low-Carb Tortillas, if desired.

14 High-protein Tortillas, page 124, OR
  Whey Tortillas, page 123
1 tbsp olive oil (15 mL)
$^1/_2$ cup chopped onion (125 mL)
4 cups diced, cooked chicken, OR (1 L)
  turkey
1 cup sour cream (250 mL)
1 cup Cheddar cheese (250 mL)
4.5 oz canned, green chilies, (127 mL)
  drained
2 tsp instant chicken stock mix (10 mL)
$1^1/_2$ cups Salsa, page 98 (375 mL)
2 cups Cheddar cheese (500 mL)

Yield: 14 servings
1 serving
234.1 calories
23.4 g protein
11.9 g fat
8.0 g carbs

In large skillet, in olive oil cook onion until tender. Remove from heat. Stir in chicken or turkey, sour cream, 1 cup (250 mL) Cheddar cheese, green chilies and instant chicken stock mix.

Fill tortillas with chicken mixture and place seam side down in 2, 2-quart (2 L) casserole dishes. Cover tortillas with Salsa, page 98 and 2 cups (500 mL) Cheddar cheese, divided between casserole dishes.

Bake in 350°F (180°C) oven 10 to 15 minutes, or just until cheese is melted. Serve with extra sour cream, if desired.

Helpful Hint: Amount of chicken is approximately 6 chicken breasts or about $1^1/_2$ lbs (0.7 kg).

CANTONESE WALNUT CHICKEN
Lots of ginger root in this recipe!

$1/4$ cup soy sauce (50 mL)
1 tbsp Worcestershire sauce (15 mL)
$1/2$ tsp Thickening Agent, page 109 (2 mL)
4 cups bite-size pieces chicken breast (1 L)
$1/4$ cup olive oil, divided (50 mL)
2 tbsp chopped ginger root (25 mL)
1 or 2 cloves garlic, crushed
2 cups mushrooms, sliced (500 mL)
2 cups snow peas (500 mL)
$1/2$ cup chopped green onion (125 mL)
$1/2$ cup walnut halves (125 mL)

Yield: 6 servings
1 serving
293.8 calories
30.6 g protein
15.7 g fat
6.1 g carbs

In small bowl, combine soy sauce, Worcestershire sauce and Thickening Agent, page 109. Add chicken and marinate 15 minutes. In wok in 2 tbsp (25 mL) olive oil, stir-fry ginger root and garlic until browning slightly. Add mushrooms and stir-fry 3 minutes. Add snow peas and green onion. Stir-fry another 3 minutes. Remove and set aside.

To wok in 2 tbsp (25 mL) olive oil, add chicken and stir-fry until cooked, about 8 minutes. Stir in vegetable mixture and walnuts and stir-fry until heated through.

Helpful Hint: Amount of chicken is approximately 6 chicken breasts or about $1^1/_2$ lbs (0.7 kg).

VEGGIE TURKEY LOAF

Really good served alongside Mexican Ratatouille, page 85.

1 tbsp olive oil (15 mL)
4 oz fresh, sliced mushrooms (113 g)
$^1/_2$ small onion, very finely chopped
$^1/_2$ red pepper, very finely chopped
1 clove garlic, crushed
1 tsp dried basil (5 mL)
$^1/_2$ tsp salt (2 mL)
$^1/_8$ tsp black pepper (0.5 mL)
3 tbsp tomato paste (45 mL)
1 tbsp white vinegar (15 mL)
1 tsp SPLENDA® Granular (5 mL)
1 lb ground turkey (0.454 kg)
$^1/_2$ cup grated Cheddar cheese (125 mL)
2 rye crisp breads, ground
1 egg
Parmesan Cheese Sprinkle, (optional)

Yield: 6 servings 1 serving 198.6 calories 20.4 g protein 9.9 g fat ***5.0 g carbs***

In large electric frying pan, in hot oil, fry mushrooms, onion and red pepper. Add garlic, basil, salt and black pepper. Stir-fry frequently until softened, about 10 minutes.

In small bowl, combine tomato paste, vinegar and SPLENDA® Granular. In large bowl, combine turkey, vegetable mixture, tomato paste mixture, Cheddar cheese, crisp bread and egg. Transfer mixture evenly into loaf pan, patting down mixture with back of spoon. Sprinkle with Parmesan Cheese, if using.

Bake in 350°F (180°C) oven 1 hour. Allow to cool 5 minutes before serving.

CHICKEN DIVAN

This is an old favorite for many people.

2 cups frozen, chopped broccoli (500 mL)
3 tbsp butter (45 mL)
$1^1/_4$ tsp Thickening Agent, page 109 (6 mL)
1 tsp instant chicken stock mix (5 mL)
1 tsp dried parsley (5 mL)
$^1/_8$ tsp white pepper (0.5 mL)
$^3/_4$ cup half-and-half cream (175 mL)
$^1/_2$ cup water (125 mL)
2 tbsp apple juice (25 mL)
$^1/_2$ cup shredded Swiss, OR (125 mL)
  Mozzarella cheese
2 cups cubed, cooked chicken, OR (500 mL)
  turkey
$^1/_4$ cup Parmesan cheese, divided (50 mL)
$^1/_4$ tsp paprika, divided (1 mL)

Yield: 4 servings
1 serving
303.8 calories
27.0 g protein
19.1 g fat
5.0 g carbs

Steam broccoli until tender, about 20 to 25 minutes, or follow package instructions. Layer broccoli on bottom of 10 x 6 x 2-inch (25 x 15 x 5 cm) baking dish.

In saucepan, melt butter. Stir in Thickening Agent, page 109, instant chicken stock mix, dried parsley and white pepper. Stir in half-and-half cream, water and apple juice. Cook until thickened and stir in Swiss or Mozzarella cheese until it melts. Pour half sauce over broccoli, and sprinkle with half Parmesan cheese. Top with cubed chicken or turkey, remaining sauce and Parmesan cheese. Sprinkle with paprika.

Bake in 350°F (180°C) oven 20 minutes, or until heated through.

SEASONED CHICKEN DRUMSTICKS

An easy, wonderful recipe to feed a crowd.

24 chicken drumsticks
$^{1}/_{2}$ cup butter (125 mL)
$^{2}/_{3}$ cup grated Parmesan cheese (150 mL)
1 tbsp dried parsley (15 mL)
$1^{1}/_{2}$ tsp paprika (7 mL)
1 tsp dried oregano (5 mL)
1 tsp dried basil (5 mL)
$^{1}/_{2}$ tsp salt (2 mL)
$^{1}/_{4}$ tsp black pepper (1 mL)

Yield: 24 servings
1 serving
196.2 calories
14.1 g protein
15.1 g fat
0.3 g carbs

In small bowl, melt butter in microwave oven. In another small bowl, combine Parmesan cheese, parsley, paprika, oregano, basil, salt and black pepper.

Dip each drumstick in butter and sprinkle seasoning mixture over with spoon. Place drumsticks in 2 greased 9 x 13-inch (3 L) glass baking dishes. Sprinkle with remaining seasoning mixture and pour remaining butter overall. Bake in 350°F (180°C) oven 1 hour.

HERBED CHICKEN BAKE

A simple, quick recipe.

10 chicken breasts, about 3 lbs (1.4 kg)
salt to taste
$1^{1}/_{4}$ cups mayonnaise (300 mL)
$^{1}/_{2}$ cup Parmesan cheese (125 mL)
2 tsp dried parsley (10 mL)
$^{1}/_{2}$ tsp dried basil (2 mL)
$^{1}/_{4}$ tsp dried oregano (1 mL)
$^{1}/_{4}$ tsp instant chicken stock mix (1 mL)

Yield: 10 servings
1 serving
368.7 calories

25.8 g fat
0.6 g carbs

In medium bowl, combine mayonnaise, Parmesan cheese, parsley, basil, oregano and instant chicken stock mix. Set aside.

Spray 9 x 13-inch (23 x 33 cm) glass baking dish with nonstick cooking spray. Place chicken breasts in baking dish. Sprinkle with salt. Bake in 350°F (180°C) oven 30 minutes. Turn chicken breasts over. Sprinkle with salt. Cover with mayonnaise mixture and bake another 25 minutes at 400°F (200°C).

FISH AND SHELLFISH

CRUNCHY TUNA PIE

This is my mother-in-law, Kay Eloff's recipe, which I modified.

Crust:
1 1/4 cups ground almonds (300 mL)
1/4 cup grated Romano cheese (50 mL)
2 tbsp soy flour, OR (25 mL)
  spelt flour
1/3 cup melted butter (75 mL)
1 egg yolk
1 tbsp water (15 mL)

Filling:
2 cans chunk light tuna, drained, flaked (133 g)
1 large onion, finely chopped
1/2 green pepper, finely chopped
1/2 red pepper, finely chopped
4 eggs
1 cup half-and-half cream (250 mL)
2 tsp prepared mustard (10 mL)
1/2 tsp black pepper (2 mL)
1/4 tsp salt (1 mL)
1/2 cup grated Cheddar cheese (125 mL)
2 tbsp grated Romano cheese (25 mL)

> **Yield:** 12 servings
> 1 serving
> 224.2 calories
> 13.9 g protein
> 16.7 g fat
> **4.2 g carbs**

Crust: In medium bowl, combine almonds, Romano cheese and soy flour or spelt flour. Stir in butter, egg yolk and water. Press into 13 x 9-inch (3 L) glass baking dish. Bake in 400°F (200°C) oven 8 minutes. Set aside.

Filling: In large bowl, combine tuna, onion, green and red pepper. In small bowl, beat eggs with fork; stir in half-and-half cream, mustard, black pepper and salt. Add to tuna-vegetable mixture. Pour over crust. Sprinkle with Cheddar cheese and Romano cheese. Bake in 400°C (200°C) oven 20 minutes, or until set.

Helpful Hint: A food processor or good blender makes short work of chopping vegetables.

SALMON BURGERS

Enjoy these on a low-carb bun, page 114 with mayonnaise and mustard, if desired.

3, 7.5 oz cans salmon, deboned (213 g)
1 cup grated old Cheddar cheese (250 mL)
$^1/_2$ cup Parmesan cheese (125 mL)
$^1/_4$ cup mayonnaise (50 mL)
$^1/_4$ cup oat bran (50 mL)
2 eggs, fork beaten
$^1/_4$ cup Healthy Butter, page 96 (50 mL)

Yield: 12 servings	
1 serving	
214.0 calories	
13.6 g protein	
17.1 g fat	
1.5 g carbs	

In large bowl, combine salmon, Cheddar cheese, Parmesan cheese, mayonnaise, oat bran and eggs. Form into 2-inch (5cm) wide patties. In electric frying pan or large skillet, fry 6 patties in 2 tbsp (25 mL) Healthy Butter, page 96 until browned underneath. Turn and fry other side until brown. Repeat.

Variation: **Tuna Burgers:** Substitute canned tuna for salmon.
Yield: 14 tuna burgers (*1.2 g Carbs*)

Cheesy Salmon Loaf: Follow recipe for Salmon Burgers, omitting Healthy Butter and place mixture in greased 9 x 5 x 3-inch (2 L) loaf pan. Sprinkle with $^1/_4$ cup (50 mL) grated Cheddar cheese. *Yield:* 8 servings. (*2.0 g Carbs*)

CREAMY POLLOCK IN CREPES

My husband raved about this.

16 Crepes, page 122
  (use 1 tsp (5 mL) SPLENDA® Granular)
White Sauce, page 93
$^1/_3$ cup canned mushrooms, (75 mL)
  drained
2 tbsp Healthy Butter, page 96 (25 mL)
1 lb pollock, broken up (0.454 kg)
grated Cheddar cheese sprinkle, (optional)

Yield: 16 servings	
1 serving	
148.8 calories	
6.7 g protein	
10.6 g fat	
6.0 g carbs	

Prepare Crepes, page 122. Set aside in casserole dish with lid and keep warm in oven or on hot plate on low heat. Prepare White Sauce, page 93, add canned mushrooms or cooked, fresh mushrooms. In large skillet, in melted Healthy Butter, page 96, cook pollock until heated through. Stir in White Sauce. Fill crepes with pollock mixture. Sprinkle with Cheddar Cheese, if desired.

FRIED SOLE OR COD WITH VEGETABLES

My youngest son, not particularly a fish lover, enjoyed this. Best served immediately.

$1^1/_2$ lb sole or cod fish fillets (680 g)
$^1/_2$ cup soy flour (125 mL)
2 tsp onion salt (10 mL)
1 tsp paprika (5 mL)
1 tsp curry powder (5 mL)
$^1/_3$ cup half-and-half cream (75 mL)
$^1/_3$ cup butter (75 mL)
2 tbsp butter (25 mL)
1 cup sliced onion (250 mL)
1 cup sliced raw mushrooms (250 mL)
1 tsp onion salt (5 mL)
$^1/_4$ tsp paprika (1 mL)
$^1/_8$ tsp curry powder (0.5 mL)
2 slices bacon, cooked

Yield: 6 servings
1 serving
296.9 calories
27.9 g protein
18.0 g fat
6.2 g carbs

Wash sole or cod fillets under running cold water. In small bowl, stir to combine soy flour, onion salt, paprika and curry powder. Spread mixture out on dinner plate. Pour half-and-half cream into medium, deep mixing bowl. Dip fish in half-and-half cream and then in soy flour mixture, turning to coat.

In large non-stick frying pan, melt some butter of $^1/_3$ cup (75 mL) measure. Cook few pieces fish (do not overcrowd pan) about 3 to 4 minutes, turning halfway. Fish will be golden brown in color and flake easily when cooked. Set aside in casserole dish on stove at low heat to keep warm. Prepare remaining fish fillets in similar manner.

In clean skillet, melt 2 tbsp (25 mL) butter. Add onion; saute until translucent. Add mushrooms; stir in onion salt, paprika and curry powder. Cook until mushrooms are soft. Chop bacon and stir in. Serve immediately with warm fish fillets.

Helpful Hint: Fried sole without vegetables. (*3.7 g Carbs*)

GARLIC BUTTER SHRIMP AND POLLOCK

I love pollock (natural and artificial lobster-flavored seafood), although it is a bit high in carbs. This way the carbs are distributed more kindly - a lovely meal with high protein content!

24 oz frozen salad shrimp (680 g)
2 cups pollock (500 mL)
$^1/_2$ cup Healthy Butter, page 96 (125 mL)
4 cloves garlic, crushed
$1^1/_2$ tsp Butter Flavor Sprinkles (7 mL)

Yield: 6 cups (1.5 L)
1 cup (250 mL) per serving
312.0 calories
29.5 g protein
17.3 g fat
7.9 g carbs

Rinse shrimp in colander over basin under cold running water 5 minutes. Break up pollock into bite size pieces; set aside.

In large skillet, in melted Healthy Butter, page 96, cook garlic until turning brown, about 1 minute. Stir in pollock. Cook 2 minutes. Stir in salad shrimp; cook another 2 minutes, or until shrimp are heated. Toss with Butter Flavor Sprinkles. Serve immediately.

SCALLOPS IN ALFREDO SAUCE

A tasty classic.

1 lb frozen small scallops (0.454 kg)
2 tbsp Healthy Butter, page 96 (25 mL)
$^1/_4$ tsp salt (1 mL)
$^1/_8$ tsp black pepper (0.5 mL)
Alfredo Sauce, page 93

Yield: 3 servings
1 serving
201.2 calories
25.5 g protein
8.8 g fat
3.6 g carbs

Thaw frozen scallops in refrigerator overnight or in bag in cold water until they are able to separate. In skillet, in Healthy Butter, page 96, cook scallops gently over medium-low heat about 5 minutes or until firm. Sprinkle with salt and pepper while cooking.

Prepare Alfredo Sauce, page 93. Pour over scallops. Serve over Low-Carb Pasta, page 127, if desired.

CHEESY POLLOCK PATTIES

I love pollock (natural and artificial lobster-flavored seafood) and I'm always looking for ways to make the carbs stretch a bit more. Super for breakfast too!

1 lb pollock (0.454 kg)
2 cups grated zucchini (500 mL)
2 cups grated Cheddar cheese (500 mL)
$1/2$ cup Parmesan cheese (125 mL)
$1/2$ cup mayonnaise (125 mL)
$1/2$ tsp garlic powder (2 mL)
$1/4$ tsp salt (1 mL)
4 eggs, fork beaten
2 tbsp butter (25 mL)

Yield: 16 servings
1 serving
162.5 calories
8.3 g protein
12.4 g fat
4.2 g carbs

Break pollock into small pieces. In large bowl, combine pollock, zucchini, Cheddar cheese, Parmesan cheese, mayonnaise, garlic powder and salt. Stir in eggs. Melt butter in large electric frying pan. Pour pollock mixture into pan to cover. Cook on medium high heat until set. Divide into 16 servings. Serve on low-carb toast, if desired.

COD FILLETS IN MUSHROOM SAUCE

This is not just any old mushroom sauce. It is quite special.

$1^1/2$ lbs cod fillets (0.680 kg)
2 tbsp butter, melted (25 mL)
$1/2$ tsp seasoning salt (2 mL)
Mushroom Sauce, page 93
  (use 2 cups (500 mL) canned mushrooms
  and half-and-half cream)
$1/2$ cup mayonnaise (125 mL)
2 tbsp chopped chives, OR (25 mL)
  green onions

Yield: 6 servings
1 serving
336.4 calories
22.8 g protein
25.7 g fat
2.4 g carbs

Spray bottom of 9 x 13-inch (23 x 33 cm) glass baking dish with nonstick cooking spray. Place cod fillets in dish. In small bowl, combine butter and seasoning salt. Brush this seasoned butter over each fillet. Bake uncovered in 400°F (200°C) oven 15 minutes, or until fish flakes easily with fork.

Prepare Mushroom Sauce, page 93, using 2 cups (500 mL) canned mushrooms. Remove from heat. Stir in mayonnaise and chives or green onions. Pour over baked cod fillets and serve immediately.

BAKED SOLE WITH LEMON SAUCE

This is an easy, quick meal.

2 lbs frozen sole, ocean perch, OR (0.9 kg)
  flounder fillets
1 tsp salt (5 mL)
$^1/_4$ tsp white pepper (1 mL)
3 tbsp butter, melted (45 mL)
Lemon Sauce:
1 tbsp butter (15 mL)
$^1/_2$ tsp Thickening Agent, page 109 (2 mL)
1 $^1/_2$ tsp instant chicken stock mix (7 mL)
$^3/_4$ cup water (175 mL)
2 tbsp lemon juice (25 mL)
2 egg yolks

Yield: 8 servings
1 serving
174.1 calories
22.4 g protein
8.5 g fat
0.9 g carbs

Arrange sole fillets in greased 9 x 13-inch (23 x 33 cm) baking dish. Sprinkle fillets with salt and pepper and drizzle butter overall. Bake in 350°F (180°C) oven 10 minutes or until fish flakes easily.

Lemon Sauce: In double boiler, over medium heat, melt butter.   Stir in Thickening Agent, page 109 and instant chicken stock mix.   Gradually stir in water and lemon juice. Cook, stirring until slightly thickened.   Place egg yolks in small bowl. Add some hot lemon sauce to egg yolks and return to double boiler, stirring constantly until thickened, however, do not boil.   Drain fillets.   Pour sauce over sole and garnish with fresh parsley or sliced pimento-stuffed olives, if desired.

Helpful Hint: This Lemon Sauce has many different uses.
Yield: 18 tbsp (270 mL), 1 tbsp (15 mL) per serving. (**0.2 g Carbs**)

SALMON PIZZA

This unusual topping for pizza is one of my favorites.

2 Whey Pizza Crusts, page 105, OR
  Pizza Crusts, page 104
Mushroom Pizza Sauce:
$^3/_4$ tsp Thickening Agent, page 109 (3 mL)
$^1/_2$ tsp dry mustard (2 mL)
$^1/_4$ tsp salt (1 mL)
$^1/_4$ tsp onion salt (1 mL)
$^1/_4$ tsp white pepper (1 mL)
$^1/_2$ cup whipping cream (125 mL)
$^1/_4$ cup water (50 mL)
2 egg yolks
$^1/_2$ cup mayonnaise (125 mL)
10 oz can sliced mushrooms (284 mL)
Topping:
3, $7^1/_2$ oz cans salmon (213 g)
$^1/_4$ cup chopped green and red peppers (50 mL)
2 green onions, chopped
2 cups Mozzarella cheese (500 mL)
1 cup Cheddar cheese (250 mL)

Yield: 24 servings
1 serving
195.9 calories
14.3 g protein
13.7 g fat
3.3 g carbs

Prepare Whey Pizza Crusts, page 105 or Pizza Crusts, page 104. Cover pizza dough on pizza pans with plastic wrap to prevent drying out. Debone salmon and set aside in small bowl.

Mushroom Pizza Sauce: In small nonstick saucepan, combine Thickening Agent, page 109, dry mustard, salt, onion salt and white pepper. In small bowl, combine whipping cream and water. Gradually add liquid to dry ingredients in saucepan, stirring with plastic whisk. Bring mixture to boil. Remove saucepan from heat. Add small amount of mixture to egg yolks; return to saucepan. Cook over low heat until thickened; do not boil. Stir in mayonnaise and mushrooms.

To assemble pizzas: Spread half Mushroom Pizza Sauce on each pizza. Divide salmon between pizzas. Divide green and red peppers and green onions between pizzas. Divide Mozzarella and Cheddar cheeses between pizzas, creating an attractive border with Cheddar Cheese.

Helpful Hint: Add ***2.6 g carbs*** per serving, if using Pizza Crusts, page 104.

VEGETABLES

EGGPLANT PARMIGIANA

A popular vegetable dish which is often served to vegetarians as the main course.

$^2/_3$ cup olive oil (150 mL)
1 large onion, chopped
1 garlic clove, minced
2 cups canned crushed tomatoes (500 mL)
2 tsp SPLENDA® Granular (10 mL)
$^1/_2$ tsp dried oregano (2 mL)
$^1/_2$ tsp dried basil (2 mL)
$^1/_2$ tsp salt (2 mL)
1 cup grated Parmesan cheese (250 mL)
2 eggs
2 tbsp water (25 mL)
1 large eggplant, cut into thin slices
3 cups grated Mozzarella cheese (750 mL)

> *Yield:* 12 servings
> 1 serving
> 241.6 calories
> 10.6 g protein
> 18.7 g fat
> *7.9 g carbs*

In large skillet, in 2 tbsp (25 mL) olive oil, cook onion and garlic until translucent and tender. Stir in crushed tomatoes, SPLENDA® Granular, oregano, basil and salt. Simmer over low heat 10 minutes. On waxed paper, spread Parmesan cheese. In small bowl, beat eggs and water together with fork. Dip eggplant in egg wash and then in Parmesan cheese. In large skillet, in about 2 tbsp (25 mL) hot oil, fry several eggplant slices until golden brown on both sides (Cover with lid – cooks faster). Add more oil and repeat.

Layer $^1/_2$ eggplant slices in 9 x 13-inch (23 x 33 cm) glass baking dish, cover with $^1/_2$ tomato mixture, sprinkle with half grated Mozzarella cheese; repeat. Bake in 350°F (180°C) oven 25 minutes.

Variation: **Fried Eggplant:** Fry eggplant as described above.
Yield: 8 servings. (*3.9 g Carbs*)

BOUNTIFUL BROCCOLI CASSEROLE

This is a special recipe which you will enjoy serving.

1 lb broccoli cut up (0.454 kg)
$^1/_4$ cup water (50 mL)
Mushroom Sauce, page 93
$^2/_3$ cup grated Cheddar cheese (150 mL)
$^1/_2$ cup mayonnaise (125 mL)
1 tbsp lemon juice (15 mL)
$^1/_3$ cup toasted slivered almonds, (75 mL)
 (optional)

> **Yield:** 8 servings
> 1 serving
> 201.0 calories
> 5.7 g protein
> 17.2 g fat
> **6.5 g carbs**

Microwave broccoli in casserole dish in water 6 minutes, or until just tender. Drain. Prepare Mushroom Sauce, page 93. Allow to cool slightly. Stir in Cheddar cheese, mayonnaise and lemon juice. Stir mushroom mixture into broccoli. Sprinkle with toasted almonds, if using. Bake in 350°F (180°C) oven 15 to 20 minutes.

Helpful Hint: To toast almonds, place in dry frying pan on medium heat, stirring until turning brown. This method increases flavor and enhances appearance.

GARLIC MUSHROOMS

Quick and easy.

6 cups raw, sliced mushrooms (1.5 L)
3 tbsp healthy butter, page 96 (45 mL)
2 cloves garlic, minced
2 tsp soy sauce (10 mL)
1 tsp dried parsley (5 mL), OR
 2 tbsp fresh parsley, chopped (25 mL)

> **Yield:** 6 servings
> 1 serving
> 69.7 calories
> 1.6 g protein
> 6.0 g fat
> **2.7 g carbs**

Wash mushrooms thoroughly. Set aside. In large skillet, over medium heat, melt butter. Add garlic; saute until browning. Add mushrooms, soy sauce and dried or fresh parsley; cook, stirring until mushrooms have softened.

TERIYAKI VEGETABLES

Delicious and children love these vegetables too!

Terikyaki Sauce:
3 tbsp SPLENDA® Granular (45 mL)
2 tbsp water (25 mL)
2 tbsp soy sauce (25 mL)
1 tsp ground ginger (5 mL)
$^1/_2$ tsp garlic powder (2 mL)
$^1/_4$ tsp Thickening Agent, page 109 (1 mL)

Stir-fry Vegetables:
2 tbsp olive oil (25 mL)
4 cups raw mushrooms, sliced (1 L)
14 oz can baby corn (398 mL)
8 oz can whole water chestnuts (227 mL)

Yield: 8 servings
1 serving
69.7 calories
2.1 g protein
3.7 g fat
4.6 g carbs

Teriyaki Sauce: In small bowl, combine SPLENDA® Granular, water, soy sauce, ginger, garlic powder and Thickening Agent, page 109.

Stir-Fry Vegetables: In hot oil in large electric frying pan, stir fry mushrooms until tender. Stir in baby corn and whole water chestnuts. Stir-fry 1 minute. Stir in Teriyaki Sauce 1 minute and serve.

Variation: Use this sauce for any frozen or fresh mixed vegetable combinations.

Helpful Hint: Make double the amount of sauce for larger quantities of vegetables.

SWEET ONION PEPPER STIR-FRY

A colorful mosaic.

3 tbsp Healthy Butter, page 96 (45 mL)
1 cup sliced onions (250 mL)
1 red pepper, sliced
1 green pepper, sliced
Sweet Mustard Sauce:
$^1/_2$ cup SPLENDA® Granular (125 mL)
1 tbsp prepared mustard (15 mL)
$1^1/_2$ tsp Worcestershire Sauce (7 mL)
$^1/_2$ tsp salt (2 mL)
$^1/_8$ tsp black pepper (0.5 mL)

Yield: 10 servings
1 serving
52.3 calories
0.7 g protein
3.6 g fat
3.8 g carbs

Sweet Mustard Sauce: In small bowl, combine SPLENDA® Granular, prepared mustard, Worcestershire Sauce, salt and pepper. Set aside.

In electric wok or large electric skillet, melt Healthy Butter, page 96. Add onions; fry until barely tender 2 minutes. Add red and green peppers; fry until barely tender 2 minutes. Stir in Sweet Mustard Sauce until heated through.

Variation: Add 1 cup (250 mL) sliced, raw mushrooms with the onions. (**4.4 g Carbs**).

ZUCCHINI SAUTE

This looks as good as it tastes.

2 tbsp olive oil (25 mL)
2 cups sliced onion (500 mL)
4 small zucchini, unpeeled and cubed
$^1/_2$ tsp salt (2 mL)
$^1/_4$ tsp black pepper (1 mL)
$^1/_4$ tsp garlic powder (1 mL)

Yield: 8 servings
1 servings
52.0 calories
1.4 g protein
3.1 g fat
3.9 g carbs

In large saucepan, in olive oil, cook onion until tender. Add zucchini, salt, pepper and garlic powder. Saute until zucchini is heated through and tender crisp.

Variation: Saute onions and 1 cup (250 mL) sliced, raw mushrooms together. (**4.3 g Carbs**)

SEASONED POTATO SKINS
These are delicious and can substitute for fries.

3 lbs potatoes (1.5 kg)
$^1/_4$ cup olive oil (50 mL)
1 tsp seasoning salt (5 mL)
$^1/_4$ tsp paprika (1 mL)

> *Yield:* 6 servings
> 1 serving
> 115.5 calories
> 1.6 g protein
> 9.1 g fat
> *5.7 g carbs*

Peel potatoes in wide strips. Set peel aside. Use peeled potatoes to make potato pie for family members or friends not on a low-carb diet.

In medium bowl, combine olive oil, seasoning salt and paprika. Toss potato skins in seasoned oil to coat well. Lay out on cookie sheets. Bake in 425°F (220°C) oven 12 to 16 minutes or until golden and crisp.

ASPARAGUS
This is an abundant spring vegetable, happily low in carbs.

1 lb asparagus (0.454 kg)

> *Yield:* 8 servings
> 1 serving
> 13.6 calories
> 1.5 g protein
> 0.2 g fat
> *1.5 g carbs*

Hold base of asparagus stalk firmly and bend stalk. End will break off at place where stalks are too tough to eat. Discard ends and trim scales if stalks are gritty. Cut asparagus diagonally crosswise in desired lengths. In large saucepan, in boiling, salted water, add stalks and bring water to boil again. Reduce heat to low; cover and simmer until tender-crisp. Whole asparagus will take about 6 to 7 minutes, cut-up stalks about 5 to 6 minutes. Season with butter, salt and pepper or Hollandaise Sauce, page 92 or Lemon Sauce, page 77.

VEGETABLES WITH SESAME CREAM CHEESE
Excellent!

4 oz light cream cheese, cubed (125 g)
$^1/_4$ cup sesame seeds, toasted (50 mL)
2 tbsp butter (25 mL)
3 cups sliced raw mushrooms (750 mL)
1 green pepper, thinly sliced
1 red pepper, thinly sliced
$^1/_2$ tsp salt (2 mL)
$^1/_4$ tsp white pepper (1 mL)

Yield: 8 servings
1 serving
137.8 calories
3.8 g protein
11.7 g fat
4.1 g carbs

Roll small cream cheese cubes in toasted sesame seeds. In wok, melt butter and add mushrooms. Stir-fry until almost tender. Add green pepper and red pepper. Sprinkle with salt and white pepper. Stir-fry vegetables until peppers are tender crisp. Drain vegetables and place in casserole dish. Add sesame cream cheese cubes and gently mix in.

Helpful Hints: To toast sesame seeds, place in dry frying pan and stir-fry over medium heat until turning brown.

FAUX MASHED POTATOES
There are many variations for this dish. Here is mine.

1.1 lb fresh cauliflower (500 g)
$^1/_4$ cup grated Cheddar, OR (50 mL)
  Mozzarella cheese
2 tbsp butter (25 mL)
1 tbsp sour cream (15 mL)
1 tbsp Parmesan cheese (15 mL)
$^1/_2$ tsp salt (2 mL)

Yield: 6 servings
1 serving
65.2 calories
2.2 g protein
5.3 g fat
1.8 g carbs

Steam cauliflower about 14 minutes, or until soft. In food processor or blender, process until smooth. Add grated Cheddar or Mozzarella cheese, butter, sour cream, Parmesan cheese and salt. Process until smooth.

Helpful Hint: If after processing product is not as smooth as desired, add 1 tbsp (15 mL) whipping cream and process at high speed until smooth.

MEXICAN RATATOUILLE

This popular, savory vegetable medley receives a flavor boost.

1 tbsp butter (15 mL)
$1/_2$ cup chopped onion (125 mL)
1 clove garlic, crushed
2 small zucchini, chopped
2 cups cubed, peeled eggplant (500 mL)
1 cup tomato sauce (250 mL)
$1/_2$ cup chopped red pepper (125 mL)
$1/_2$ cup water (125 mL)
3 tbsp medium-hot Salsa (45 mL)
1 tsp dried basil (5 mL)
$1/_2$ tsp salt (2 mL)
$1/_8$ tsp black pepper (0.5 mL)
8 tsp Parmesan cheese (40 mL)

Yield: 8 servings
1 serving
39.0 calories
2.3 g protein
0.8 g fat
5.4 g carbs

In large electric frying pan, over high heat and in melted butter, fry onion and garlic until tender. Add zucchini, eggplant, tomato sauce, red pepper, water, Salsa, basil, salt and black pepper. Bring to boiling, reduce heat and simmer 20 minutes. Cook uncovered 5 or 10 minutes more, stirring occasionally, until thickened. Sprinkle each serving with Parmesan cheese.

GREEN BEANS IN LEMON SAUCE

A fabulous new flavor addition.

1 lb frozen green beans (0.454 kg)
Lemon Sauce, page 77
2 tbsp sesame seeds, toasted (25 mL)
  (optional)

Yield: 8 servings
1 serving
44.6 calories
1.6 g protein
2.8 g fat
2.4 g carbs

In steamer, steam green beans until tender. Prepare Lemon Sauce, page 77 and pour over green beans. Sprinkle with toasted sesame seeds, if desired.

CAULIFLOWER PUFF

This looks impressive for a lowly vegetable dish.

1 large head cauliflower
Cheese Sauce, page 88
$^1/_4$ tsp salt (1 mL)
$^1/_8$ tsp pepper (0.5 mL)
4 eggs
$^1/_4$ tsp lemon juice (1 mL)
$^1/_8$ tsp paprika (0.5 mL)

Yield: 8 servings
1 serving
189.5 calories
9.9 g protein
15.0 g fat
3.4 g carbs

Break cauliflower into florets. In large casserole dish, place cauliflower and a little water. Microwave on high power 9 minutes or just until tender. Drain well. Place in greased 9 x 13-inch (3 L) glass dish. Prepare Cheese Sauce, page 88. Add extra salt and pepper to Cheese Sauce (see ingredients above).

In food processor or electric mixer, beat egg whites with lemon juice until stiff. Add egg yolks one at a time, while beating until thick and creamy. Fold egg mixture into Cheese and pour over cauliflower. Sprinkle with paprika and bake in 350°F (180°C) oven 20 minutes.

SEASONED FRIED TOMATOES

This is my favorite way to eat tomatoes. Serve them for breakfast alongside a bacon and cheese omelet, if desired.

2 tomatoes
3 tbsp butter, or Healthy Butter, (45 mL)
 page 96
2 tbsp Parmesan cheese (25 mL)
$^1/_4$ tsp onion salt (1 mL)
$^1/_8$ tsp black pepper (0.5 mL)

Yield: 4 servings
1 serving
129.0 calories
2.0 g protein
12.7 g fat
2.3 g carbs

Cut tomatoes into thin slices. In large frying pan, fry tomato slices in melted butter until soft. In small bowl, combine Parmesan cheese, onion salt and black pepper. Sprinkle over tomatoes and cook a little longer.

CHINESE VEGETABLE STIR-FRY

Bright, healthy vegetables with the wonderful flavor of fresh ginger root.

$1/4$ cup orange juice (50 mL)
2 tbsp Worcestershire sauce (25 mL)
1 tbsp water (15 mL)
$1/4$ tsp Thickening Agent, page 109 (1 mL)
2 tbsp olive oil (25 mL)
1 tbsp ginger root (15 mL)
2 cups chopped broccoli florets (500 mL)
1 red pepper, sliced thinly
1 cup sliced canned water chestnuts (250 mL)
2 tbsp walnut halves (25 mL)

| *Yield:* 8 servings |
| 1 serving |
| 67.2 calories |
| 1.9 g protein |
| 4.7 g fat |
| *4.5 g carbs* |

In small bowl, combine orange juice, Worcestershire sauce, water and Thickening Agent, page 109. Set aside. In wok, heat olive oil and add ginger root. Stir-fry ginger root until it just begins to brown. Add broccoli florets and red pepper. Stir-fry 3 to 4 minutes until vegetables are tender-crisp. Stir in water chestnuts.

Whisk sauce and stir in along with walnuts. Stir-fry another minute. Serve.

Helpful Hints: This sauce does not darken the vegetables, as soy sauce has a tendency to do. The vegetables remain bright and colorful. Make twice the amount of sauce for larger quantities of vegetables.

This stir-fry sauce may be used with your own vegetable combinations. Be creative, and use those low-carb vegetables, which you happen to have on hand or the ones, which you happen to prefer.

SAUCES, JAMS, CHUTNEYS AND DRESSINGS

CHEESE SAUCE

A rich, thick sauce.

$^{1}/_{2}$ tsp dry mustard (2 mL)
$^{1}/_{4}$ tsp xanthan or guar gum (1 mL)
$^{1}/_{4}$ tsp salt (1 mL)
$^{1}/_{4}$ tsp white pepper (1 mL)
$^{1}/_{2}$ cup whipping cream (125 mL)
$^{1}/_{4}$ cup water (50 mL)
2 egg yolks, fork beaten
2 cups grated Cheddar cheese (500 mL)

Yield: $1^{1}/_{3}$ cups (325 mL)
2 tbsp (25 mL) per serving
98.1 calories
3.9 g protein
9.0 g fat
0.6 g carbs

In small nonstick saucepan, stir together dry mustard, xanthan gum, salt and white pepper. In small bowl, combine whipping cream and water. Gradually add whipping cream mixture to saucepan, stirring with whisk. Bring mixture to boil. Remove saucepan from heat. Add small amount of mixture to egg yolks; return to saucepan. Stir in cheese. Cook over very low heat until cheese melts. Do not boil. Remove from heat, if necessary.

Variation: **Thinner Cheese Sauce:** Use 1 cup (250 mL) cheddar cheese. (*0.5 g Carbs*)

Helpful Hint: Half-and-half cream may be used instead of cream. Refrigerate main recipe until cold. It makes a very good spreadable processed cheese.

SPLENDA KETCHUP

My youngest son, Jonathan, prefers using the spicy dressing below instead.

$5^{1}/_{2}$ oz tomato paste (156 mL)
$^{1}/_{2}$ cup water (125 mL)
$^{1}/_{3}$ cup SPLENDA® Granular (75 mL)
3 tbsp white vinegar (45 mL)
$^{1}/_{2}$ tsp onion salt (2 mL)
$^{1}/_{2}$ tsp salt (2 mL)
$^{1}/_{4}$ tsp garlic powder (1 mL)
$^{1}/_{8}$ tsp black pepper (0.5 mL)

Yield: $1^{1}/_{4}$ cups (300 mL)
1 tbsp (15 mL) per serving
8.7 calories
0.3 g protein
0.1 g fat
1.7 g carbs

In blender, combine tomato paste, water, SPLENDA® Granular, white vinegar, onion salt, salt, garlic powder and black pepper. Blend until smooth. (Or simply combine by whisking with wire whisk)

Variation: **Spicy California-Style Dressing:** Use $^{2}/_{3}$ cup (150 mL) vinegar, $^{1}/_{2}$ cup (125 mL) SPLENDA® Granular and $^{1}/_{4}$ cup (50 mL) water.
Yield: 28 tbsp, 1 tbsp (15 mL) per serving. (*1.6 g Carbs*)

Barbecue Sauce: Use Splenda Ketchup recipe above, and add 3 tbsp (45 mL) white vinegar, 1 tbsp (15 mL) Worcestershire sauce, 1 tsp (5 mL) onion salt, $^{1}/_{8}$ tsp (0.5 mL) Hickory Liquid Smoke (optional) and 4 drops Tabasco sauce.
Yield: $1^{1}/_{2}$ cups (375 mL), 1 tbsp (15 mL) per serving. (*1.5 g Carbs*)

TARTAR SAUCE

An easy, quick recipe. Serve with fish or seafood.

$^{1}/_{2}$ cup mayonnaise (125 mL)
$^{1}/_{4}$ cup sour cream (50 mL)
2 tbsp pickle relish (25 mL)
1 tbsp chopped chives, (optional) (15 mL)
1 tbsp lemon juice (15 mL)

Yield: $^{3}/_{4}$ cup (175 mL)
1 tbsp (15 mL) per serving
78.0 calories
0.3 g protein
8.1 g fat
1.3 g carbs

In small bowl, combine mayonnaise, sour cream, pickle relish, chives (if using) and lemon juice.

SPICY BARBECUE SAUCE

This began with my marinade, which my husband doctored one day to make a very tasty all-purpose barbecue sauce.

$^1/_2$ cup SPLENDA® Granular (125 mL)
$^1/_4$ cup soy sauce (50 mL)
2 tbsp red wine vinegar (25 mL)
2 tsp ground ginger (10 mL)
1 tsp garlic powder (5 mL)
$5^1/_2$ oz tomato paste (156 mL)
$^1/_2$ cup water (125 mL)
2 tbsp red wine vinegar (25 mL)
2 tsp seasoning salt (10 mL)
$^1/_2$ tsp salt (2 mL)
$^1/_4$ tsp liquid smoke, (optional) (1 mL)

Yield: $1^2/_3$ cups (400 mL)
1 tbsp (15 mL) per serving
8.9 calories
0.3 g protein
0.1 g fat
1.8 g carbs

In medium bowl, combine SPLENDA® Granular, soy sauce, red wine vinegar, ginger and garlic powder. Stir in tomato paste, water, red wine vinegar, seasoning salt, salt and liquid smoke (if using) with whisk. Store in an empty, clean ketchup or barbecue sauce bottle in refrigerator.

Variation: **Marinade:** In small bowl, combine SPLENDA® Granular, soy sauce, red wine vinegar, ginger and garlic powder.
Yield: $^1/_2$ cup (125 mL). (*22 g Total Carbs*)

Helpful Hints: Also see Barbecue Sauce, page 89. The above marinade is good for steak, veal, spareribs, pork or lamb. This marinade works very well as a Chinese stir-fry sauce. Use 2 tbsp (25 mL) or more chopped fresh ginger and 4 small cloves garlic, crushed, if desired, instead of ground ginger and garlic powder. Also see excellent marinade for chicken and pork, page 66 and a spicy marinade for lamb, page 45.

PEACH-NECTARINE JAM

Imagine buttering rye crisp bread, low-carb crackers or a slice of fresh low-carb bread and spreading a teaspoon (5 mL) of this delicious jam on it.

4 cups chopped ripe peaches (1 L)
2 cups chopped ripe nectarines (500 mL)
3 tbsp lemon juice (45 mL)
3 cups SPLENDA® Granular (750 mL)
1 package No Sugar Needed (49 g)
  Fruit Pectin (Bernardin)
1 cup water (250 mL)
$^1/_2$ tsp butter (2 mL)

Yield: $5^1/_2$ cups (1.375 L)
1 tsp (5 mL) per serving
4.1 calories
0.0 g protein
0.0 g fat
0.9 g carbs

In 9 x 13-inch (23 x 33 cm) glass baking dish, cover six 1-cup (250 mL) jars, lids and rings, a large long-handled spoon and a pair of tongs with boiling water to sterilize. In large kettle, combine peaches and nectarines. Stir in lemon juice. Add SPLENDA® Granular and stir in well. Stir in pectin gradually. Stir in water. Cook over medium high heat and as fruit softens, mash with potato masher (fruit will mostly still be in tiny chunks). Bring to full rolling boil, stirring constantly. Add butter. Boil 1 minute. Remove from heat. Skim off any foam with long-handled spoon.

Carefully pick up jar with tongs and tip water out. Place jar on saucer and spoon hot jam to within $^1/_2$-inch (1cm) of rim. Pick up lid with tongs; place on jar. Pick up ring with tongs and screw on jar tightly, using a clean dish towel. Allow to cool. Refrigerate up to 1 year or freeze for much longer storage.

Variations: **Strawberry Jam:** Use 8 cups (2 L) frozen unsweetened strawberries and 2 tbsp (25 mL) lemon juice. (***0.8 g Carbs***)

Strawberry-Rhubarb Jam: Use 6 cups (1.5 L) frozen unsweetened strawberries and 2 cups (500 mL) frozen unsweetened, chopped rhubarb, 1 cup (250 mL) water plus 3 tbsp (45 mL) extra water. Omit lemon juice. Chop rhubarb as it cooks and softens. (***0.7 g Carbs***)

Raspberry or Blueberry Jam: Use 8 cups (2 L) frozen unsweetened raspberries or blueberries, in addition to, 1 tbsp (15 mL) lemon juice. (**Raspberry:** ***0.7 g Carbs***) (**Blueberry:** ***0.8 g Carbs***)

Helpful Hint: If you're unable to find the particular pectin which is to be used with low-calorie sweeteners, then use light pectin and stir in 1 envelope (15 mL) gelatin softened in 2 tbsp (25 mL) water at end of cooking. Use jam fairly quickly after opening. It should last about 1 month in the refrigerator.

TOFU MAYONNAISE

This mayonnaise-type sauce has no raw eggs or sugar.

1 cup silken tofu, crumbled, (250 mL)
  (extra-firm)
$^1/_4$ cup olive oil (50 mL)
$^1/_4$ cup sour cream (50 mL)
1 small clove garlic, crushed
$1^1/_2$ tbsp SPLENDA® Granular (22 mL)
1 tbsp lemon juice (15 mL)
1 tbsp chopped chives, optional (15 mL)
2 tsp white vinegar (10 mL)
$1^1/_2$ tsp mustard powder (7 mL)
1 tsp dried parsley OR (5 mL)
  2 tsp fresh, finely chopped parsley (10 mL)
$^1/_2$ tsp salt (2 mL)
black pepper to taste, (optional)

> **Yield:** $1^1/_2$ cups (375 mL)
> 1 tbsp (15 mL) per serving
> 48.1 calories
> 2.1 g protein
> 4.2 g fat
> *0.9 g carbs*

Place tofu, olive oil, sour cream, garlic, SPLENDA® Granular, lemon juice, chives, white vinegar, mustard powder, dried parsley and salt in blender. Blend until smooth and creamy. Stir in black pepper, if using.

HOLLANDAISE SAUCE

This sauce is useful for serving over poached eggs, asparagus, green beans or fish.

3 egg yolks
$1^1/_2$ tbsp lemon juice (22 mL)
$^1/_2$ cup butter (125 mL)

> **Yield:** $^2/_3$ cup (150 mL)
> 2 tsp (10 mL) per serving
> 66.5 calories
> 0.6 g protein
> 7.2 g fat
> *0.2 g carbs*

In double boiler over hot water (not boiling), whisk eggs and lemon juice. Add one third of butter, whisk constantly until melted; repeat with remaining butter. Remove from heat as mixture thickens and is completely heated.

WHITE SAUCE

A versatile sauce. Serve hot on cooked vegetables, poultry, fish or seafood.

$^2/_3$ cup whipping cream (150 mL)
$^1/_3$ cup water (75 mL)
2 tbsp butter (25 mL)
$^3/_4$ tsp Thickening Agent, page 109, (3 mL)
  OR 2 tbsp soy flour (25 mL)
$^1/_2$ tsp salt (2 mL)
$^1/_8$ tsp white pepper (0.5 mL)
$^1/_8$ tsp paprika (0.5 mL)
2 egg yolks, fork beaten

> **Yield:** 1 cup (250 mL)
> 2 tbsp (25 mL) per serving
> 105.9 calories
> 1.2 g protein
> 11.1 g fat
> *0.7 g carbs*

In small bowl, combine whipping cream and water. Set aside. In double boiler or heavy saucepan, melt butter over low heat. Add soy flour (if using), salt, pepper and paprika to melted butter. Over low heat, stir together until smooth. Gradually stir in cream and water mixture, using a whisk. Use wooden spoon to incorporate any flour mixture around sides of saucepan. Increase heat to medium. If using Thickening Agent, page 109 instead of soy flour, sprinkle over sauce gradually and whisk in. Stir constantly with whisk, heating to scalding and until thickened.

Stir some of hot liquid into beaten egg yolks. Pour into saucepan and stir until sauce thickens. Do not boil. Remove from heat. If sauce develops lumps, which is unlikely, pour through sieve.

Variations: **Alfredo Sauce:** Prepare as above, however, use unsalted butter (and less salt) and add $^1/_4$ tsp (1 mL) garlic powder and $^1/_3$ cup (75 mL) Parmesan cheese. *Yield:* 1 cup (250 mL), 2 tbsp (25 mL) per serving. (*0.9 g Carbs*)

Mushroom Sauce: Add 1, 10 oz (284 mL) can sliced mushrooms, drained.
Yield: $1^1/_2$ cups (375 mL), 2 tbsp (25 mL) per serving. (*0.7 g Carbs*)

Bechamel Sauce: Prepare as above, but use $^1/_2$ cup (125 mL) whipping cream and $^1/_2$ cup (125 mL) chicken broth. Reduce salt to taste.
Yield: 1 cup (250 mL), 2 tbsp (25 mL) per serving. (*0.6 g Carbs*)

Cheese Sauce: Use $^1/_4$ tsp (1 mL) salt. Stir in 1 cup (250 mL) grated Cheddar Cheese. *Yield:* $1^1/_2$ cups (375 mL), 2 tbsp (25 mL) per serving. (*0.6 g Carbs*)

Helpful Hint: Half-and-half cream may be used instead of whipping cream for negligible carbohydrate differences. Reduce salt to $^1/_4$ tsp (1 mL), if desired. Add half amount of salt, taste, then add the remaining salt as desired.

BEEF GRAVY

A handy recipe.

2 tbsp pan drippings, (25 mL)
 and/or scrapings
1 cup ice cold water (250 mL)
$^3/_4$ tsp Thickening Agent, page 109 (3 mL)
$1^1/_2$ tsp instant beef stock mix (7 mL)
$^1/_8$ tsp cayenne pepper (0.5 mL)

> **Yield:** $1^1/_4$ cups (300 mL)
> 2 tbsp (25 mL) per serving
> 20.6 calories
> 0.0 g protein
> 2.3 g fat
> *0.0 g carbs*

Scrape pan drippings from skillet after draining excess liquid or oil. If there are only scrapings, add 2 tbsp (25 mL) water and scrape pan.

In small saucepan, combine pan drippings and remaining ice cold water. Skim excess fat. Add instant beef stock mix and cayenne pepper. Sprinkle Thickening Agent, page 109 over gravy. Bring to boil, stirring with whisk over medium-high heat. Sieve, if necessary.

Variations: **Lamb Gravy:** Use $1^1/_2$ tsp (7 mL) instant vegetable stock mix. Omit cayenne pepper. (*0.0 g Carbs*)

Chicken Gravy: Use $1^1/_2$ tsp (7 mL) instant chicken stock mix. Omit cayenne pepper. Use $^1/_4$ tsp (1 mL) paprika. (*0.0 g Carbs*)

Helpful Hints: Gravies are a wonderful way to add interest and delicious flavor to meat, as well as disguising the fact that a roast beef, for instance, may have dried out a bit too much in the oven.

CRANBERRY-PINEAPPLE CHUTNEY

This is a sweet, mildly spicy chutney, which goes well with poultry or pork. My sons love it!

2 cooking apples
2 tbsp seedless raisins (25 mL)
3 cups frozen cranberries (750 mL)
2 tbsp water (25 mL)
2, 14-oz cans crushed pineapple, (398 mL)
 in juice
1 cup SPLENDA® Granular (250 mL)
1 tsp ground ginger (5 mL)
$^1/_2$ tsp ground cinnamon (2 mL)
$^1/_4$ tsp ground allspice, (1 mL)
 (optional)

Yield: 5 cups (1.25 L)
1 tbsp (15 mL) per serving
10.2 calories
0.1 g protein
0.0 g fat
2.2 g carbs

In 9 x 13-inch glass dish, cover five 1-cup (250 mL) jars, lids, rings, large long-handled spoon and pair of tongs with boiling water to sterilize.

Peel, core and dice apples. Place apples in medium bowl; add water to cover. Microwave 2 minutes; drain and set aside. With kitchen scissors, snip raisins in half or smaller. In large kettle, cook cranberries and 2 tbsp (25 mL) water over medium heat until cranberries pop, about 15 minutes. Stir in crushed pineapple, diced apple, snipped raisins, SPLENDA® Granular, ginger, cinnamon and allspice, if using. Bring to full rolling boil, stirring constantly. Boil until apples are softened and chutney is thickened. Remove from heat and ladle chutney into hot, sterilized jars, sealing with lids and rings. Refrigerate when cool.

Helpful Hint: For extra precautions to ensure longest storage, boil in water bath canner 15 minutes, covering jars with at least 1-inch (2.5 cm) of water. I discovered as long as the jars are refrigerated, this step can generally be omitted.

HEALTHY BUTTER

This is a clever way to make butter healthier and higher in monounsaturated fats. The taste is superb, plus it spreads easily straight from the refrigerator. My friend, Mary Converse from Great Falls in Montana, gave me this idea.

1 lb butter, softened (0.454 kg)
$1^1/_3$ cups light-tasting olive oil (325 mL)

> **Yield:** 3 cups (750 mL)
> 1 tsp (5 mL) per serving
> 40.2 calories
> 0.0 g protein
> 4.5 g fat
> *0.0 g carbs*

In blender, process butter and olive oil until soft, creamy and smooth. Turn out into plastic bowl with lid and refrigerate until firm.

RASPBERRY VINAIGRETTE

A delightfully, different and colorful dressing.

1 cup frozen raspberries (250 mL)
  (unsweetened)
2 tbsp water (25 mL)
$^1/_2$ cup SPLENDA® Granular (125 mL)
$^1/_2$ cup light-tasting olive oil (125 mL)
$^1/_3$ cup cider vinegar (75 mL)
1 tsp crushed garlic (5 mL)

> **Yield:** 1 cup (250 mL)
> 1 tbsp (15 mL) per serving
> 67.4 calories
> 0.1 g protein
> 6.8 g fat
> *1.6 g carbs*

In small bowl, combine raspberries and water. Microwave on high power one minute; mash and sieve. In blender, blend pureed raspberries, SPLENDA® Granular, olive oil, cider vinegar and garlic. Refrigerate leftovers. To reuse, heat 30 seconds in microwave oven. Let stand at room temperature until serving time.

ZUCCHINI MARMALADE

This marmalade caused much mirth in our household, however, everyone ate it and said it tasted just like marmalade.

5 cups finely grated zucchini (1.25 L)
  (about 3 ½ medium zucchini)
2 unpeeled oranges, finely chopped
$^1/_2$ cup canned crushed pineapple, (125 mL)
  drained
$^1/_2$ cup pineapple juice (125 mL)
$^1/_2$ cup water (125 mL)
3 tbsp lemon juice (45 mL)
$^2/_3$ cup water (150 mL)
5$^1/_2$ cups SPLENDA® Granular (1.375 L)
1 package No Sugar Needed Fruit Pectin (49 g)
  (Bernardin)
$^1/_2$ tsp butter (2 mL)

Yield: 5 cups (1.25 L)
1 tsp (5 mL) per serving
4.2 calories
0.0 g protein
0.0 g fat
1.0 g carbs

In large canning pot, combine grated zucchini (use food processor), finely chopped oranges, crushed pineapple, pineapple juice, $^1/_2$ cup (125 mL) water and lemon juice. Over high heat while stirring, bring to boil. Simmer 10 minutes over medium-low heat, stirring occasionally. Add $^2/_3$ cup (150 mL) water, bring to boil and simmer, covered, over medium-low heat another 10 minutes (stirring occasionally) or until orange peel is soft. Add SPLENDA® Granular; stir well. Add pectin; stir well. Stir in butter.

Bring to full rolling boil. Boil 1 minute. Spoon jam into hot, sterilized jars and seal.

Helpful Hint: The color of this marmalade is light green. If you can get past that, you'll enjoy this very much.

MEDIUM-HOT SALSA

An easy-to-make Salsa, without sugar added. Excellent!

2 lbs ripe plum tomatoes (0.9 kg)
$^1/_2$ cup finely chopped onion (125 mL)
2 garlic cloves, crushed
$^1/_3$ cup apple cider vinegar (75 mL)
3 tbsp tomato paste (45 mL)
1 tbsp SPLENDA® Granular (15 mL)
2 tsp dried oregano (10 mL)
$^3/_4$ tsp salt (3 mL)
2 drops Tabasco Sauce
3 jalapeno chilies, chopped very finely
with some seeds

> **Yield:** 3 cups (750 mL)
> 1 tbsp (15 mL) per serving
> 6.3 calories
> 0.2 g protein
> 0.1 g fat
> *1.1 g carbs*

Coarsely chop tomatoes and place in large canning pot along with onion, garlic, apple cider vinegar, tomato paste, SPLENDA® Granular, oregano, salt and Tabasco sauce. Over medium-high heat, bring to boil. Boil hard 3 minutes, stirring occasionally. Reduce heat to medium-low. Simmer 10 minutes. Add jalapeno chilies and continue cooking 20 minutes, stirring occasionally. Fill 1, 2-cup (500 mL) sterilized glass jar and 1, 1-cup (250 mL) sterilized glass jar.

Helpful Hints: This Salsa should keep one month in refrigerator and longer in the freezer. For longer storage, process in boiling water bath (on rack in canning pot) 25 minutes. If this method is chosen, double this recipe to make the effort worthwhile. Increase or decrease the heat in this Salsa, by increasing or decreasing the number of jalapeno chilies by one, or increase heat by adding more Tabasco Sauce.

Apparently, studies have shown that Salsa will boost your metabolism significantly, as will drinking 8 glasses of ice cold water a day!

CUCUMBER-AND-PINEAPPLE PICKLE

A lovely flavor and texture blend of cucumber, onion and pineapple. Serve alongside fancy cheeses and low-carb crackers or low-carb bread.

1 x 10-inch (25 cm) cucumber
1 large onion, finely cubed
1 cup canned pineapple chunks, (250 mL)
  finely cubed
1 cup SPLENDA® Granular (250 mL)
1 cup red wine vinegar (250 mL)
2 tsp salt (10 mL)
1 tsp curry powder (5 mL)
1 tsp ground turmeric (5 mL)
$^3/_4$ tsp Thickening Agent, page 109 (3 mL)

Yield: $3^1/_2$ cups (875 mL)
1 tbsp (15 mL) per serving
7.3 calories
0.1 g protein
0.0 g fat
1.8 g carbs

Halve cucumber, remove seeds and cut up cucumber into small cubes. Place in large, heavy-bottomed saucepan, along with onion, pineapple, SPLENDA® Granular, red wine vinegar, salt, curry powder and turmeric. Bring to boil over high heat, stirring. Reduce heat to medium. Simmer 15 minutes, stirring occasionally. Sprinkle Thickening Agent, page 109 over and stir into cucumber-and-pineapple pickle; simmer 3 minutes longer. Spoon into hot, sterilized jars.

BUTTERMILK-PARMESAN DRESSING

A delicious dressing for garden salads.

$^3/_4$ cup sour cream (175 mL)
$^2/_3$ cup mayonnaise (150 mL)
$^2/_3$ cup buttermilk (150 mL)
$^1/_4$ cup grated Parmesan cheese (50 mL)
2 tbsp white vinegar (25 mL)
1 tbsp light-tasting olive oil (15 mL)
$1^1/_2$ tsp ground black pepper (7 mL)
1 tsp dried parsley, OR (5 mL)
 2 tbsp fresh parsley (25 mL)
1 tsp lemon juice (5 mL)
$^1/_2$ tsp dry mustard powder (2 mL)
$^1/_4$ tsp onion salt (1 mL)
$^1/_4$ tsp garlic powder (1 mL)

> **Yield:** $2^1/_4$ cups (550 mL)
> 2 tbsp (25 mL) per serving
> 92.7 calories
> 1.2 g protein
> 9.2 g fat
> *1.0 g carbs*

In medium bowl, combine sour cream, mayonnaise, buttermilk, Parmesan cheese, white vinegar, olive oil, black pepper, dried or fresh parsley, lemon juice, dry mustard powder, onion salt and garlic powder. Stir well to combine.

Variation: **Buttermilk-Feta Dressing:** Replace Parmesan cheese with crumbled Feta cheese. (*1.1 g Carbs*)

THOUSAND ISLAND DRESSING

A classic - it is fun to serve one's own version.

1 cup mayonnaise (250 mL)
2 tbsp tomato paste (25 mL)
2 tbsp minced green pepper (25 mL)
1 tsp grated onion (5 mL)
1 tsp dried parsley (5 mL)
$^1/_8$ tsp hot chili powder (0.5 mL)

> **Yield:** $1^1/_3$ cups (325 mL)
> 1 tbsp (15 mL) per serving
> 87.4 calories
> 0.2 g protein
> 8.4 g fat
> *0.4 g carbs*

In medium bowl, combine mayonnaise, tomato paste, green pepper, onion, parsley and hot chili powder.

Russian Dressing: Use 1 cup (250 mL) mayonnaise, 3 tbsp (45 mL) tomato paste, 1 tsp (5 mL) chopped chives or minced onion and $^1/_4$ tsp (1 mL) hot chili powder. ***Yield:*** 1 cup (250 mL) dressing. (*0.5 g Carbs*)

CRANBERRY SAUCE

This is an excellent sauce as an accompaniment to turkey or chicken dinners.

$1^1/_2$ cups SPLENDA® Granular (375 mL)
$1^1/_4$ cups water (300 mL)
1 pkg frozen cranberries (600 g)

Yield: $3^2/_3$ cups (900 mL)
1 tbsp (15 mL) per serving
7.6 calories
0.0 g protein
0.0 g fat
1.5 g carbs

In medium saucepan, dissolve SPLENDA® Granular in water; add cranberries. Over medium heat, bring to boil and cook until cranberries pop (about 20 minutes). Lower heat and simmer 10 minutes more. Allow to cool. Cover and refrigerate.

Variations: **Smooth Cranberry Sauce:** Cook as above, except omit simmering step. Stir 2 tsp (10 mL) unflavored gelatin softened in 2 tbsp (25 mL) water into sauce. Pour into strainer over bowl. Mash cranberries with back of spoon, frequently scraping outside of strainer until no pulp is left. Stir contents of bowl. Pour into serving container. Cover and cool completely at room temperature. Refrigerate. *Yield:* 3 cups (750 mL), 1 tbsp (15 mL) per serving. (*1.6 g Carbs*)

Jellied Cranberry Sauce: Prepare as for Smooth Cranberry Sauce above. In small bowl, combine 2 tbsp (25 mL) unflavored gelatin and $^1/_4$ cup (50 mL) water. Microwave 40 seconds on high power to dissolve. Stir into sauce. Refrigerate until set.
Yield: 3 cups (750 mL), 1 tbsp (15 mL) per serving. (*1.6 g Carbs*)

Cranberry Fruit Spread: As for Smooth Cranberry Sauce above. Use as fruit spread on low-carb toast or crackers.
Yield: $3^1/_4$ cups (800 mL), 1 tsp (5 mL) per serving. (*0.5 g Carbs*)

BLUEBERRY JELLY JAM

Delicious! Try other berries, such as raspberries, Saskatoon berries or strawberries.

3 lb frozen blueberries (1.4 kg)
2 cups water (500 mL)
1 pkg No Sugar Needed Fruit Pectin (49 g)
1 cup SPLENDA® Granular (250 mL)

Yield: 4 cups (1 L)
1 tsp (5 mL) per serving
2.3 calories
0.0 g protein
0.0 g fat
0.6 g carbs

In large kettle, combine blueberries and water. Bring to boil and boil gently 10 minutes. Drip through cheesecloth for several hours. In large kettle, pour 4 cups (1 L) blueberry juice. Gradually stir in pectin. Stir in SPLENDA® Granular. Bring to full rolling boil and boil hard 1 minute. Remove from heat, skim any foam and spoon hot jelly into sterilized jars.

Helpful Hint: Make sure you have 4 cups (1 L) of juice. If necessary, pour extra hot water over fruit as it drips through cheesecloth. With this particular jam, I squeeze the bag (as clarity is not an issue here), and I usually end up with just over 4 cups (1 L) blueberry juice.

MICROWAVE PEACH CHUTNEY

This chutney is a snap to make in the microwave oven.

4 peaches, peeled and chopped
¼ cup very finely chopped onion (50 mL)
1 tbsp water (15 mL)
½ cup SPLENDA® Granular (125 mL)
¼ cup red wine vinegar (50 mL)
2 tsp soy sauce (10 mL)
¼ tsp salt (1 mL)
⅛ tsp Tabasco Sauce (0.5 mL)

Yield: 1 cup (250 mL)
2 tsp (10 mL) per serving
9.2 calories
0.1 g protein
0.0 g fat
2.1 g carbs

Place peaches, onion and water in large, deep casserole dish. Microwave covered on high power 4 minutes. Mash fruit with potato masher. Microwave uncovered on high power 6 minutes. Mash again. Add SPLENDA® Granular, red wine vinegar, soy sauce, salt and Tabasco Sauce. Uncover and cook 10 minutes longer until fairly thick. Pour into sterilized 1 cup (250 mL) glass jar. Refrigerate.

BREADS AND OTHER BAKING

PANCAKES

Lovely, tender little pancakes. I like these with strawberries and whipped cream, however, you may prefer Maple Syrup, page 172.

1 cup ricotta cheese (250 mL)
4 eggs
3 tbsp soy flour, OR (45 mL)
 spelt flour
1 tbsp spelt, OR all-purpose flour (15 mL)
1 tbsp SPLENDA® Granular (15 mL)
$^1/_4$ tsp salt (1 mL)
3 tbsp olive oil (45 mL)

Yield: 16 servings
1 pancake
61.6 calories
3.8 g protein
4.6 g fat
1.5 g carbs

In blender, blend ricotta cheese until smooth. Add eggs, soy or spelt flour, spelt or all-purpose flour, SPLENDA® Granular and salt; blend. Drop mixture by 2 tbsp (25 mL) onto oiled, hot, nonstick frying pan or electric frying pan. Do 4 at a time. When bubbles form, flip to cook topside. Scrape pan with lifter to make sure all batter is removed from pan, before flipping pancake.

Helpful Hints: I use $^1/_4$ cup (50 mL) measure and pour half mixture out onto pan for each pancake. If using a previously opened tub of ricotta cheese, drain any liquid first. These uniform pancakes may be served as appetizers with a variety of savory toppings. Pancakes with spelt flour instead of soy flour: (*2.0 g Carbs*).

PIZZA CRUSTS

A lovely crust recipe (enough for 2 pizzas), which rolls out easily.

7 ½ fluid oz warm water (235 mL)
  (1 tbsp (15 mL) shy of 1 cup (250 mL))
1¼ cups whole wheat (300 mL)
  pastry flour, OR whole spelt flour
¾ cup soy flour (175 mL)
½ cup ground almonds (125 mL)
¼ cup unflavored whey powder (50 mL)
2 tbsp SPLENDA® Granular (25 mL)
2 tbsp butter (25 mL)
4 tsp vital wheat gluten (20 mL)
4 tsp skim milk powder (20 mL)
1 tbsp bread machine yeast (15 mL)
1 tsp granulated sugar (5 mL)
1 tsp salt (5 mL)

Yield: 24 servings
1 serving
51.8 calories
2.9 g protein
2.3. g fat
5.2 g carbs

In bread machine pan, place water (warmed in microwave oven 1 minute 40 seconds), whole wheat pastry flour or whole spelt flour, soy flour, ground almonds, unflavored whey powder, SPLENDA® Granular, butter, vital wheat gluten, skim milk powder, yeast, sugar and salt. Program bread machine to knead and first rise (pizza dough setting). When ready, remove dough and divide in half. On floured surface (use soy protein isolate, if desired), roll each half to fit greased 12-inch (30 cm) pizza pans. Use hard, flat spatula or piece of stiff, thin cardboard to lift dough onto pizza pan. Roll out further using small rolling pin or cylindrical-shaped object.

Cover with sauce, toppings and grated cheese (see examples in this book). Bake at 375°F (190°C) 20 to 25 minutes. For crispier crust, use pizza pan with holes in bottom, or place on lowest rung in oven and bake normal time, then cover loosely with foil and bake another 10 minutes.

Variation: Traditional Method: This recipe may be made without a bread machine. See Oat Bran Bread, page 118. Use 3 tbsp (45 mL) less water and add during the mixing stage as required. One rising required.

WHEY PIZZA CRUSTS

Thanks go to my husband, Ian, for this recipe! Makes 2 large pizzas.

Almond Whey Bake Mix #1:
$1^1/_3$ cups ground almonds (325 mL)
$^3/_4$ cup whey protein powder (175 mL)
  (natural)
$^1/_2$ cup unbleached spelt, OR (125 mL)
  all-purpose flour
1 tbsp vital wheat gluten (15 mL)

Pizza Crusts:
$^3/_4$ cup water, LESS 1 tbsp (160 mL)
2 tbsp olive oil (25 mL)
$1^1/_2$ cups Almond Whey Bake Mix #1 (375 mL)
$^2/_3$ cup 75% vital wheat gluten (150 mL)
$^1/_2$ cup wheat bran (125 mL)
$^1/_3$ cup natural whey protein powder (75 mL)
2 tbsp SPLENDA® Granular (25 mL)
1 tbsp spelt flour (15 mL)
1 tbsp sugar (15 mL)
1 tbsp skim milk powder (15 mL)
1 tbsp bread machine yeast (15 mL)
1 tsp salt (5 mL)

Yield: 24 servings
1 serving
63.2 calories
6.1 g protein
3.1 g fat
2.6 g carbs

Almond Whey Bake Mix #1: In medium bowl, combine almonds, whey protein powder, spelt or all-purpose flour and vital wheat gluten. Store in airtight container at room temperature and use as required.
Yield: 3 cups (750 mL), $^1/_4$ cup (50 mL) per serving. (**4.7 g Carbs**)

Pizza Crusts: In bread machine pan, place water (warmed in microwave oven 1 minute 30 seconds), olive oil, Almond Whey Bake Mix #1, vital wheat gluten (75% not 80% to reduce elasticity), wheat bran, natural whey protein powder, SPLENDA® Granular, spelt flour, sugar, skim milk powder, yeast and salt. Program bread machine to pizza dough setting, or knead and first rise. When ready, remove dough and divide in half. On lightly floured surface, roll out each ball as much as possible. Cover with towel and allow to rest 10 to 20 minutes between rolling. Place on 2 greased 12-inch (30 cm) pizza pans. Roll out dough to fit pan, using small rolling pin or small cylindrical object. Cover with pizza sauce, toppings and grated cheese. Bake on lowest oven rack at 375°F (190°C) 20 to 25 minutes or until browned.

Helpful Hints: My small rolling pin I acquired through the Pampered Chef (similar to Tupperware-type parties). It has 2 dissimilar sized rolling pins on either end of a rod.

WHEY BAKE MIX

An alternative bake mix, useful in many of the recipes in this book.

Almond Whey Bake Mix #2:
$1^1/_3$ cups ground almonds (325 mL)
$^3/_4$ cup spelt flour (175 mL)
$^1/_2$ cup whey protein powder, (125 mL)
 (natural)
$^1/_4$ cup 80% vital wheat gluten (50 mL)

> **Yield:** 3 cups (750 mL)
> $^1/_3$ cup (75 mL) serving
> 164.9 calories
> 11.2 g protein
> 9.4 g fat
> *8.4 g carbs*

In medium bowl, combine almonds, spelt flour, natural whey protein powder and vital wheat gluten. Stir well with wooden spoon until well mixed. Store in airtight container at room temperature and use as required.

Variations: **Walnut Whey Bake Mix:** Use walnuts instead of almonds. (*8.5 g Carbs*)

Hazelnut Whey Bake Mix: Use hazelnuts instead of almonds. (*9.1 g Carbs*)

Pecan Whey Bake Mix: Use pecans instead of almonds. (*9.1 g Carbs*)

Helpful Hint: This bake mix produces baked goods that taste very similar to what we are used to, however, they're mostly less moist than those made with the soy bake mix.

Typically, less liquid is required with this bake mix than with the soy bake mix, however, if you find the baked product a little dry, cautiously adjust the moisture next time around, by using a little more liquid or one extra small egg.

Whole spelt flour or whole wheat flour or whole wheat pastry flour (quite a bit lower in carbs than any of the other options!) may be substituted for spelt flour, however, only in some applications. Breads or muffins, for instance, would be a good application, whereas cakes would not. I have not tested the recipes using these options, however, I cannot see any reason why they wouldn't work just as well.

BAKE MIX

Using the basic techniques outlined in my recipes, experiment with other nuts for negligible carbohydrate differences (except for cashews), to come up with your own unique recipes.

Almond Bake Mix:
*$1^1/_3$ cups blanched almonds, (325 mL) ground
$^1/_2$ cup unbleached spelt, OR (125 mL) all-purpose flour
$^1/_2$ cup soy flour (125 mL)
1 tbsp vital wheat gluten (15 mL)

> **Yield:** $2^2/_3$ cups, (650 mL)
> $^1/_3$ cup (75 mL) per serving
> 159.2 calories
> 7.9 g protein
> 10.6 g fat
> **8.7 g carbs**

In medium bowl, stir to combine ground almonds, spelt or all-purpose flour, soy flour and vital wheat gluten. Blend in small batches in food processor food mill, coffee grinder or blender until fine.

If using walnuts or any nuts that produce a lumpy bake mix, do the following extra step:

Sift over medium bowl. Any mixture that does not sift through, grind or blend again and stir into sifted product. Store in airtight container at room temperature and use as required.

Variations: Walnut Bake Mix: Use walnuts instead of almonds. (**8.8 g Carbs**)

Hazelnut Bake Mix: Use hazelnuts instead of almonds. (**9.4 g Carbs**)

Pecan Bake Mix: Use pecans instead of almonds. (**9.5 g Carbs**)

Helpful Hints: *For convenience, purchased ground almonds may be used instead of grinding your own, in which case, use an extra 2 tbsp (25 mL) ground almonds. One tbsp (15 mL) blanched almonds, ground, produces about 1.3 tbsp (20 mL) ground almonds which accounts for the yield shown above. Whole spelt flour, whole wheat flour, or whole wheat pastry flour may be used for bread recipes, muffins, loaves, etc., if desired. See Helpful Hints, page 106.

ULTIMATE BAKE MIX

This bake mix may be substituted cup-for-cup for all-purpose white wheat flour. It may be used to reduce carbohydrates in the recipes in my books, Splendid Desserts and More Splendid Desserts by 50 to 65%.

Soy Ultimate Bake Mix:
1 cup ground almonds (250 mL)
$^2/_3$ cup spelt or all-purpose flour (150 mL)
$^2/_3$ cup soy flour (150 mL)
$^1/_4$ cup 80% vital wheat gluten (50 mL)

Yield: $2^3/_4$ cups (675 mL)
$^1/_4$ cup (50 mL) per serving
115.4 calories
7.7 g protein
6.1 g fat
8.0 g carbs

In medium bowl, combine almonds, spelt flour, soy flour and vital wheat gluten. Stir with wooden spoon to mix very well.

Variations: **Self-Raising Soy Ultimate Bake Mix/Whey Ultimate Bake Mix:** To convert Ultimate Bake Mix into a substitute for self-raising cake and pastry flour, use this recipe for equally good results: 1 cup (250 mL) Ultimate Bake Mix, $1^1/_2$ tsp (7 mL) baking powder, $^1/_3$ tsp (1.5 mL) salt. Therefore, for instance, when substituting Ultimate Bake Mix for $2^1/_2$ cups (625 mL) self-raising cake and pastry flour, use $2^1/_2$ cups (625 mL) Ultimate Bake Mix, $3^3/_4$ tsp (19 mL) baking powder and $^3/_4$ tsp (3 mL) salt to convert to self-raising.

Whey Ultimate Bake Mix (soy-free): Combine 1 cup (250 mL) ground almonds, 1 cup (250 mL) spelt or all-purpose flour, $^2/_3$ cup (150 mL) natural whey protein powder and 6 tbsp (90 mL) vital wheat gluten.
Yield: 3 cups (750 mL), $^1/_4$ cup (50 mL) per serving. (*7.9 g Carbs*)

Helpful Hints: When substituting Ultimate Bake Mix for all-purpose flour or cake and pastry flour in cake, loaf and muffin recipes, typically use about $^1/_4$ cup (50 mL) or up to $^1/_2$ cup (125 mL) less liquid. Add liquid cautiously! If there is liquid added to a cookie recipe, add gradually, until correct cookie dough consistency is achieved. If a dry, powdery texture occurs in your baked cookies, replace some of the butter with whipping cream. Do not use in cream pies or to thicken sauces. Recipes made with these bake mixes are usually quite successful, however, cakes do not always rise as high as with white flour. Depending on the application, whole spelt flour or whole wheat flour may be used instead. You will find practically endless ideas for using this bake mix in your own recipes.

Look for more recipes using the Ultimate Bake Mix in follow-up cookbooks. Its purpose is to make this WOL really livable as some of our old favorite recipes become possible once again with an easy, simple substitution for white flour.

THICKENING AGENT

This is useful to use instead of pure cornstarch or flour in thickening sauces.

$8^1/_2$ tsp xanthan gum (42 mL)
$4^1/_2$ tsp guar gum (22 mL)
$2^1/_4$ tsp corn starch (11 mL)

> *Yield:* $^1/_3$ cup (75 mL)
> 1 tsp (5 mL) per serving
> 1.5 calories
> 0.0 g protein
> 0.0 g fat
> *0.4 g carbs*

In small plastic container with lid, combine xanthan gum, guar gum and cornstarch; seal. Sprinkle over warm sauces and cook until thickened.

Helpful Hint: Substitute thickening agent for cornstarch, using $^1/_4$ as much and substitute Thickening Agent for flour, using $^1/_8$ as much to achieve approximately the same results.

This Thickening Agent must be used in small quantities to avoid a "gummy" texture. For instance, do not use in quantities greater than $^1/_2$ tsp (2 mL) for thickening sauces for stir-fried vegetables. You may use only guar gum or only xanthan gum, if one or the other is not available.

"GRANOLA"

Delicious topping for yogurt – nicer than granola and healthier! Flax seeds are nature's Tomoxifen (anti-cancer drug), latest studies reveal.

$1^1/_4$ cups SPLENDA® Granular (300 mL)
1 cup unsweetened coconut (250 mL)
$^3/_4$ cup whole roasted almonds, (175 mL)
   finely chopped
$^2/_3$ cup flax seeds, ground (150 mL)
$^1/_8$ tsp salt (0.5 mL)
$^1/_3$ cup Healthy Butter, page 96 (75 mL)
   melted

> *Yield:* 4 cups (1 L)
> 2 tbsp (25 mL) per serving
> 76.1 calories
> 1.3 g protein
> 6.6 g fat
> *2.1 g carbs*

In large bowl, combine SPLENDA® Granular, coconut, almonds, flax seeds and salt. Stir in Healthy Butter, page 96.

Spread on two greased cookie sheets. Spray "granola" with nonstick cooking spray. Bake in 300°F (150°C) oven 25 to 30 minutes. Granola on top oven rack may be baked an extra 5 minutes.

BRAN BREAD MACHINE BREAD

This bread rises high and is airy and light when fresh, becoming more dense when refrigerated.

$1^1/_4$ cups water (300 mL)
2 tbsp olive oil (25 mL)
1 cup Almond Bake Mix, (250 mL)
  page 107, OR
  *Almond Whey Bake Mix #2, page 106
1 cup 80% vital wheat gluten (250 mL)
$^1/_2$ cup wheat bran (125 mL)
$^1/_3$ cup soy, OR spelt flour (75 mL)
2 tbsp SPLENDA® Granular (25 mL)
1 tbsp granulated sugar (15 mL)
1 tbsp skim milk powder (15 mL)
1 tbsp bread machine yeast (15 mL)
1 tsp salt (5 mL)

Yield: 18 large slices
1 slice
79.4 calories
7.8 g protein
3.6 g fat
4.2 g carbs

In cereal bowl, heat water in microwave oven 1 minute and 40 seconds. In bread pan, place water, olive oil, Almond Bake Mix, page 107 or Almond Whey Bake Mix #2, page 106, vital wheat gluten, wheat bran, soy or spelt flour, SPLENDA® Granular, sugar, skim milk powder, yeast and salt. Program bread machine to Bread Rapid setting and color of bread to medium. Bake bread, removing 30 to 35 minutes before end of baking time or when golden brown in color.

Variations: **Croutons:** Cut loaf into 9 thick slices and into $^3/_4$-inch (2 cm) cubes (25 cubes per slice). In large skillet, melt $^1/_2$ cup (125 mL) butter and stir in $^1/_4$ cup (50 mL) Parmesan cheese. Add bread cubes and stir until coated. Spread cubes on cookie sheet. Bake in 300°F (150°C) oven 10 minutes. Stir. Bake 5 minutes more, or until crisp. ***Yield:*** 5 croutons per serving. (***1.7 g Carbs***)

Low-Carb Breadcrumbs: Toast 1 slice of bread. Blend in blender with salt and pepper to taste. Freeze any leftover breadcrumbs in sealed plastic bag. ***Yield:*** $^2/_3$ cup (150 mL). (***4.2 g Carbs***)

Loaf Pan Bread: See Flax Bread Machine Bread, page 115 .
Yield: 24 slices. **Soy Option:** (***3.2 g Carbs***) **Whey Option:** (***3.9 g Carbs***)

Helpful Hints: *Use 1 cup (250 mL) water, plus 1 tbsp (15 mL) and spelt flour instead of soy flour option in recipe. This Bread made with whey protein does not rise quite as high, (bigger than medium-sized), however, refrigerate and cut into same number of slices. The taste is wonderful – similar to 60% whole wheat! (***4.9 g Carbs***) In addition, if you refrigerate bread made with principal recipe, it will divide into 24 slices. (***3.2 g Carbs***)

CHEESE BREAD

This is an attractive-looking bread.

*Bran Bread Machine Bread, page 110
1 cup grated Cheddar cheese, (250 mL)
  divided
nonstick cooking spray

Yield: 24 slices
1 slice
71.3 calories
6.6 g protein
3.7 g fat
3.2 g carbs

Follow instructions for Bran Bread Machine Bread, page 110 for loading bread pan. Program bread machine to pizza dough setting or to knead and one rise. When cycle is done, remove bread dough. Knead briefly on lightly floured surface. Fashion with hands into 12-inch (30 cm) roll, 3-inches (8 cm) wide. Using a long, sharp, serrated bread knife, cut a $1/2$-inch (1 cm) deep slit vertically down center of loaf. Fill with half amount Cheddar cheese.

Place loaf on greased cookie sheet. Spray loaf with nonstick cooking spray. Cover loosely with foil. Allow bread to double in size in 200°F (93°C) preheated oven, which has been switched off. Remove, keeping covered and away from drafts. Heat oven to 350°F (180°C). Sprinkle remaining cheese over loaf and bake on middle shelf 20 minutes. Cover loosely with foil and bake 5 minutes more.

Variation: ****Soy-free Cheese Bread:*** *(A milder tasting bread)* Use Almond Whey Bake Mix #2, page 106 and $1/3$ cup (75 mL) spelt flour instead of soy flour. Use 1 cup (250 mL) water plus 1 tbsp (15 mL). (***3.9 g Carbs***)

Oat Bran Cheese Bread: *(Denser than principal recipe, however, it makes extraordinarily good toast)* Use Oat Bran Bread, page 118. Use bread machine yeast and do not place yeast in direct contact with water. Follow directions as for Cheese Bread above.

GARLIC BREAD

Great for barbecues! Most of the work is done in the bread machine.

*Bran Bread Machine Bread, page 110
1 tbsp Parmesan Cheese, (15 mL)
 (optional)
Garlic Butter:
1 cup butter, softened (250 mL)
2 to 4 garlic cloves, crushed

Yield: 10 slices per loaf
1 slice, 1-inch (2.5 cm) thick
153.2 calories
7.1 g protein
12.5 g fat
3.8 g carbs

Follow instructions for Bread Machine Bread, page 110 for loading bread pan. Program bread machine to pizza dough setting or to knead and one rise. When cycle is done, remove bread dough. On floured surface, punch down dough. On greased cookie sheet, form two, 9-inch (23 cm) or one 18-inch (45 cm) French loaf shape. Spray loaves with nonstick cooking spray. Cover loosely with foil.

Place in preheated 200°F (93°C) oven, which has been switched off. Allow to rise 30 minutes or until doubled in size. Remove, keeping covered and away from drafts. Spray loaves with nonstick cooking spray. Sprinkle with Parmesan cheese, if using. Bake bread in 375°F (190°C) oven 15 to 20 minutes or until golden brown.

Remove bread. Slice bread horizontally in half (like a hot dog bun), however, not right through. Open loaves, place face down on wire rack and allow to cool.

Garlic Butter: Combine butter and garlic cloves. Spread cool loaf halves inside with garlic butter. Cover each loaf completely in foil. Bake in 400°F (200°C) oven 10 minutes. Cut into 10 thick slices per loaf. Serve immediately.

Variation: French Toast: Omit garlic butter. Do not cut loaves open. Slice French loaves into 15 slices per loaf. In small bowl beat together 2 extra-large eggs, $^2/_3$ cup (150 mL) half-and-half cream, 1 tbsp (15 mL) SPLENDA® Granular and $^1/_4$ tsp (1 mL) vanilla extract. Serve with Maple Syrup, page 172, if desired. **Yield:** 30 slices, 1 slice per serving. (**2.8 g Carbs**, without Syrup)

*Soy-free Garlic Bread:** Use Almond Whey Bake Mix #2, page 106 and $^1/_3$ cup (75 mL) spelt flour instead of soy flour. Use 1 cup (250 mL) water plus 1 tbsp (15 mL). (**4.5 g Carbs**)

Helpful Hint: The garlic bread may be made one or two days before and then baked just before serving.

FOCACCIA

This is a tasty Italian bread, which can have many different toppings.

*Bran Bread Machine Bread, page 110
$^1/_4$ cup Parmesan cheese (50 mL)
1 tsp seasoned herb medley (5 mL)
$^1/_2$ tsp parsley (2 mL)
4 tbsp olive oil (50 mL)

Yield: 24 slices
1 slice
59.5 calories
5.9 g protein
2.7 g fat
3.2 g carbs

Follow instructions for Bread Machine Bread, page 110 for loading bread pan. Program bread machine to pizza dough setting or to knead and one rise. When cycle is done, remove bread dough. Knead briefly on lightly floured surface. Form into two 8-inch (20 cm) circles. Place on cookie sheet and spray circles with nonstick cooking spray. Cover loosely with foil.

Place in preheated 200°F (93°C) oven, which has been switched off. Allow to rise 30 minutes or until doubled in size. Remove, keeping covered and away from drafts. Without piercing dough, make fairly deep dimples all over with fingertips. Sprinkle each bread with 1 tbsp (15 mL) olive oil. In small bowl, combine Parmesan cheese, seasoned herb medley and parsley. Sprinkle half Parmesan mixture over both breads.

Bake on center rack in 400°F (200°C) oven 10 to 15 minutes. Remove and sprinkle with remaining olive oil and Parmesan cheese mixture.

***Variation:* *Soy-free Focaccia:** Use Almond Whey Bake Mix #2, page 106 and $^1/_3$ cup (75 mL) spelt flour instead of soy flour. Use 1 cup (250 mL) water plus 1 tbsp (15 mL). (*3.7 g Carbs*)

HAMBURGER BUNS

Warm, homemade crusty buns! These are large buns, suitable for hamburgers or dinner rolls.

$1^1/_8$ cups (9 fl oz) water (280 mL)
2 tbsp olive oil (25 mL)
1 cup Almond Bake Mix, (250 mL)
  page 107, OR
 *Almond Whey Bake Mix #2, page 106
1 cup 80% vital wheat gluten (250 mL)
$^1/_2$ cup wheat bran (125 mL)
$^1/_3$ cup soy, OR spelt flour (75 mL)
2 tbsp SPLENDA® Granular (25 mL)
1 tbsp granulated sugar (15 mL)
1 tbsp skim milk powder (15 mL)
1 tbsp bread machine yeast (15 mL)
1 tsp salt (5 mL)

Yield: 10 Hamburger Buns
1 hamburger bun
142.9 calories
14.1g protein
6.5 g fat
7.5 g carbs

In cereal bowl, heat water in microwave oven 1 minute and 40 seconds. In bread pan, place water, olive oil, Almond Bake Mix, page 107 or Almond Whey Bake Mix #2, page 106, vital wheat gluten, wheat bran, soy or spelt flour, SPLENDA® Granular, sugar, skim milk powder, yeast and salt. Set bread machine to pizza dough setting or to knead and one rise. When cycle is done, remove bread dough. Knead briefly on lightly floured surface. Form into 10 hamburger buns.

Place on greased pizza pan. Spray buns with nonstick cooking spray. Cover loosely with foil and place in 200°F (93°C) preheated oven, which has been switched off. Allow buns to double in size, about 40 minutes. Remove foil, leave buns inside, heat oven to 350°F (180°C) and set timer (from the start of heating oven) for 20 to 25 minutes or until buns are browned.

Variation: ****Soy-Free Hamburger Buns:*** *(Great Taste!)* Use Almond Whey Bake Mix #2 and spelt flour instead of soy flour in above recipe. Also, use 1 cup (250 mL) water, plus 1 tbsp (15 mL). ***Yield:*** 9 hamburger buns. (***9.8 g Carbs***)

Low-Carb Hamburger Buns are $^1/_4$ the carbohydrates of a regular white bun:

Usable Carbs

Regular White Bun	30.4 g
Low-Carb Bun	7.5 g
	22.9 g *less*

FLAX BREAD MACHINE BREAD

This is a delicious, large bread – like a health bread from a special bakery.

$1^1/_4$ cups water (300 mL)
2 tbsp olive oil (25 mL)
1 cup Almond Bake Mix (250 mL)
  page 107, OR
  *Almond Whey Bake Mix #2, page 106
1 cup 80% vital wheat gluten (250 mL)
$^1/_3$ cup flax seeds, ground (75 mL)
$^1/_3$ cup soy flour, OR (75 mL)
  spelt flour
2 tbsp SPLENDA® Granular (25 mL)
1 tbsp granulated sugar (15 mL)
1 tbsp skim milk powder (15 mL)
1 tbsp bread machine yeast (15 mL)
1 tsp salt (5 mL)

Yield: 18 large slices
1 slice
89.2 calories
8.0 g protein
4.5 g fat
4.3 g carbs

In cereal bowl, heat water in microwave oven 1 minute and 40 seconds. In bread pan, place water, olive oil, Almond Bake Mix, page 107 or Almond Whey Bake Mix #2, page 106, vital wheat gluten, ground flax seeds, soy or spelt flour, SPLENDA® Granular, sugar, skim milk powder, yeast and salt. Program bread to Bread Rapid setting and color of bread to medium. Bake bread, removing 30 to 35 minutes before end of baking time or when golden brown in color. Remove bread and cut slices with good quality, sharp, serrated bread knife.

Variation: **Loaf Pan Bread:** Program bread machine to pizza dough setting or to knead and one rise. Remove dough, knead briefly on lightly floured surface and form into loaf shape to fit 9 x 5 x 3-inch (2 L) well-greased loaf pan. Cover lightly with foil and allow to rise 40 minutes in preheated 200°F (93°C) oven, which has been switched off. Leave loaf inside, remove foil and heat oven to 350°F (180°C). Set timer from start of heating oven and bake 20 to 25 minutes or until golden brown.
Yield: 24 slices. **Soy Option:** (*3.1 g Carbs*) **Whey Option:** (*3.8 g Carbs*)

Helpful Hint: *If using whey protein option, bread will not rise quite as high, however, the flavor is wonderful. Use spelt flour option instead of soy flour and 1 cup (250 mL) water plus 1 tbsp (15 mL). Refrigerate and cut into same number of slices. (*5.0 g Carbs*) Loaf Pan Bread is the best way to make the Soy-Free Flax Bread.

CINNAMON-SWIRL EGG BREAD

Lovely loaf reminiscent of cinnamon buns! Soy-free analysis is given second.

Flax Bread Machine Bread, page 115
   (use 1 cup (250 mL) water, and
   1 large egg, OR with soy-free option
   use $^3/_4$ cup (175 mL) water and 1
   large egg)
Cinnamon Butter:
$^1/_3$ cup Healthy Butter, page 96, (75 mL)
   OR softened butter
3 tbsp whipping cream (45 mL)
1 cup SPLENDA® Granular (250 mL)
2 tsp ground cinnamon (10 mL)

Yield: 28 slices
1 slice
84.4 calories
5.2 g protein
5.5 g fat
3.7 g/4.2 g carbs

In small bowl, warm water in microwave oven 1 minute 40 seconds. In bread pan, place water, olive oil, Almond Bake Mix, page 107 or Almond Whey Bake Mix #2, page 106, vital wheat gluten, ground flax seeds, soy or spelt flour, SPLENDA® Granular, sugar, skim milk powder, yeast, salt and egg. Program bread machine to pizza dough setting or to knead and one rise. When cycle is done, remove bread dough. Knead a few minutes on lightly floured surface. Roll out to 16 x 13-inch (40 x 33 cm) rectangle. Let dough rest 10 minutes under clean towel, if it resists rolling out. Roll out and allow to rest again as necessary.

Cinnamon Butter: In food processor with sharp blade or in blender, process Healthy Butter, page 96 and whipping cream. Add SPLENDA® Granular and cinnamon; process until smooth.

Assembly: Spread dough with Cinnamon Butter almost to edges. Roll from one long side. Seal seam tightly by pinching dough and place seam side down on greased cookie sheet. Cover loosely with foil. Allow to rise 30 minutes in 200°F (93°C) preheated oven, which has been switched off. Bake in 375°F (190 °C) oven 15 minutes. Cover loosely with foil and bake another 5 minutes. Serve with extra Cinnamon Butter or Frost with Cream Cheese Frosting, page 157.

Variation: With Cream Cheese Frosting: *(4.2 g/4.6 g Carbs)*

Helpful Hint: This bread may be made the traditional way (see Oat Bran Bread, page 118) using only Almond Bake Mix option, page 107, in combination with the soy flour option, using traditional active dry yeast. Allow to rise 1 hour in preheated oven and then roll out, spread with Cinnamon Butter, roll up and cover loosely with foil. Allow to rise again in warm oven 30 minutes. Then bake as directed above. The best method is the former as the loaf rises very much bigger. For former method, 75% vital wheat gluten will also work just fine.

BRAIDED FLAX BREAD

A very attractive-looking bread and so easy to make.

*Flax Bread Machine Bread, page 115

Yield: 28 slices
1 slice
56.1 calories
5.2 g protein
2.8 g fat
2.7 g carbs

In small bowl, warm water in microwave oven 1 minute 40 seconds. In bread pan, place water, olive oil, Almond Bake Mix, page 107, or *Almond Whey Bake Mix #2, page 106, vital wheat gluten, ground flax seeds, soy or spelt flour, SPLENDA® Granular, sugar, skim milk powder, yeast and salt. Program bread machine to pizza dough setting or to knead and one rise. When cycle is done, remove bread dough. On floured surface, punch down dough and divide into 3 equal portions. Form 3 smooth balls. Cover balls with clean tea towel and let rest 10 minutes.

Alternately squeeze and roll balls with both hands to form 3 smooth 16-inch (40 cm) ropes of even thickness. Allow ropes to rest again, if dough is too elastic. Place 3 ropes an inch (2.5 cm) apart on greased cookie sheet. Braid by bringing left rope underneath center rope, then lay it down. Then bring right rope under new center rope and lay it down. Repeat to end, braiding fairly loosely to allow bread room to expand. Pinch ends together firmly to seal. Spray braid with nonstick cooking spray.

Cover loosely with foil. Allow to rise 30 minutes in 200°F (93°C) preheated oven, which has been switched off. Remove foil, leave loaf inside and heat oven to 375°F (190°C). Set timer from the start of heating oven. Bake 15 to 20 minutes, or until turning brown, cover loosely with foil and bake 5 minutes more. Serve with Cinnamon Butter, page 116, if desired.

Variations: **Braided Flax Raisin Bread:** Add $^1/_3$ cup (75 mL) seedless raisins to bread pan ingredients. Raisins may be snipped in half, if desired, for more evenly distributed sweetness. (***4.1 g Carbs***)

*Soy-free Braided Flax Bread: Use spelt flour option instead of soy flour and 1 cup (250 mL) water plus 1 tbsp (15 mL). (***3.2 g Carbs***)

OAT BRAN BREAD

Excellent bread – more flavorful than white bread any day! It makes great toast.

1^1/$_8$ cup (9 fl oz) water (280 mL)
1 tbsp granulated sugar (15 mL)
1 tbsp traditional active dry yeast (15 mL)
2 tbsp olive oil (25 mL)
1^2/$_3$ cups Almond Bake Mix (400 mL)
 page 107
^{2}/$_3$ cup vital wheat gluten (150 mL)
^{1}/$_3$ cup oat bran (75 mL)
^{1}/$_3$ cup soy flour (75 mL)
2 tbsp SPLENDA® Granular (25 mL)
1 tbsp skim milk powder (15 mL)
1 tsp salt (5 mL)

Yield: 24 slices
1 slice
69.6 calories
4.3 g protein
3.6 g fat
3.8 g carbs

In large electric mixer bowl, pour warm water, 105 to 115°F (40 to 45°C). Dissolve sugar in water. Sprinkle yeast over water. Allow to sit 3 to 5 minutes, then stir to dissolve completely. Add olive oil, Almond Bake Mix, page 107, vital wheat gluten, oat bran, soy flour, SPLENDA® Granular, skim milk powder and salt. Using dough blades, mix with electric mixer, scraping sides occasionally, until dough is moist and elastic. (Mix by hand with wooden spoon, if you do not have an electric mixer.)

On lightly floured surface, knead dough briefly and form into a loaf shape to fit a 9 x 5 x 3-inch (2 L) well-greased loaf pan. Cover loosely with foil. Allow to double in size 1 hour in 200°F (93°C) preheated oven, which has been switched off. Turn heat up to 350°F (180°C), setting timer for 25 minutes.

Variation: **Brown Bread:** Use Walnut Bake Mix, page 107 instead of Almond Bake Mix. ***Yield:*** 24 thin, uniform slices. (***3.8 g Carbs***)

Imitation Corn Bread (soy-free): *(This coarse-crumbed bread is reminiscent of corn bread. If desired, add a couple of drops yellow food coloring. Best eaten when warm. Microwave cooled loaf briefly.)* Use ^{2}/$_3$ cup (150 mL) water and Whey Almond Bake Mix #1, page 105, instead of Almond Bake Mix and ^{1}/$_3$ cup (75 mL) spelt flour instead of soy flour. Bake 18 to 20 minutes, or until evenly browned all over. (***3.8 g Carbs***) This bread does not rise high.

Helpful Hint: To warm cold water to correct temperature, in cereal bowl, microwave water on high power, 1 minute 40 seconds. Stir water and check temperature with instant-read thermometer. This loaf doubles in size, but that only brings the loaf to just below the loaf pan ridge. It has a dense, moist texture and a great taste, which I really like. Enjoy buttered with grated Cheddar cheese.

APPLE-CINNAMON LATTICE LOAF

My sons love this! Oat Bran version may be made in bread machine. See below.

Oat Bran Bread, page 118
Apple Filling:
2 cups finely chopped apples (500 mL)
2 tbsp water (25 mL)
1 tbsp lemon juice (15 mL)
$^1/_4$ cup SPLENDA® Granular (50 mL)
1 tsp cinnamon (5 mL)
$^1/_8$ tsp Thickening Agent, (0.5 mL)
  page 109
2 tbsp butter, softened (25 mL)
1 tbsp SPLENDA® Granular (15 mL)
$^1/_4$ tsp cinnamon (1 mL)

Yield: 2 loaves, 2x12 slices
1 slice per serving
84.2 calories
5.3 g protein
4.6 g fat
5.6 g carbs

See Oat Bran Bread, page 118. In large electric mixer bowl, pour water, 105 to 115°F (40 to 45°C). Dissolve sugar in water. Sprinkle yeast over water. Allow to sit 3 to 5 minutes; stir to dissolve completely. Add olive oil, Almond Bake Mix, page 107, vital wheat gluten, oat bran, soy flour, SPLENDA® Granular, skim milk powder and salt. Using dough blades, mix with electric mixer until all ingredients are moistened well. On floured surface, knead dough briefly and form into large ball. Place in large, greased bowl, covered loosely with foil. Allow to rise 1 hour in 200°F (93°C) preheated oven, which has been switched off.

Apple Filling: In small bowl, combine chopped apples, water and lemon juice. Microwave on high power 2 minutes. Drain. Stir in $^1/_4$ cup (50 mL) SPLENDA® Granular, 1 tsp (5 mL) cinnamon and Thickening Agent, page 109. Remove dough and place on floured surface. Punch down and roll into two, 9-inch (23 cm) squares. (Dough will resist rolling. Roll out and then allow to rest 10 minutes; repeat.) Spread each with butter. Place half filling down center of each square (keeping 1 tbsp (15 mL) for garnish), leaving a space at top and bottom. Make cuts at an angle on either side of filling about 1 inch (2.5 cm) apart, cutting just to filling. Fold up top and bottom ends, placing strips neatly down sides of filling (encasing filling). Now fold over strips from alternating sides until all strips are folded over. Tuck strips in where necessary. Fill spaces here and there with remaining apple pieces. In small bowl, combine 1 tbsp (15 mL) SPLENDA® Granular and $^1/_4$ tsp (1 mL) cinnamon; sprinkle over loaves. Place on greased cookie sheets. Cover loosely with foil. Allow to rise 30 minutes in 200°F (93°C) preheated oven, which has been switched off. Bake in 350°F (180 °C) oven 20 to 25 minutes, or until golden. Serve with Cinnamon Butter, page 116, if desired.

Variation: **Soy-free Loaf:** Use Flax Bread Machine Bread, page 115 on pizza dough setting, 75% gluten, bread machine yeast and 1 oven rising. (***5.4 g Carbs***)

CARROT BREAD MACHINE BREAD

Warm, crusty bread! It is important to age the grated carrot one week in the refrigerator, as the bread will turn a lovely, golden color.

$1^1/_8$ cups (9 fl. oz) water, PLUS (280 mL)
 1 tbsp water (15 mL)
2 tbsp olive oil (25 mL)
$1^1/_2$ cups Almond Bake Mix, (375 mL)
 page 107
$^2/_3$ cup vital wheat gluten (150 mL)
$^1/_2$ cup wheat bran (125 mL)
$^1/_3$ cup soy flour (75 mL)
$^1/_4$ cup grated carrot, (50 mL)
 (aged 1 week in refrigerator)
2 tbsp SPLENDA® Granular (25 mL)
1 tbsp granulated sugar (15 mL)
1 tbsp skim milk powder (15 mL)
1 tbsp bread machine yeast (15 mL)
1 tsp salt (5 mL)

Yield: 14 slices
1 large slice per serving
108.7 calories
8.7 g protein
5.7 g fat
5.9 g carbs

In cereal bowl, heat water in microwave oven 1 minute and 40 seconds. In bread pan, place water, olive oil, Almond Bake Mix, page 107, vital wheat gluten, wheat bran, soy flour, grated carrot, SPLENDA® Granular, sugar, skim milk powder, yeast and salt. Place pan in bread machine. Program bread machine to Bread Rapid setting and color of bread to medium setting. Bake bread, removing 30 to 40 minutes before end of baking time or when golden brown in color. Remove from bread pan and cut slices with good quality, sharp, serrated bread knife.

Helpful Hint: Bread slices more easily when cold. Refrigerate bread and when completely cool, cut into 20 thin slices. (***4.1 g Carbs***)

YEAST-FREE FLAX BREAD

Easy-to-make bread, without using yeast or baking powder. This bread slices thinly very easily and reaches a nice height.

1³/₄ cups Almond Bake Mix, (425 mL)
   page 107, OR
   *Almond Whey Bake Mix #2, page 106
2 tbsp SPLENDA® Granular (25 mL)
¹/₄ tsp salt (1 mL)
¹/₃ cup butter, softened (75 mL)
¹/₄ cup flax seeds, ground (50 mL)
6 extra-large eggs, separated
¹/₄ tsp lemon juice (1 mL)
1 tsp vanilla extract (5 mL)

Yield: 32 slices
1 slice
63.7 calories
2.7 g protein
5.0 g fat
1.9 g carbs

In large bowl, combine Almond Bake Mix, page 107, or Almond Whey Bake Mix #2, page 106, SPLENDA® Granular and salt. Rub in butter. Stir in flax seeds.

In large bowl, beat egg whites with lemon juice until stiff. While beating, add yolks one at a time until thick and creamy. Make well in center of Bake Mix mixture. Pour in egg mixture and vanilla extract; fold in. Pour into greased 9 x 5 x 3-inch (2 L) loaf pan.

Bake in 350°F (180°C) oven 25 minutes. Loosen edges and invert.

Variation: ***Yeast-Free Flax Bread (without soy flour):** Use Almond Whey Bake Mix #2, page 106 and 5 extra-large eggs. (***1.9 g Carbs***)

Sunshine Bread: Use 6 tbsp (90 mL) sunflower seeds, ground, instead of flax seeds.

CREPES

Everyone in the family loves these. No noticeable soy aftertaste! Serve with Maple Syrup, page 172 and fresh lemon juice or simply butter and enjoy!

$^1/_2$ cup table cream, 18 % B.F. (125 mL)
$^1/_2$ cup water (125 mL)
$^3/_4$ cup Almond Bake Mix, (175 mL)
  page 107, OR
  Almond Whey Bake Mix #2, page 106
2 tbsp soy, OR spelt flour (25 mL)
2 tbsp spelt flour (25 mL)
2 tbsp SPLENDA® Granular (25 mL)
2 extra-large eggs
2 tsp vanilla extract (10 mL)
$^1/_8$ tsp salt (0.5 mL)
2 tbsp Healthy Butter, page 96 (25 mL)

> **Yield:** 16 servings
> 1 crepe
> 66.2 calories
> 2.6 g protein
> 5.0 g fat
> **2.7 g carbs**

In blender, combine table cream, water, Almond Bake Mix, page 107 or Almond Whey Bake Mix #2, page 106, soy or spelt flour, spelt flour, SPLENDA® Granular, eggs, vanilla extract and salt. Blend until completely combined. Using small nonstick pan or wok {inside diameter measures 5 inches (13 cm)}, melt small amount of Healthy Butter, page 96 over medium heat.

Measure 2 tbsp (25 mL) batter into $^1/_4$ cup (50 mL) measure. Pour into greased pan and tilt to cover evenly. Cook 1 minute; flip with flexible spatula and cook other side 30 seconds. Repeat. If mixture gets thick, add $1^1/_2$ tsp (7 mL) water and blend again.

Variation: **Filled Crepes with Strawberry Sauce:** *Filling:* In blender, blend 4 oz (125 g) light cream cheese (softened), 3 tbsp (45 mL) SPLENDA® Granular and 2 tbsp (25 mL) sour cream. Spread some cheese filling on each crepe and roll. Pour some Strawberry Sauce, page 149 over each serving. (*4.5 g Carbs*)

Soy-free Crepes: *(These are slightly thinner crepes.)* Use Almond Whey Bake Mix #2, page 106 instead. Use spelt flour instead of soy flour in recipe. (*3.0 g Carbs*)

Helpful Hint: These may also be used for savory fillings; just reduce sweetener to 1 tsp (5 mL), or leave out altogether.

WHEY TORTILLAS

These are easy to make and last a long time in the refrigerator or freezer.

$^3/_4$ cup water (175 mL)
1 tbsp sugar (15 mL)
1 tbsp traditional yeast (15 mL)
2 tbsp olive oil (25 mL)
$1^1/_3$ cups Almond Whey Bake
  Mix #2, page 106 (325 mL)
$^2/_3$ cup 75% vital wheat gluten (150 mL)
$^1/_2$ cup wheat bran (125 mL)
$^1/_3$ cup spelt flour (75 mL)
2 tbsp SPLENDA® Granular (25 mL)
1 tbsp sugar (15 mL)
1 tbsp skim milk powder (15 mL)
1 tsp salt (5 mL)

Yield: 20 Tortillas
1 Tortilla
74.5 calories
6.2 g protein,
3.4 g fat
4.4 g carbs

In large electric mixer bowl, pour warm water, 105 to 115°F (40 to 45°C). (To warm water: microwave water 1 minute and 20 seconds.) Dissolve sugar in water. Sprinkle yeast over water. Allow to sit 3 to 5 minutes, then stir to dissolve completely. Add olive oil, Almond Whey Bake Mix #2, page 106, vital wheat gluten, wheat bran, spelt flour, SPLENDA® Granular, skim milk powder and salt. Using dough blades, mix with electric mixer, scraping sides occasionally until dough is moist and elastic. (Mix by hand with wooden spoon, if you do not have an electric mixer.)

On lightly floured surface, knead dough briefly and place in greased bowl. Cover loosely with foil. Allow to double in size 1 hour in 200°F (93°C) preheated oven, which has been switched off. Remove, punch down and break off 20 small balls of dough. Cover with clean towel to prevent drying out. Roll each in a paper thin circle on lightly floured surface. In nonstick dry skillet, cook briefly on both sides until brown spots appear. Place in plastic bag to keep tortillas supple. Refrigerate. Freeze for longer storage.

Helpful Hints: These, in my humble opinion, taste better than the regular, almost tasteless white flour tortillas we used to buy. I sometimes use them as a flat bread with butter and fruit spread or grated cheese.

These tortillas cannot be made using a bread machine. The dough will be too elastic to roll out and even if you do manage to roll them out, significant shrinkage will occur in the skillet.

HIGH-PROTEIN TORTILLAS

Detailed instructions on how to make these present a task no more difficult than making crepes – in fact, in my opinion, these are more fun to make!

$^3/_4$ cup oat bran (175 mL)
$^1/_2$ cup whole wheat pastry flour, OR
  whole spelt flour (125 mL)
$^1/_2$ cup soy protein isolate (125 mL)
$^1/_3$ cup ground almonds (75 mL)
1 tbsp vital wheat gluten (15 mL)
1 tbsp SPLENDA® Granular (15 mL)
1 tsp salt (5 mL)
1 cup hot water (250 mL)

Yield: 14 Tortillas
1, 6-inch (15 cm) Tortilla
93.8 calories
12.1 g protein
2.7 g fat
4.7 g carbs

In medium bowl, combine oat bran, whole wheat pastry flour or whole spelt flour, soy protein isolate, ground almonds, vital wheat gluten, SPLENDA® Granular and salt. With wooden spoon, stir in hot water all at once. Knead dough briefly. Form 14 small equal-sized balls. Keep balls of dough in plastic bag to prevent drying out.

Roll each ball on lightly "floured" (use soy protein isolate) countertop to 6-inches (15 cm) in diameter or slightly bigger, making dough as thin as possible for maximum flexibility. "Flour" rolling pin, if necessary, with soy protein isolate. To ensure delicate Tortilla dough does not fall apart in transfer to skillet, use piece of light cardboard (such as one side of Splenda box) and gently slide non-shiny side underneath one edge. If dough sticks to countertop at any point, approach from other side, until it is loosened and sitting squarely on cardboard. Gently lower Tortilla off cardboard onto dry skillet over medium heat.

Cook until brown spots appear underneath; flip and cook other side. Remove skillet from heat; dust with soft, clean towel. Place Tortillas in plastic bag to keep them soft and supple (they will become even more supple).

Helpful Hints: Edges of Tortillas will appear irregular, but once filled, they will look quite acceptable. Occasionally, a crack might occur in Tortilla as it is placed in skillet. If this should happen, simply, press down with flexible spatula to seal.

SUNFLOWER CHEESE CRACKERS

These delicate crunchy, tasty crackers are a snap to make. Homemade crackers taste so much nicer than store bought crackers, in my opinion. My favorite are the Sesame Cheese Crackers.

2 cups Cheddar cheese (500 mL)
$1^1/_4$ cups Almond Bake Mix,(300 mL)
  page 107, OR
  Almond Whey Bake Mix #2, page 106
$^2/_3$ cup salted sunflower seeds (150 mL)
$^1/_2$ cup grated Parmesan cheese (125 mL)
$^1/_2$ cup unsalted butter, softened (125 mL)
$^1/_2$ cup Minute oats (125 mL)
$^1/_4$ cup wheat bran (50 mL)
3 tbsp water (45 mL)
1 tbsp SPLENDA® Granular (15 mL)
$^1/_8$ tsp salt (0.5 mL)

Yield: 70 crackers
1 cracker
43.6 calories
1.7 g protein
3.5 g fat
1.4 g carbs

In large bowl, combine Cheddar cheese, Almond Bake Mix, page 107 or Almond Whey Bake Mix #2, page 106, sunflower seeds, Parmesan cheese, unsalted butter, Minute oats, wheat bran, water, SPLENDA® Granular and salt.

Form into 2, 6-inch (15 cm) long rolls, wrap in wax paper and freeze $^1/_2$ hour, or until firm. Slice thinly with sharp, serrated knife. Place on well-greased cookie sheets and flatten each cracker slightly, sealing any cracks that may form. Bake in 400°F (200°C) oven 8 to 10 minutes or until golden brown underneath. Remove crackers from cookie sheets and cool on wire racks.

Variation: **Sesame Cheese Crackers:** Omit Minute oats. Use 1 cup (250 mL) sesame seeds instead of sunflower seeds and salted butter. Use 2 tbsp (25 mL) water to form a cohesive dough. Bake 10 minutes.
Yield: 70 crackers. (*0.9 g Carbs*)

Helpful Hint: These crackers keep very well. They work well with Walnut Bake Mix as well. They are not ideal for spreads as they are too delicate. See Flax Seed Crackers or Sunflower Seed Crackers, page 126 for crackers more suitable for spreads.

FLAX SEED CRACKERS

Flax seeds – nature's Tomoxifen – in strong, crunchy crackers.

$^1/_2$ cup soy flour, OR (125 mL)
  whole wheat pastry flour, OR whole spelt
$^1/_2$ cup flax seeds, ground (125 mL)
$^1/_2$ cup grated Parmesan, OR (125 mL)
  Romano cheese
2 tbsp spelt, OR (25 mL)
  whole wheat pastry flour
2 tbsp SPLENDA® Granular (25 mL)
$^1/_4$ tsp baking soda (1 mL)
$^1/_4$ tsp salt (1 mL)
5 tbsp water (75 mL)
3 tbsp olive oil (45 mL)

Yield: 40 crackers	
1 cracker	
29.1 calories	
1.4 g protein	
2.1 g fat	
1.1 g carbs	

In medium bowl, combine soy or whole spelt flour or whole wheat pastry flour, ground flax seeds, grated Parmesan or Romano cheese, spelt flour or whole wheat pastry flour, SPLENDA® Granular, baking soda and salt; stir. Make well in center of dry ingredients. Pour water and olive oil into center. Stir with fork to combine. Turn out on countertop. Knead lightly.

Line 11 x 17-inch (28 x 43 cm) jelly roll pan with foil. Spray with nonstick cooking spray. Press dough onto foil and flatten out with hands across pan, ignoring big spaces that form. Use small rolling pin or nonstick cooking spray bottle (or any small cylindrical shape) to roll out dough toward edges of pan. Dip rolling pin in soy protein isolate (zero carbs) or soy flour, as needed, to prevent sticking to dough. If dough bunches up at edges or gets too thick there, use knife to neatly cut edges. Reuse dough where necessary. Roll dough thinly to cover entire pan evenly. Prick dough with fork and score 8 vertical x 5 horizontal cuts.

Bake 13 minutes in 400°F (200°C) oven, cover loosely with foil and bake 2 minutes more. Allow to cool 5 minutes before cutting along scored areas. For crispier crackers, remove outside edge crackers and bake middle crackers a further 5 minutes. Store uncovered in cupboard. As crackers dry out overnight, they become even more crisp.

Variation: **Sunflower Seed Crackers:** Use $^2/_3$ cup (150 mL) unsalted sunflower seeds, ground, instead of flax seeds. Add the last tablespoon (15 mL) water gradually as needed until dough holds together. (***1.0 g Carbs***)

Soy-free Crackers: Use whole spelt flour or whole wheat pastry flour instead of soy flour. (***1.5 g Carbs***)

LOW-CARB PASTA

This is not bad for a substitute. My son, Jonathan, who is real picky and not a low-carber, asked at lunch time whether there would be more Scallops and Alfredo Sauce over Low-Carb Pasta for his supper that night.

$^1/_3$ cup soy protein isolate (75 mL)
3 tbsp kamut, OR spelt flour (45 mL)
1 tbsp vital wheat gluten (15 mL)
1 tbsp soy flour (15 mL)
$^1/_2$ tsp salt (2 mL)
1 egg
$^1/_4$ cup water (50 mL)

Yield: 3 servings
1 serving
197.7 calories
35.9 g protein
3.8 g fat
6.7 g carbs

In small bowl, combine soy protein isolate, kamut or spelt flour, vital wheat gluten, soy flour and salt. In cereal bowl, beat egg with fork, stirring in water. Stir into dry ingredients a little at a time until dough holds together.

Form 3 balls of dough. Roll each ball out very thinly on lightly "floured" surface (use soy protein isolate) and cut into strips of any size. Use firm, flat spatula to carefully remove dough strips off counter top surface. Drop in deep pot (to prevent water boiling over) with rapidly boiling water and set timer for 2 minutes. Place pasta in sieve or colander. Rinse under running hot water. Butter and salt to taste and serve with Spaghetti meat sauce, page 53, Scallops in Alfredo Sauce, page 75 or Tuna cheese sauce, page 42.

Variation: **Lasagna:** Make one batch Low-Carb Pasta recipe. Roll each ball thinly and divide into 4 vertical strips. Divide each vertical strip horizontally in half for easier handling. Don't be concerned about ragged edges, as it will not be detected in lasagna. Prepare as above. See Lasagna, page 48.

Helpful Hints: Kamut flour, available in most upscale health food stores, is wonderfully suited to making pasta, however, spelt flour may be substituted. Use a deep pot for boiling pasta, otherwise water will boil over. If this should happen, quickly spoon out excess water with large spoon.

A manual pasta maker is a super investment. Make pasta dough as before. Form into 3 balls and follow manufacturer's instructions to produce uniform spaghetti or fettuccini. Cook as directed above for tender pasta. Do not dry pasta overnight as it will be too rubbery upon cooking. Fresh pasta is best.

BRAN MUFFINS

These are for those morning persons who like a bran muffin and coffee! Omit wheat bran, hot water, sour cream and raisins in variations below.

1$\frac{1}{2}$ cups Almond Whey Bake, (375 mL)
  Mix #2, page 106, OR
  *Almond Bake Mix, page 107
$\frac{1}{2}$ cup SPLENDA® Granular (125 mL)
1 tbsp baking powder (15 mL)
$\frac{1}{4}$ tsp baking soda (1 mL)
$\frac{1}{8}$ tsp salt (0.5 mL)
$\frac{1}{4}$ cup butter, softened (50 mL)
$\frac{3}{4}$ cup wheat bran (175 mL)
$\frac{1}{2}$ cup hot water (125 mL)
2 tbsp sour cream (25 mL)
2 tbsp raisins, snipped, optional (25 mL)
2 tsp vanilla extract (10 mL)
5 eggs, separated
$\frac{1}{4}$ tsp lemon juice (1 mL)

> *Yield:* 18 muffins
> 1 muffin
> 100.1 calories
> 4.5 g protein
> 7.2 g fat
> *3.9 g carbs*

In large bowl, combine Almond Whey Bake Mix #2, page 106 or Almond Bake Mix, page 107 *(use 6 eggs), SPLENDA® Granular, baking powder, baking soda and salt. Rub in butter. In small bowl, combine wheat ban, hot water, sour cream, raisins, if using, and vanilla extract. In medium bowl, beat egg whites and lemon juice until stiff. While beating, add egg yolks one at a time until thick and creamy. Stir bran mixture into dry ingredients. Fold in egg mixture. Fill 18 greased muffin cups half full. Place muffin pans next to each other in middle of oven. Bake in 350°F (180°C) oven 15 to 20 minutes or until light brown.

Variations: **Cranberry Orange Muffins:** Use 1$\frac{3}{4}$ cups (425 mL) *Almond Bake Mix, page 107 or Almond Whey Bake Mix #2, page 106, $\frac{1}{2}$ cup (125 mL) butter and $\frac{2}{3}$ cup (150 mL) SPLENDA® Granular. Stir in $\frac{3}{4}$ cup (175 mL) frozen unsweetened cranberries (finely chopped in blender or food processor), 2 tbsp (25 mL) finely grated orange rind, 2 tbsp (25 mL) fresh orange juice and 1 tsp (5 mL) orange extract. (*4.2 g Carbs*)

Banana Walnut Muffins: Use 1$\frac{3}{4}$ cups (425 mL) *Walnut Bake Mix or Walnut Whey Bake Mix pages 107 or 106, $\frac{1}{2}$ cup (125 mL) butter, $\frac{1}{2}$ banana (mashed), $\frac{1}{4}$ cup (50 mL) chopped walnuts and 1 tsp (5 mL) banana extract. (*4.5 g Carbs*)

Apple Hazelnut Muffins: Use 1$\frac{3}{4}$ cups (425 mL) *Hazelnut Bake Mix, page 107 or Hazelnut Whey Bake Mix, page 106, $\frac{1}{2}$ cup (125 mL) butter, 1 apple grated and 1 tsp (5 mL) vanilla extract. Sprinkle $\frac{1}{4}$ cup (50 mL) flaked hazelnuts over muffins before baking. (*4.9 g Carbs*)

GLAZED LEMON LOAF
This is a lovely loaf with a tender crumb texture.

1³/₄ cups Almond Whey Bake Mix #2,
  page 106, OR (425 mL)
  *Almond Bake Mix, page 107
1 cup SPLENDA® Granular (250 mL)
1 tbsp baking powder (15 mL)
¹/₄ tsp baking soda (1 mL)
¹/₈ tsp salt (0.5 mL)
¹/₂ cup unsalted butter, softened (125 mL)
2 tbsp finely grated lemon rind (25 mL)
4 eggs, separated
¹/₄ tsp lemon juice (1 mL)
1 tsp lemon or vanilla extract (5 mL)
Glaze:
3 tbsp SPLENDA® Granular (45 mL)
2 tbsp lemon juice (25 mL)
¹/₈ tsp Thickening Agent, page 109 (0.5 mL)

Yield: 18 slices	
1 slice	
123.0 calories	
5.1 g protein	
9.3 g fat	
4.6 g carbs	

In large bowl, combine Almond Whey Bake Mix #2, page 106, or Almond Bake Mix, page 107, SPLENDA® Granular, baking powder, baking soda and salt. Rub in butter until mixture resembles coarse crumbs. Stir in lemon rind. In medium bowl, beat egg whites with lemon juice until stiff. While beating, add egg yolks one at a time until thick and creamy. Make well in center of dry ingredients and fold in egg mixture and lemon extract. Pour into 9 x 5 x 3-inch (2 L), well-greased loaf pan.

Bake in 350°F (180°C) oven 25 to 30 minutes or until cake tester comes out clean. Cool on wire rack 20 minutes. Loosen edges and invert.

Glaze: In small saucepan, combine SPLENDA® Granular, lemon juice and Thickening Agent, page 109. Over medium heat, bring to boil. With pastry brush, spread glaze over loaf.

Variation: **Frosted Banana Loaf:** Use ¹/₃ cup (75 mL) butter, 2 tsp (10 mL) banana extract (omit vanilla) and ¹/₃ cup (75 mL) mashed banana. Use Cream Cheese Frosting, page 157. (*5.6 g Carbs*)

Helpful Hint: *If using Almond Bake Mix, page 107, use 5 eggs, separated. In comparing this Lemon Loaf to my regular Lemon Loaf in *"More Splendid Desserts,"* it is 14 grams carbohydrate less per slice!!! It is, however, possible by substituting my tasty Ultimate Bake Mix for all-purpose flour to reduce the regular Lemon Loaf to less than half the original carbs (6.8 g down from 18.8 g).

CHOCOLATE ECLAIRS

No one will guess these are low-carb! Easy and fun to make!

1 cup water (250 mL)
$^1/_2$ cup butter (125 mL)
$^1/_8$ tsp salt (0.5 mL)
$1^1/_2$ cups Whey Ultimate Bake (375 mL)
  Mix, page 108
2 eggs
$1^3/_4$ cups Crème Fraiche, (425 mL)
  page 172

Chocolate Drizzle:
1 tbsp unsalted butter (15 mL)
1 tbsp whipping cream (15 mL)
$^1/_4$ tsp vanilla extract (1 mL)
$^1/_2$ cup SPLENDA® Granular (125 mL)
$^1/_2$ oz unsweetened baking chocolate, melted (15 g)

> **Yield:** 9 Eclairs
> 1 Éclair
> 231.5 calories
> 6.1 g protein
> 20.3 g fat
> **6.9 g carbs**

Spray cookie sheet with nonstick cooking spray; set aside. In medium saucepan, combine water, butter and salt; bring to boil. Stir in Whey Ultimate Bake Mix all at once. Stir in eggs 1 at a time, beating with wooden spoon after each addition until smooth.

Spoon into pastry bag with $^1/_2$-inch (1 cm) front opening; secure bag with ring, if necessary. Cut a straw to measure 4 inches (10 cm). For each éclair, next to straw, pipe 2 strips 4 inches long (10 cm) and $^1/_2$ inch (1 cm) wide side by side, on cookie sheet. Pipe another 2 strips on top. Bake in 450°F (230°C) oven 15 minutes. Reduce heat to 350°F (180°C) and bake a further 10 minutes or until puffed and golden brown. Cool completely on wire rack. Split in half and remove soft dough from inside. Fill each with Crème Fraiche, page 172 and drizzle with Chocolate Drizzle. Refrigerate or serve immediately at room temperature.

Chocolate Drizzle: In small bowl, melt butter in microwave oven. Stir in cream, vanilla extract and SPLENDA® Granular until smooth. Stir in chocolate. If necessary, microwave 10 seconds until molten. Use teaspoon to drizzle chocolate over eclairs.

Variation: Chocolate Cream Puffs: Pipe sixteen 2-inch (5 cm) rounds onto prepared cookie sheet. Bake, fill and drizzle with chocolate as directed.
Yield: 16 Cream Puffs. (**3.9 g Carbs**)

CINNAMON DONUT STRIPS

My sons and husband made short work of these, so they were a hit!

$^2/_3$ cup water (150 mL)
4 tbsp butter (60 mL)
6 tbsp SPLENDA$^{®}$ Granular (90 mL)
$^1/_2$ cup spelt flour (125 mL)
$^1/_2$ cup soy flour (125 mL)
2 eggs

Cinnamon-Splenda Sprinkle:
$^1/_4$ cup SPLENDA$^{®}$ Granular (50 mL)
$^1/_2$ tsp cinnamon (1 mL)

Yield: 36 Donuts
1 Cinnamon Donut Strip
30.1 calories
1.3 g protein
1.9 g fat
2.3 g carbs

In medium saucepan, combine water, butter and SPLENDA$^{®}$ Granular. Bring to the boil. Stir in spelt flour and soy flour all at once, using wooden spoon, until smooth ball forms. Allow to cool 5 minutes. In food processor with dough blade or in electric mixer, add eggs to dough and beat until smooth.

Spoon mixture into pastry bag with $^1/_2$-inch (1 cm) front opening; secure bag with ring. Cut a straw to measure $2^1/_2$ inches (6 cm). Line cookie sheet with wax paper. For each donut strip, pipe one strip next to straw on wax paper. Make 36 donut strips and freeze 10 minutes or until strips remove easily from wax paper. Fry in deep fat fryer at 375°F (190°C) until golden brown. Drain on paper towel. Roll in Cinnamon-Splenda Sprinkle.

Cinnamon-Splenda Sprinkle: In small bowl, combine SPLENDA$^{®}$ Granular and cinnamon.

FROZEN DESSERTS, POPSICLES, JELLIES AND PUDDINGS

LIGHT VANILLA ICE CREAM

I love the rich ice creams, page 137, however, sometimes I prefer lighter fare.

3 eggs
2 cups half-and-half cream (500 mL)
$^3/_4$ cup SPLENDA® Granular (175 mL)
1 envelope unflavored gelatin
2 tbsp butter (25 mL)
1 tbsp vanilla extract (15 mL)
$^1/_8$ tsp salt (0.5 mL)

> *Yield:* 4 cups (1 L)
> $^1/_2$ cup (125 mL) per serving
> 138.3 calories
> 4.2 g protein
> 10.8 g fat
> *5.4 g carbs*

In double boiler, combine eggs, 1 cup (250 mL) half-and-half cream, SPLENDA® Granular, gelatin and butter. Over simmering water, stir with wire whisk (scrape sides occasionally with spatula) almost constantly, about 10 minutes, until mixture thickens. Remove from heat. Sieve, if necessary, and whisk in remaining half-and-half cream, vanilla extract and salt. Cover surface with plastic wrap and refrigerate just until cool.

Freeze in ice cream maker according to manufacturer's instructions.

Variations: Lemon Ice Cream: Stir $^1/_3$ cup (75 mL) lemon juice and also $^1/_2$ tsp (2 mL) lemon extract into ice cream custard. Omit vanilla extract.
Yield: $4^1/_2$ cups (1 L), $^1/_2$ cup (125 mL) per serving. (*5.4 g Carbs*)

Strawberry-Lemon Ice Cream: Stir 2 cups (500 mL) frozen unsweetened strawberries, thawed and pureed with $^1/_2$ cup (125 mL) ice cream custard in blender, into Lemon Ice Cream custard above.
Yield: 6 cups (1.5 L), $^1/_2$ cup (125 mL) per serving. (*5.2 g Carbs*)

Helpful Hint: Don't refrigerate custard too long, or it will begin to set. Variations for Rich Vanilla Ice Cream, page 137, also apply.

KOOL-AID JELLY

This is a handy recipe for the strict dieting phase. The iced mocha jelly is different and a great way to use leftover coffee.

$^3/_4$ cup SPLENDA® Granular (175 mL)
3 envelopes unflavored gelatin (45 mL)
1 envelope Kool-Aid (4.5 g)
  (sugar-free, if possible)
2 cups boiling water (500 mL)
2 cups ice cold water (500 mL)

Yield: 6 servings
1 serving
25.1 calories
3.0 g protein
0.0 g fat
3.2 g carbs

In medium bowl, combine SPLENDA® Granular and gelatin. Pour boiling water over and stir until gelatin is dissolved. Stir in ice cold water. Stir in Kool-Aid. Pour jelly into 8-inch (20 cm) square casserole dish. Refrigerate until set.

Variations: **Dry Diet Jelly Mix:** $^1/_2$ cup (125 mL) SPLENDA® Granular, $1^1/_2$ envelopes unflavored gelatin (22 mL), $^1/_2$ envelope (7 mL) Kool-Aid. Combine. Substitute in recipes calling for diet jelly. *Yield:* 1 batch. (***13.1 g Carbs***)

Diet Popsicles: Reduce unflavored gelatin to $1^1/_2$ envelopes (22 mL) and add 1 tbsp (15 mL) lemon juice. To release popsicles, place base under hot, running water. Microwave frozen popsicle 15 seconds on high power, if desired. *Yield:* 16 popsicles. (***1.3 g Carbs***)

Iced Mocha Jelly: Combine $^1/_2$ cup (125 mL) SPLENDA® Granular and 1 tbsp (15 mL) cocoa. Gradually whisk in 1 cup (250 mL) whipping cream and $1^1/_2$ tsp (7 mL) vanilla extract. Sprinkle 3 envelopes gelatin (45 mL) over cream. Stir in 3 cups (750 mL) hot prepared coffee. Sieve. *Yield:* 6 servings. (***3.9 g Carbs***)

Lemon or Lime Jelly: Combine $^1/_3$ cup (75 mL) lemon or lime juice, $^1/_2$ cup (125 mL) SPLENDA® Granular, $1^1/_2$ envelopes (22 mL) unflavored gelatin and 1 cup (250 mL) boiling water. Stir in 1 cup (250 mL) cold water. *Yield:* 4 servings. (***4.6 g Carbs***)

RASPBERRY TRIFLE

English trifle is a classic and beautiful dessert.

2 tbsp raspberry fruit spread (25 mL)
1 tbsp pineapple juice (15 mL)
1 tbsp water (15 mL)
1 tsp SPLENDA® Granular (5 mL)
20 Lady Fingers, page 183
1^1/$_2$ cups raspberries (375 mL)
1^1/$_2$ cups Delicious Pouring Custard,
  page 138 (375 mL)
^{2}/$_3$ cup Crème Fraiche, page 172, (150 mL)
  (prepared with Thickening Agent, page 109)
^{1}/$_2$ cup Crème Fraiche, page 172 (125 mL)

Yield: 10 to 12 servings
1 serving
170.9 calories
5.2 g protein
12.7 g fat
8.3 g carbs/6.9 g carbs

In small bowl, combine raspberry fruit spread, pineapple juice, water and SPLENDA® Granular. Spread one Lady Finger, page 183 with raspberry mixture and top with another Lady Finger; repeat with remaining Lady Fingers. Cover bottom of 8-cup (2 L) trifle bowl with Lady Fingers. Pour remaining raspberry mixture over Lady Fingers. Sprinkle 1 cup (250 mL) raspberries over top.

In medium bowl, combine Delicious Pouring Custard, on page 138 and ^{2}/$_3$ cup (150 mL) Crème Fraiche, page 172 with wire whisk until smooth. Pour over raspberries. Garnish top with remaining raspberries and pipe ^{1}/$_2$ cup (125 mL) Crème Fraiche around perimeter and with "spokes of a wheel" coming in to meet a "pool" of raspberries in center. If desired, put a raspberry between each spoke of the wheel as well. Refrigerate at least 6 hours before serving.

Helpful Hints: To make this dessert easier, if time is a factor on the day guests are expected, prepare Ladyfingers, Delicious Pouring Custard and Crème Fraiche the day before; then assemble first thing the next morning. Prepare Crème Fraiche, page 172 with ^{1}/$_2$ tsp (2 mL) Thickening Agent, page 109. Use a commercial Splenda-sweetened raspberry spread or Raspberry Jam, page 91.

CREAMY STRAWBERRY POPSICLES

For creamier results, allow to thaw 5 minutes, then loosen under hot water.

$1^1/_2$ cups plain yogurt (375 mL)
1 cup whipping cream (250 mL)
$^2/_3$ cup SPLENDA® Granular (150 mL)
$^1/_2$ cup frozen strawberries, (125 mL)
   (unsweetened)
$^1/_4$ tsp strawberry Kool-Aid (1 mL)

> *Yield:* 13 popsicles
> 1 popsicle
> 86.8 calories
> 1.6 g protein
> 7.4 g fat
> *2.7 g carbs*

In blender, blend yogurt, whipping cream, SPLENDA® Granular, strawberries and Kool-Aid until smooth. Pour into popsicle molds.

Variations: **Creamy Orange Popsicles:** In blender, combine as for above recipe, omitting strawberries and Kool-Aid, using instead 2 tbsp (25 mL) orange juice from concentrate (undiluted), 2 tsp (10 mL) lemon juice and $^1/_4$ tsp (1 mL) orange extract. *Yield:* 13 popsicles. (*3.3 g Carbs*)

Coconut Banana Cream Popsicles: In blender, blend 1, 14-oz can (400 mL) unsweetened coconut milk, 1 cup (250 mL) yogurt, 1 cup (250 mL) SPLENDA® Granular, $^2/_3$ cup (150 mL) whipping cream, 1 medium banana, sliced and $^1/_2$ tsp (2 mL) banana or vanilla extract until smooth. *Yield:* 16 popsicles. (*4.7 g Carbs*)

INSTANT STRAWBERRY ICE CREAM

This ice cream tastes very fruity.

$1^1/_2$ cups frozen strawberries, (375 mL)
   (unsweetened)
$^3/_4$ cup whipping cream (175 mL)
$^1/_2$ cup SPLENDA® Granular (125 mL)
$^1/_4$ cup sour cream or plain yogurt (50 mL)

> *Yield:* $2^1/_2$ cups (625 mL)
> $^1/_2$ cup (125 mL) per serving
> 84.8 calories
> 1.7 g protein
> 5.4 g fat
> *6.9 g carbs*

In colander, rinse strawberries very briefly under running cold water to remove any ice crystals. In food processor with sharp blade or blender, process strawberries on slowest speed until coarsely chopped. Add whipping cream, SPLENDA® Granular and sour cream. Process, increasing speed gradually until smooth. Freeze leftovers in sealed plastic container. Microwave briefly and enjoy again.

CREAMY DELIGHT ORANGE MOUSSE

My son Daniel, not really a dessert person, likes this. Try other flavors.

8 oz light cream cheese, softened (250 g)
2 cups whipping cream (500 mL)
³/₄ cup SPLENDA® Granular (175 mL)
1 envelope unflavored gelatin (15 mL)
1 tsp orange-flavored Kool-Aid (5 mL)
  (sugarless, if possible)
1 cup boiling water (250 mL)

> **Yield:** 10 servings
> 1 serving
> 222.1 calories
> 3.4 g protein
> 21.8 g fat
> *4.0 g carbs*

In food processor with sharp blade, blender or in bowl with electric mixer, process cream cheese. Add whipping cream and SPLENDA® Granular; process until smooth and thickened. In small bowl, stir gelatin into boiling water. Add to cream cheese mixture along with Kool-Aid; process on slow speed until well combined. Pour into 9-inch (23 cm) pie dish. Chill a few hours until set.

Variation: **Chocolate Mousse:** Add ¹/₃ cup (75 mL) cocoa to processed cream cheese; increase SPLENDA® Granular to 1 cup (250 mL) and add 1¹/₂ tsp (7 mL) vanilla extract. Continue as above; omit Kool-Aid. Sprinkle with 1 tsp (5 mL) grated unsweetened chocolate, if desired. (*4.9 g Carbs*)

THREE-LAYER JELLY

Tired of plain jelly? This one makes a nice change. It separates into 3 layers.

³/₄ cup SPLENDA® Granular (175 mL)
3 envelopes unflavored gelatin (45 mL)
2 cups boiling water (500 mL)
3 oz cream cheese, softened (85 g)
2 cups cold water (500 mL)
1 envelope sugarless Kool-Aid (4.5 g)
¹/₃ cup whipping cream (75 mL)

> **Yield:** 8 servings
> 1 serving
> 77.2 calories
> 3.3 g protein
> 5.2 g fat
> *3.0 g carbs*

In medium bowl, combine SPLENDA® Granular and gelatin. Pour boiling water over mixture; stir to dissolve. Add cream cheese and beat until frothy. Stir in cold water and Kool-Aid. Whip cream until stiff and whisk into jelly mixture. Pour into 8-inch (2L) square, deep glass baking dish. Chill until firm.

VANILLA ICE CREAM

Drizzle with Hardening Chocolate, page 171, if desired.

$^3/_4$ cup SPLENDA® Granular (175 mL)
$^1/_2$ cup half-and-half cream (125 mL)
5 egg yolks
1 egg
$1^1/_2$ cups whipping cream (375 mL)
1 tbsp vanilla extract (15 mL)
$^1/_8$ tsp salt (0.5 mL)

Yield: 4 cups (1 L)
$^1/_2$ cup (125 mL) per serving
224.3 calories
3.9 g protein
21 g fat
4.7 g carbs

In double boiler, combine SPLENDA® Granular and half-and-half cream. Heat until scalding. Stir into eggs and return mixture to double boiler. Heat until custard is hot and coats metal spoon. Do not boil or eggs will scramble. Over medium bowl, strain through sieve. Stir in whipping cream, vanilla extract and salt. Cover surface with plastic wrap and refrigerate until cold or freeze half an hour. Freeze in ice cream maker as manufacturer directs.

Variations: **Chocolate Ice Cream:** Use 1 cup (250 mL) SPLENDA® Granular, 1 tsp (5 mL) vanilla extract, omit salt and sift $^1/_4$ cup (50 mL) cocoa over *hot* custard; whisk in. *Yield:* $4^1/_2$ cups (1.125 L). (*5.5 g Carbs*)

Chocolate Mint Ice Cream: As above. Omit salt and vanilla extract. Add 2 tsp (10 mL) peppermint extract. *Yield:* $4^1/_2$ cups (1 L). (*5.5 g Carbs*)

Strawberry or Raspberry Ice Cream: Use 1 cup (250 mL) frozen unsweetened strawberries or raspberries, slightly thawed. In blender, blend strawberries with custard, adding few drops red food coloring and 1 tsp (5 mL) vanilla extract. Microwave raspberries 2 minutes and press through sieve, then blend with custard, red food coloring and vanilla.
Yield: 5 cups (1.25 L). (*4.4 g Carbs*)

Maple Walnut Ice Cream: Use $1^1/_2$ tbsp (22 mL) maple extract instead of vanilla extract and $^2/_3$ cup (150 mL) walnut pieces.
Yield: $4^1/_2$ cups (1.125 mL). (*5.5 g Carbs*)

Cappuccino Ice Cream: Use 1 tsp (5 mL) vanilla and also 1 tbsp (15 mL) instant coffee dissolved in 2 tbsp (25 mL) hot whipping cream.
Yield: 4 cups (1 L). (*4.6 g Carb*)

Peach Vanilla Ice Cream: Use 1 cup (250 mL) canned peaches, chopped, and 1 tbsp (15 mL) vanilla extract. *Yield:* $5^1/_2$ cups (1.38 L). (*4.5 g Carbs*)

BAKED CUSTARD

A creamy, rich comfort dessert! It may be enjoyed either warm or cold.

3 eggs
1$^1/_2$ cups half-and-half cream (375 mL)
$^1/_2$ cup whipping cream (125 mL)
$^1/_2$ cup SPLENDA$^®$ Granular (125 mL)
1 tbsp vanilla extract (15 mL)
$^1/_8$ tsp ground nutmeg, for garnish (0.5 mL)

Yield: 8 servings
1 serving
140.8 calories
4.0 g protein
11.6 g fat
4.4 g carbs

In medium bowl, beat eggs, half-and-half cream, whipping cream, SPLENDA$^®$ Granular and vanilla extract in bowl until combined. Pour into 8-inch (2 L) deep glass baking dish. Place baking dish in larger, shallow baking dish and pour boiling water into it, about halfway up side of glass baking dish. Sprinkle custard with nutmeg.

Bake uncovered in 350°F (180°C) oven 15 minutes. Reduce heat to 300°F (150°C) and bake 25 minutes more. Custard will be slightly wobbly when dish is shaken lightly. Remove from water bath immediately. Serve with warm Maple Syrup, page 172, if desired.

Variations: **Coconut Custard Pie:** Pour custard mixture into cooked Coconut Pie Crust, page 145. Bake as above. *Yield:* 10 servings. (*5.7 g Carbs*)

Delicious Pouring Custard: In double boiler, combine half-and-half cream, whipping cream and SPLENDA$^®$ Granular. When scalding, pour cream mixture into small bowl with 6 egg yolks; stir. Return to double boiler and stir constantly until custard begins to thicken (about 5 minutes) and coats metal spoon easily. Sieve. Stir in 1 tbsp (15 mL) vanilla extract. Pour into small glass jug. Cover surface with plastic wrap; refrigerate until ready to serve.
Yield: 2$^1/_2$ cups (625 mL), 2 tbsp (25 mL) per serving. (*1.7 g Carbs*)

INSTANT CHOCOLATE PUDDING

Quick and easy substitute for instant diet commercial puddings.

1 cup whipping cream (250 mL)
$^3/_4$ cup SPLENDA® Granular (175 mL)
$^1/_2$ cup water (125 mL)
$^1/_2$ cup sour cream (125 mL)
2 tbsp cocoa (25 mL)
1 tsp Thickening Agent, page 109 (5 mL)
1 tsp vanilla extract (5 mL)

Yield: 6 servings
1 serving
176.8 calories
1.8 g protein
16.7 g fat
5.3 g carbs

In food processor or blender, beat whipping cream, SPLENDA® Granular, water, sour cream, cocoa, Thickening Agent, page 109 and vanilla extract on slow speed until thickened, about 1 minute. Beat on high speed about 1 minute, scraping edges of bowl once or twice.

Variations: **Vanilla Pudding:** Use $^2/_3$ cup (150 mL) SPLENDA® Granular, 1 tbsp (15 mL) custard powder and 1 tbsp (15 mL) vanilla extract. Omit cocoa. Beat all ingredients in above recipe and these modified ingredients together until just combined, then add 1 tbsp (15 mL) butter, melted, and beat until thickened. (*6.2 g Carbs*)

Strawberry or Cherry Pudding: Use $^2/_3$ cup (150 mL) SPLENDA® Granular, 1 tbsp (15 mL) custard powder and $^1/_2$ tsp (2 mL) sugarless strawberry or cherry-flavored Kool-Aid. Omit cocoa and vanilla extract. Follow directions for Vanilla Pudding, adding 1 tbsp (15 mL) butter, melted. (*6.0 g Carbs*)

Pudding in a Cloud: Prepare Chocolate Pudding above and Crème Fraiche, page 172. Using about $^1/_3$ cup (75 mL) Crème Fraiche for each of 6 pretty wine glasses, spread on bottom and sides. Fill centers with Chocolate Pudding. (*8.7 g Carbs*)

Helpful Hint: Pudding in a Cloud turns ordinary pudding into company fare.

LEMON SHERBET

With each mouthful, flavor bursts forth in the most refreshing way! These carbohydrate values were calculated based on the Go-Diet authors' laboratory-proven values for carbohydrates in yogurt and buttermilk with live cultures.

$1^1/_2$ cups buttermilk (375 mL)
$1^1/_2$ cups yogurt (375 mL)
$^3/_4$ cup SPLENDA® Granular (175 mL)
$^3/_4$ cup ice cold water (175 mL)
$^1/_3$ cup lemon juice (75 mL)
1 envelope unflavored gelatin
$^1/_4$ cup water (50 mL)
$^1/_2$ tsp lemon extract (2 mL)

Yield: $6^1/_2$ cups (1.625 L)
$^1/_2$ cup (125 mL) per serving
41.6 calories
2.7 g protein
1.2 g fat
2.9 g carbs

In large bowl, stir buttermilk, yogurt, SPLENDA® Granular, $^3/_4$ cup (175 mL) water and lemon juice together. In cereal bowl, stir unflavored gelatin into $^1/_4$ cup (50 ml) water. Microwave 40 seconds and stir into sherbet mixture, along with lemon extract. Freeze in ice cream maker according to manufacturer's instructions.

Variations: **Lime Sherbet:** Use lime juice instead of lemon juice, omitting lemon extract. (***2.9 g Carbs***)

Lemon-Lime Sherbet: Use 2 tbsp (25 mL) lemon juice, 3 tbsp (45 mL) lime juice and 1 tsp (5 mL) lemon extract. (***2.8 g Carbs***)

Orange Sherbet: Use 1 cup (250 mL) water, 1 tbsp (15 mL) orange concentrate, 1 tsp (5 mL) orange extract and $^1/_8$ tsp (0.5 mL) orange Kool-Aid. Omit lemon extract. (***2.9 g Carbs***)

Cranberry-Raspberry Sherbet: Use $^2/_3$ cup (150 mL) Splenda Cranberry Cocktail Juice, use $^1/_2$ cup (125 mL) water instead of $^3/_4$ cup (175 mL) water and 1 tsp (5 mL) raspberry Kool-Aid. Omit lemon extract. (***2.8 g Carbs***)

STRAWBERRY FROZEN YOGURT

These good-for-you frozen yogurts can be eaten every day on this diet. Use yogurt made with live bacterial cultures and one that is not too sour.

1 cup frozen strawberries, (250 mL)
  (unsweetened)
2 cups plain yogurt (500 mL)
$^3/_4$ cup SPLENDA® Granular (175 mL)
$^1/_2$ cup whipping cream (125 mL)
1 tsp vanilla extract (5 mL)

> *Yield:* 5 cups (1.25 L)
> $^1/_2$ cup (125 mL) each
> 87.0 calories
> 2.4 g protein
> 5.8 g fat
> ***4.1 g carbs***

In small bowl, microwave strawberries on high power 1 minute. Chop strawberries and mash. In medium bowl, combine yogurt, strawberries, SPLENDA® Granular, whipping cream and vanilla extract. Freeze in ice cream maker according to manufacturer's instructions.

Variations: **Blueberry:** Use $^3/_4$ cup (175 mL) frozen unsweetened blueberries. In small bowl, microwave blueberries 1 minute.
Yield: 5 cups (1.25 L). (***4.0 g Carbs***)

Raspberry: Use 1 cup (250 mL) frozen unsweetened raspberries plus another 2 tbsp (25 mL). In small bowl, microwave raspberries and 1 tbsp (15 mL) water 1 minute 50 seconds. Mash with fork and press through sieve.
Yield: 5 cups (1.25 L). (***3.8 g Carbs***)

Maple Walnut: Omit vanilla extract. Use 2 tbsp (25 mL) maple extract and $^1/_2$ cup (125 mL) walnut pieces. *Yield:* $4^1/_2$ cups (1.125 L). (***4.2 g Carbs***)

Cappuccino: Use 1 tbsp (15 mL) instant coffee stirred into 2 tbsp (25 mL) cream; microwave 20 seconds to dissolve. Use $^1/_2$ tsp (2 mL) vanilla extract.
Yield: 4 cups (1 L). (***3.9 g Carbs***)

Peach Vanilla: Use 1 cup (250 mL) canned unsweetened peaches in juice, drained and chopped and use 1 tbsp (15 mL) vanilla extract.
Yield: 5 cups (1.25 L). (***4.4 g Carbs***)

Fruit Cocktail: Use 1 cup (250 mL) canned unsweetened fruit cocktail in juice, drained. *Yield:* 5 cups (1.25 L). (***4.7 g Carbs***)

Lemon or Lime: Use $^1/_3$ cup (75 mL) lemon or lime juice and $^1/_2$ tsp lemon extract. Omit vanilla extract. *Yield:* $4^1/_2$ cups (1.125 L). (***3.7 g Carbs***)

STRAWBERRY SORBET

Another name for this sorbet would be fruit ice. It is especially nice to enjoy this low-calorie treat out on the deck on a hot, sunny day.

1 envelope unflavored gelatin
$^2/_3$ cup SPLENDA® Granular (150 mL)
$2^1/_4$ cups water (550 mL)
2 cups frozen strawberries, (500 mL)
  thawed and pureed, (unsweetened)
2 tbsp lemon juice (25 mL)

> *Yield:* 4 cups (1 L)
> $^1/_2$ cup (125 mL) per serving
> 24.4 calories
> 1.0 g protein
> 0.2 g fat
> *4.4 g carbs*

In medium saucepan, combine unflavored gelatin, SPLENDA® Granular and 1 cup (250 mL) water. Dissolve gelatin over medium heat. Remove from heat and pour into large bowl. Allow to cool to room temperature. Stir in remaining water, pureed strawberries and lemon juice. Freeze until firm.

In food processor with sharp blade, process mixture until smooth. Freeze again until firm. Microwave briefly and enjoy. Freeze leftovers.

Variations: **Peach Sorbet:** Use $1^1/_4$ cups (300 mL) canned unsweetened peaches in juice, drained and pureed with $^1/_4$ cup (50 mL) lemon juice in blender. *Yield:* $3^1/_2$ cups (875 mL), 6 servings. (*5.2 g Carbs*)

Raspberry Sorbet: In blender, blend 2 cups (500 mL) raspberries with 2 tbsp (25 mL) lemon juice and 2 tbsp (25 mL) water. Press through sieve. *Yield:* $3^1/_4$ cups (800 mL), 6 servings. (*5.4 g Carbs*)

Helpful Hint: You may want to try other low-carb fruits, if desired.

FROZEN STRAWBERRY CREAM SQUARES

A lovely dessert! The surprise here is that these frozen squares are thawed to room temperature before serving.

Almond Crust:
$^2/_3$ cup ground almonds (150 mL)
2 tbsp SPLENDA® Granular (25 mL)
1 tbsp soy flour, OR spelt flour (15 mL)
1 tbsp butter, melted (15 mL)
1 egg yolk
Filling:
$1^3/_4$ cups Crème Fraiche, (425 mL)
  page 172
2 cups frozen unsweetened strawberries (500 mL)

Yield: 20 squares
1 square
78.9 calories
1.6 g protein
7.0 g fat
2.5 g carbs

Almond Crust: In small bowl, combine almonds, SPLENDA® Granular, soy or spelt flour, butter and egg yolk. Spread in 8-inch (20 cm) square glass baking dish. Cover with plastic wrap. Press crust out evenly; remove wrap. Bake in 350°F (180°C) oven 10 minutes. Set aside to cool.

Filling: Prepare Crème Fraiche, page 172. Thaw strawberries slightly, just enough to slice and without the juices beginning to run. Fold strawberries into Crème Fraiche. Spread over cooled crust. Freeze 2 hours or until frozen. Thaw to room temperature before serving. Refrigerate any leftovers.

Variations: Frozen Raspberry Cream Squares: (*2.3 g Carbs*)

Helpful Hint: If you like your dessert quite sweet and you have the carb budget, sprinkle strawberries with 2tbsp (25 mL) SPLENDA® Granular and toss to combine.

CHEESECAKES

CREATE-A-FLAVOR CHEESECAKE

Easy and very quick to assemble.

8 oz light cream cheese, softened (250 g)
2 cups whipping cream (500 mL)
$^3/_4$ cup SPLENDA® Granular (175 mL)
$^1/_4$ cup water (50 mL)
2 envelopes gelatin (25 mL)
1 tsp any-flavor Kool-Aid, (5 mL)
  (sugarless)

Yield: 12 servings
1 serving
187.0 calories
3.3 g protein
18.2 g fat
3.3 g carbs

In food processor with sharp blade, blender or in bowl with electric mixer, process cream cheese, cream and SPLENDA® Granular.

In small saucepan, heat water and gelatin, until gelatin dissolves. Add to cream cheese mixture, together with Kool-Aid; process until smooth. Pour into 9-inch (23 cm) glass pie dish. Chill until set.

Helpful Hints: If desired, omit the crusts in the other cheesecakes to bring the carbohydrate count down by 2 to 3 grams.

If possible, rather choose sugarless Kool-Aid, even although it does not come in as many flavors.

COCONUT STRAWBERRY CHEESECAKE
Simple, tasty and quick.

Coconut Crust:
1 cup medium-flaked coconut, (250 mL)
  (unsweetened)
3 tbsp SPLENDA® Granular (45 mL)
2 tbsp sour cream (25 mL)
1 egg white

Strawberry Cheese Filling:
4 large frozen unsweetened strawberries,
  slightly thawed
8 oz light cream cheese, softened (250 g)
$^1/_2$ cup SPLENDA® Granular (125 mL)
$^1/_2$ cup sour cream (125 mL)
3 tbsp whipping cream (45 mL)
1 envelope unflavored gelatin (15 mL)
$^1/_3$ cup water (75 mL)
$^1/_2$ tsp cherry extract, (optional) (2 mL)

Yield: 12 servings
1 serving
131.1 calories
3.2 g protein
11.1 g fat
3.2 g carbs

Coconut Crust: In medium bowl, combine coconut and SPLENDA® Granular. Stir in sour cream and egg white. Spread in 9-inch (23 cm) glass pie dish. Cover with plastic wrap. Press coconut crust out evenly; remove wrap. Microwave 2 minutes, pat down and microwave another minute or until set.

Strawberry Cheese Filling: In food processor with sharp blade or blender, process strawberries until coarsely chopped. Add cream cheese; process. Add SPLENDA® Granular, sour cream and cream; process. In cereal bowl, soften gelatin in $^1/_3$ cup (75 mL) water. Microwave 40 seconds, stir and add to strawberry cheese filling, along with cherry extract, if using; process. Pour over coconut crust. Place in freezer half an hour, then refrigerate. Sprinkle with grated, unsweetened chocolate, if desired.

Variations: Chocolate Truffle Cheesecake: Omit strawberries. Use 16 oz (500 g) light cream cheese, softened $1^1/_4$ cups (300 mL) SPLENDA® Granular and 1 tbsp (15 mL) vanilla extract. Cover set cheesecake with Dipping Chocolate, page 175. (*8.5 g Carbs*)

Strawberry Truffle Cheesecake: Use 8 medium unsweetened, frozen strawberries, 16 oz (500 g) light cream cheese and $1^1/_4$ cups (300 mL) SPLENDA® Granular. Cover set cheesecake with Dipping Chocolate, page 175. (*9.5 g Carbs*)

BUTTERSCOTCH PECAN CHEESECAKE
A soft set cheesecake (really creamy).

2 tbsp butter (25 mL)
$^1/_3$ cup water (75 mL)
$^1/_4$ cup SPLENDA® Granular (50 mL)
1 egg yolk
1 envelope unflavored gelatin (15 mL)
2 tsp butterscotch extract (10 mL)
8 oz light cream cheese, softened (250 g)
1 cup whipping cream (250 mL)
$^1/_2$ cup SPLENDA® Granular (125 mL)
Butterscotch Pecan Topping:
2 tbsp butter (25 mL)
$^3/_4$ cup finely chopped pecans (175 mL)
3 tbsp SPLENDA® Granular (45 mL)

> **Yield:** 12 servings
> 1 serving
> 189.4 calories
> 3.2 g protein
> 18.1 g fat
> ***4.0 g carbs***

In medium saucepan, melt butter. Add water, SPLENDA® Granular, egg yolk and gelatin. Stir over medium-low heat with wire whisk until gelatin dissolves. Remove from heat and stir in butterscotch extract. Allow to cool slightly.

In food processor with sharp blade, blender or in bowl with electric mixer, process cream cheese until smooth. Add whipping cream and SPLENDA® Granular; process until smooth. Add gelatin mixture; process. Pour into 9-inch (23 cm) glass pie dish. Add Butterscotch Pecan Topping. Freeze half an hour and refrigerate.

Butterscotch Pecan Topping: Melt butter in small saucepan. Stir in pecans and SPLENDA® Granular. Remove from heat.

Variations: **Maple Walnut Cheesecake:** Use 1 tbsp (15 mL) maple extract . (***4.0 g Carbs***)

Pecan Butterscotch Cheesecake: Simply a different spin on the above cheesecake. For crust use $1^1/_4$ cups (300 mL) pecans, chopped, 3 tbsp (45 mL) SPLENDA® Granular and 2 tbsp (25 mL) butter, melted. Omit Butterscotch Pecan Topping. (***4.6 g Carbs***). Ground pecan crust, page 150 may be used instead. (***4.1 g Carbs***)

RASPBERRY SWIRL CHEESECAKE

Excellent and what a pretty cheesecake!

Almond Crust, page 149
Raspberry Sauce:
2 cups frozen raspberries, (500 mL)
  (unsweetened)
$^1/_4$ cup SPLENDA$^®$ Granular (50 mL)
2 tbsp water (25 mL)
$^3/_4$ tsp Thickening Agent, page 109 (3 mL)
Filling:
16 oz light cream cheese, softened (500 g)
$1^1/_4$ cups SPLENDA$^®$ Granular (300 mL)
$^1/_2$ cup whipping cream (125 mL)
$^1/_2$ cup sour cream (125 mL)
2 tbsp lemon juice (25 mL)
*2 envelopes unflavored gelatin (25 mL)
$^1/_3$ cup water (75 mL)

Yield: 12 servings
1 serving
265.5 calories
7.0 g protein
21.8 g fat
8.1 g carbs

Almond Crust: Prepare Almond Crust, page 149 in 9-inch (23 cm) glass pie dish.

Raspberry Sauce: In small saucepan, combine raspberries, SPLENDA$^®$ Granular and water. Sprinkle Thickening Agent over warm berry sauce. Stir constantly over medium-low heat until boiling and thickened. Mash and sieve.

Filling: In food processor with sharp blade, blender or in bowl with electric mixer, process cream cheese until smooth. Add SPLENDA$^®$ Granular, whipping cream, sour cream and lemon juice; process. In small bowl, sprinkle gelatin over water, stir and microwave 40 seconds. Add to cheesecake batter; process. Pour over crust. Place large blobs of raspberry sauce on top. Using knife with sharp tip, swirl to combine. Freeze one hour and serve or refrigerate for later.

Helpful Hint: *Use 1 tsp (5 mL) gelatin less for a creamier, slightly sweeter cheesecake as gelatin tends to cut sweetness somewhat. If using sauce (also try other berries) for other uses, use only $^1/_2$ tsp (2 mL) Thickening Agent, page 109 and 3 tbsp (45 mL) water. 1 tbsp (15 mL) Sauce will typically be just under 1 gram carbohydrate.

FRUIT COCKTAIL CHEESECAKE

A fruity, pretty cheesecake, popular with friends and family.

Coconut Almond Crust:
$^2/_3$ cup ground almonds (150 mL)
$^1/_3$ cup SPLENDA® Granular (75 mL)
$^1/_4$ cup medium-flaked coconut, (50 mL)
  (unsweetened)
2 tbsp soy, OR spelt flour (25 mL)
3 tbsp butter, melted (45 mL)
1 egg yolk
Filling:
16 oz light cream cheese, softened (500 g)
1 cup sour cream (250 mL)
1 cup SPLENDA® Granular (250 mL)
1 envelope unflavored gelatin
2 tbsp water (25 mL)
$1^1/_4$ cups canned fruit cocktail in unsweetened juice (300 mL)
1 tsp vanilla extract (5 mL)

> **Yield:** 12 servings
> 1 serving
> 232.7 calories
> 6.3 g protein
> 19.3 g fat
> **8.5 g carbs**

Coconut Almond Crust: In medium bowl, combine ground almonds, SPLENDA® Granular, coconut and soy or spelt flour. Stir in butter and egg yolk. Press into 9-inch (23 cm) glass pie dish and also up sides about $^1/_2$-inch (1.5 cm). Bake in 350°F (180°C) oven 10 minutes.

Filling: In food processor with sharp blade, blender or in bowl with electric mixer, process cream cheese until smooth. Add sour cream and SPLENDA® Granular; process. In small saucepan, combine gelatin and water. Dissolve gelatin over medium heat. Add to cheesecake mixture; process briefly. Make sure there is no more than $^1/_2$ cup (125 mL) liquid with canned fruit. Stir fruit and vanilla extract into cheesecake mixture. Pour over prepared crust. If desired, garnish top with few more pieces of fruit, pressing fruit into cheesecake slightly. Chill until set.

BLUE RIBBON CHEESECAKE

This firm, extra-special cheesecake only gets better as it ages.

Crust:
$^1/_2$ cup ground almonds (125 mL)
2 tbsp SPLENDA® Granular (25 mL)
1 tbsp soy, OR spelt flour (15 mL)
2 tbsp butter, melted (25 mL)
1 egg yolk

Filling:
16 oz light cream cheese, softened (500 g)
8 oz regular cream cheese, softened (250 g)
$1^1/_4$ cups SPLENDA® Granular (300 mL)
$^1/_3$ cup unsalted butter, melted (75 mL)
3 eggs
2 tbsp vanilla extract (25 mL)

Raspberry or Strawberry Sauce:
$1^1/_2$ cups frozen unsweetened raspberries, OR (375 mL)
  strawberries
$^1/_4$ cup SPLENDA® Granular (50 mL)
3 tbsp water (45 mL)
$^1/_2$ tsp Thickening Agent, page 109 (2 mL)

Yield: 12 servings
1 serving
286.8 calories
7.7 g protein
24.7 g fat
7.4 g carbs

Crust: In medium bowl, combine ground almonds, SPLENDA® Granular and soy or spelt flour. Stir in butter and egg yolk. Sprinkle in 9-inch (23 cm) glass pie dish or springform pan. Cover with plastic wrap and press crust out evenly; remove plastic wrap. Bake in 350°F (180°C) oven 10 minutes or until turning brown at edges.

Filling: In food processor with sharp blade, blender or in bowl with electric mixer, process cream cheeses until smooth. Add SPLENDA® Granular, butter, eggs and vanilla extract; process until smooth. Pour over crust. Bake in 350°F (180°C) oven 35 to 40 minutes. Cool to room temperature. Cover cheesecake in center with slightly cooled Raspberry or Strawberry Sauce. Refrigerate. Later garnish perimeter with piped Crème Fraiche, page 172, if desired.

Raspberry or Strawberry Sauce: In medium saucepan, combine raspberries or strawberries, SPLENDA® Granular and water. Sprinkled Thickening Agent, page 109 over warm berry sauce. Cook over medium heat until boiling and thickened.

Variation: Blue Ribbon Maple Walnut Cheesecake: Use walnuts and maple extract. Omit Strawberry Sauce. Garnish with Crème Fraiche, page 172.
(5.6 g Carbs)

PRALINES 'N CHOCOLATE CREAM CHEESECAKE

A marbled beauty - my husband's favorite!

Pecan Crust
$^2/_3$ cup unsalted pecan halves, (150 mL)
  ground
2 tbsp soy, OR spelt flour (25 mL)
2 tbsp SPLENDA® Granular (25 mL)
2 tbsp butter, melted (25 mL)
1 egg yolk

Filling:
$^1/_2$ cup coarsely chopped pecans (125 mL)
2 tbsp butter, melted (25 mL)
2 tbsp SPLENDA® Granular (25 mL)
16 oz light Philadelphia Cream Cheese, softened (500 g)
$1^1/_4$ cups SPLENDA® Granular (300 mL)
$^1/_2$ cup half-and-half cream (125 mL)
$^1/_2$ cup whipping cream (125 mL)
$^1/_4$ cup water (50 mL)
$1^1/_2$ envelopes gelatin (22 mL)
2 oz unsweetened baking chocolate, melted (60 g)
$^1/_2$ cup SPLENDA® Granular (125 mL)
$^2/_3$ cup sour cream (150 mL)

Yield: 12 servings
1 serving
291.6 calories
6.8 g protein
26.4 g fat
8.9 g carbs

Pecan Crust: In small bowl, combine pecans, soy or spelt flour, SPLENDA® Granular, butter and egg yolk. Press into bottom of 9-inch (23 cm) glass pie dish or springform pan. Bake in 350°F (180°C) oven 10 minutes or microwave 2 minutes. (The baked crust holds together slightly better.)

Filling: In small bowl, combine pecans, butter and 2 tbsp (25 mL) SPLENDA® Granular; set aside. In food processor with sharp blade, blender or in bowl with electric mixer, process cream cheese until smooth. Add $1^1/_4$ cups (300 mL) SPLENDA® Granular, half-and-half cream and whipping cream; process. In small saucepan, combine water and gelatin. Dissolve gelatin over medium heat (or microwave 40 seconds). Add dissolved gelatin to cream cheese mixture; process.

Stir chocolate and $^1/_2$ cup (125 mL) SPLENDA® Granular into $1^1/_2$ cups (375 mL) batter. To remaining batter, add sour cream and process until smooth. Spread all but $^3/_4$ cup (175 mL) plain batter over crust. Sprinkle praline mixture over plain batter. Spread chocolate cheese mixture over pralines. Now spoon several dollops of plain batter on top of chocolate layer. Using paring knife with sharp tip, swirl to marble. Chill several hours.

ALMOND MILK CHOCOLATE CHEESECAKE

This cheesecake is so firm that it tastes like a baked cheesecake.

*Sliced Almond Crust:
$1^1/_3$ cups sliced almonds, (325 mL)
 (blanched)
$^1/_3$ cup SPLENDA® Granular (75 mL)
3 tbsp butter, melted (45 mL)
1 egg yolk

Milk Chocolate Filling:
$^1/_2$ cup Confectioner's Sugar (125 mL)
 Substitute, page 173
$^1/_4$ cup cocoa (50 mL)
1 envelope gelatin (15 mL)
$^3/_4$ cup whipping cream (175 mL)
$^1/_4$ cup water (50 mL)
$^1/_2$ tsp vanilla extract (2 mL)
12 oz light cream cheese, softened (375 g)
$^1/_2$ cup SPLENDA® Granular (125 mL)
$^1/_4$ cup water (50 mL)

Yield: 12 servings
1 serving
281.6 calories
11.2 g protein
24.1 g fat
6.3 g carbs

Sliced Almond Crust: In medium bowl, combine almonds, SPLENDA® Granular, melted butter and egg yolk. Press into 9-inch (23 cm) deep, glass pie dish or springform pan. Bake in 350°F (180°C) oven 10 minutes.

Milk Chocolate Filling: In medium saucepan, combine Confectioner's Sugar Substitute, page 173, cocoa and gelatin. Gradually whisk in whipping cream and $^1/_4$ cup (50 mL) water. Whisk over medium-low heat just until gelatin dissolves. Do not boil. Remove from heat. Stir in vanilla extract.

In food processor with sharp blade, blender or in a bowl with electric mixer, process cream cheese until smooth. To cream cheese, add SPLENDA® Granular and $^1/_4$ cup (50 mL) water; process. Add milk chocolate sauce; process until smooth. Fill prepared crust. Sprinkle with teaspoon (5 mL) grated, unsweetened chocolate, if desired. Refrigerate.

Helpful Hint: For a different garnish, omit grated chocolate. Allow cheesecake to set. Garnish with Drizzling Chocolate (see Chocolate-Drizzled Marshmallows, page 168). *This cheesecake is also wonderful with Nanaimo crust, page 185. (**7.8 g Carbs**)

CITRUS CHEESECAKE
Bursting with strong, citrus flavor!

Coconut Almond Crust:
$^2/_3$ cup ground almonds (150 mL)
$^1/_3$ cup SPLENDA® Granular (75 mL)
$^1/_4$ cup medium-flaked coconut, (50 mL)
  (unsweetened)
2 tbsp soy, OR spelt flour (25 mL)
3 tbsp butter, melted (45 mL)
1 egg yolk

Filling:
16 oz light cream cheese, softened (500 g)
$1^1/_4$ cups SPLENDA® Granular (300 mL)
1 cup sour cream (250 mL)
2 eggs
2 tbsp soy, OR spelt flour (25 mL)
1 tbsp grated lemon rind (optional) (15 mL)
1 tbsp lemon juice (15 mL)
2 tsp lime juice (10 mL)

Topping:
Crème Fraiche, page 172, (halve all ingredients)

Yield: 12 servings
1 serving
266.5 calories
7.8 g protein
22.6 g fat
8.8 g carbs

Coconut Almond Crust: In medium bowl, combine almonds, SPLENDA® Granular, coconut and soy or spelt flour. Stir in butter and egg yolk. Press into 9-inch (23 cm) springform pan, lined with wax paper. Bake in 350°F (180°C) oven 10 minutes.

Filling: In food processor with sharp blade, blender or in bowl with electric mixer, process cream cheese until smooth. Add SPLENDA® Granular, sour cream, eggs, soy or spelt flour, lemon rind, lemon juice and lime juice. Process until smooth. Pour over prepared crust. Bake in 350°F (180°C) oven 35 to 40 minutes.

Topping: Prepare Crème Fraiche, page 172 (halve all ingredients) and spread over cheesecake. Garnish center of cheesecake with thin lemon slice, twisted decoratively, if desired.

CREAMY STRAWBERRY CHEESECAKE

A fabulous, creamy cheesecake with plenty of flavor.

Coconut Almond Crust:
$^2/_3$ cup ground almonds (150 mL)
$^1/_3$ cup SPLENDA® Granular (75 mL)
$^1/_4$ cup medium-flaked coconut, (50 mL)
  (unsweetened)
2 tbsp soy, OR spelt flour (25 mL)
3 tbsp butter, melted (45 mL)
1 egg yolk

Filling:
$^2/_3$ cup strawberries, hulled and thinly sliced (150 mL)
16 oz light cream cheese, softened (500 g)
1 cup SPLENDA® Granular (250 mL)
$^1/_2$ cup whipping cream (125 mL)
$^1/_4$ cup water (50 mL)
2 envelopes unflavored gelatin (25 mL)
1 cup frozen unsweetened strawberries (250 mL)
$^1/_2$ cup water (125 mL)
red food coloring, if desired

Yield: 12 servings
1 serving
234 calories
6.5 g protein
20.1 g fat
7.0 g carbs

Coconut Almond Crust: In medium bowl, combine ground almonds, SPLENDA® Granular, flaked coconut and soy or spelt flour. Stir butter and egg yolk in with fork. Press into 9-inch (23 cm) springform pan. Bake in 350°F (180°C) oven 10 minutes. Allow to cool slightly and arrange sliced strawberries on crust. Line sides of pan with strip of wax paper wide enough to reach top.

Filling: In food processor with sharp blade, blender or in bowl with electric mixer, process cream cheese until smooth. Add SPLENDA® Granular and whipping cream; process. In small saucepan, combine $^1/_4$ cup (50 mL) water and gelatin; dissolve over medium heat. In blender, blend frozen unsweetened strawberries, $^1/_2$ cup (125 mL) water and 1 cup (250 mL) cheesecake batter. Add to remaining cheesecake batter along with gelatin; process until smooth. Pour over crust and chill several hours. Remove pan rim from cheesecake and remove wax paper. Garnish with strawberry fan and whipped cream or Crème Fraiche, page 172, if desired.

Helpful Hints: This method with wax paper lining a springform pan may be used for any of the gelatin cheesecakes. To make strawberry fan, use one large strawberry and cut several vertical slits, without cutting right through. Gently spread open to form fan.

CAKES

CHOCOLATE STRAWBERRY TORTE
This cake has a light, moist texture.

5 extra-large eggs, separated
$^1/_4$ tsp lemon juice (1 mL)
$1^1/_4$ cups almonds, ground (300 mL)
1 cup SPLENDA® Granular (250 mL)
$^1/_4$ cup cocoa (50 mL)
2 tbsp spelt flour, OR (25 mL)
 all-purpose flour
$2^1/_2$ tsp baking powder (12 mL)
$^1/_4$ cup sour cream (50 mL)
1 tsp vanilla extract (5 mL)
$^1/_2$ cup strawberries, sliced (125 mL)
Chocolate Cream Frosting:
1 cup whipping cream (250 mL)
$^1/_2$ cup SPLENDA® Granular (125 mL)
$^1/_4$ cup cocoa (50 mL)
$^1/_2$ tsp vanilla extract (2 mL)

Yield: 12 servings
1 serving
200.3 calories
6.5 g protein
16.3 g fat
6.7 g carbs

In large bowl, beat egg whites with lemon juice until stiff. While beating, add egg yolks one at time until thick and creamy. In medium bowl, combine almonds, SPLENDA® Granular, cocoa, spelt flour or all-purpose flour and baking powder. Make well in center and fold in egg mixture, sour cream and vanilla extract.

Pour into two greased 8-inch (20 cm) cake pans. Bake in 350°F (180°C) oven 20 minutes or until cake tester comes out clean. Allow to cool on cake rack.

Chocolate Cream Frosting: In medium bowl, beat whipping cream, SPLENDA® Granular, cocoa and vanilla extract until stiff.

Frost cooled cake layers in center and on top. Place sliced strawberries on top of frosting on bottom layer. Sprinkle top layer with 1 tsp (5 mL) grated unsweetened chocolate, if desired. This gives frosting a deep chocolate color after a few hours.

BASIC SPONGE CAKE

My son, Jonathan, loves this cake.

6 extra-large eggs, separated
$^1/_4$ tsp lemon juice (1 mL)
$1^3/_4$ cups ground almonds (425 mL)
1 cup SPLENDA® Granular (250 mL)
2 tbsp spelt, OR soy flour (25 mL)
2 tsp baking powder (10 mL)
1 tsp vanilla extract (5 mL)
Creamy Lemon Frosting, page 173

Yield: 16 servings
1 serving
158.7 calories
5.9 g protein
12.9 g fat
4.4 g carbs

In large bowl, beat egg whites with lemon juice until stiff. While beating, add egg yolks one at a time until thick and creamy. In medium bowl, combine almonds, SPLENDA® Granular, spelt or soy flour and baking powder. Make well in center. Pour in egg mixture and vanilla extract; fold in. Pour into well-greased 10-inch (25 cm) nonstick tube pan and bake in 350°F (180°C) oven 20 minutes, or until golden and cake tester comes out clean.

Prepare Creamy Lemon Frosting, page 173. Slice tube cake in half. Frost bottom and top layers.

Variation: **Lemony Cake:** Use $1^1/_4$ cups (300 mL) SPLENDA® Granular, add 2 tbsp (25 mL) finely grated lemon rind and sprinkle 1 tbsp (15 mL) lemon juice over dry ingredients. Frost as above. (*5.1 g Carbs*)

Helpful Hint: The principal cake recipe above lends itself to just about any frosting of your choice.

STRAWBERRY CREAM SWISS ROLL
Always an elegant dessert!

4 eggs, separated
$^1/_4$ tsp lemon juice (1 mL)
$^2/_3$ cup SPLENDA® Granular (150 mL)
1 cup ground almonds (250 mL)
2 tbsp spelt, OR soy flour (25 mL)
$2^1/_2$ tsp baking powder (12 mL)
1 tsp vanilla extract (5 mL)
Strawberry Cream Filling:
2 cups Crème Fraiche, page 172 (500 mL)
1 cup fresh strawberries, sliced (250 mL)

> **Yield:** 12 servings
> 1 serving
> 171.0 calories
> 5.1 g protein
> 14.1 g fat
> **5.6 g carbs**

In medium bowl, beat egg whites with lemon juice until soft peaks form. Add SPLENDA® Granular, beating until stiff. While beating, add egg yolks one at a time until thick and creamy. In large bowl, combine almonds, spelt or soy flour and baking powder. Make well in center of dry ingredients. Pour in egg mixture and vanilla extract; fold in. Line 15 x 10-inch (38 x 25 cm) jelly roll pan with greased and lightly floured wax paper and spread out cake mixture evenly.

Place in 400°F (200°C) oven, reduce heat to 350°F (180°C) and bake 10 minutes. Loosen edges of cake from pan; invert onto clean towel. Remove paper; trim any brown, crusty edges. Carefully roll up towel and cake together; place seam side down on wire rack. Set aside to cool completely.

Strawberry Cream Filling: Prepare Crème Fraiche, page 172. Unroll cake, remove towel and spread cooled cake with 2 cups (500 mL) Crème Fraiche, leaving $^1/_4$-inch (0.5 cm) border. Place sliced strawberries on Crème Fraiche. Roll up gently from one short side without towel.

Variation: Chocolate Cream Swiss Roll: Add 3 tbsp (45 mL) cocoa, use spelt or all-purpose flour (not soy flour), $^3/_4$ cup (175 mL) SPLENDA® Granular and fold in $^1/_4$ cup (50 mL) whipping cream as well as egg mixture into dry ingredients. Fill with Crème Fraiche, page 172, roll up and drizzle with Chocolate Drizzle (under Chocolate-Drizzled Marshmallows, page 168). (**6.5 g Carbs**)

CARROT CAKE

This is a special cake with bits of carrot and raisins showing. Garnish with Marzipan "carrots," page 174, if desired.

1²/₃ cups ground walnuts (400 mL)
1 cup SPLENDA® Granular (250 mL)
2 tbsp soy, OR spelt flour (25 mL)
2 tbsp spelt, OR soy flour (25 mL)
2¹/₂ tsp baking powder (12 mL)
¹/₈ tsp salt (0.5 mL)
1 medium carrot
2 tbsp raisins, snipped (25 mL)
5 extra-large eggs separated
¹/₄ tsp lemon juice (1 mL)
Cream Cheese Frosting:
4 oz light cream cheese, softened (125 g)
¹/₃ cup SPLENDA® Granular (75 mL)
2 tbsp butter, softened (25 mL)
1 tbsp whipping cream (15 mL)
1 tsp vanilla extract (5 mL)

Yield: 16 servings
1 serving
156.6 calories
6.3 g protein
12.4 g fat
5.8 g carbs

In large mixing bowl, combine walnuts, SPLENDA® Granular, soy or spelt flour, spelt or soy flour, baking powder and salt. Stir well. Slice carrot and coarsely chop carrot in blender. Stir carrot and raisins into dry ingredients. In food processor or electric mixer, beat egg whites with lemon juice until stiff. While beating, add egg yolks one at a time until thick and creamy. Make well in center of dry ingredients. Pour in beaten eggs and fold into dry ingredients just until moistened. Scoop into well-greased 10-inch (4 L) nonstick tube pan and bake in 350°F (180°C) oven 30 minutes or until cake tester comes out clean. Invert on wire rack to cool. Carefully, turn cake right side up and frost top.

Cream Cheese Frosting: In food processor with sharp blade or blender, process cream cheese, SPLENDA® Granular, butter, whipping cream and vanilla extract until smooth.

Variation: Banana Walnut Cake: Instead of carrot, use one medium banana, mashed. Omit raisins. Use 1 tbsp (15 mL) baking powder. Use same frosting as above. (**6.0 g Carbs**)

Helpful Hints: Grind walnuts in blender in small batches. Small pieces of walnuts visible in ground product are acceptable. A coffee or nut grinder will produce a finer product. Carrots will be coarsely chopped into small pieces.

APPLE WALNUT TORTE

A special occasion dessert.

6 extra-large eggs, separated
$^1/_4$ tsp lemon juice (1 mL)
$1^2/_3$ cups walnuts, ground, OR (400 mL)
 hazelnuts, ground
1 cup SPLENDA® Granular (250 mL)
1 tbsp soy, OR spelt flour (15 mL)
1 tbsp spelt flour (15 mL)
1 tbsp baking powder (15 mL)
$^1/_8$ tsp salt (0.5 mL)
1 tsp vanilla extract (5 mL)
1 apple
2 tbsp SPLENDA® Granular (25 mL)
2 tbsp water (25 mL)
2 tsp lemon juice (10 mL)
Creamy Vanilla Frosting, page 173

Yield: 12 servings
1 serving
227.7 calories
8.9 g protein
18.3 g fat
7.6 g carbs

In large bowl, beat egg whites with lemon juice until stiff. While beating, add egg yolks one at a time until thick and creamy. In large bowl, combine walnuts or hazelnuts, 1 cup (250 mL) SPLENDA® Granular, soy or spelt flour, spelt flour, baking powder and salt. Make well in center of dry ingredients. Pour in egg mixture and vanilla extract; fold in. Pour into two very well greased 8-inch (20 cm) nonstick cake pans. Bake in 350°F (180°C) oven 25 to 30 minutes or until cake pulls away from sides of pan. Cool on wire racks.

Peel, core and slice apple into thin wedge slices. Place apple wedges in small cereal bowl with saucer for lid. Sprinkle 2 tbsp (25 mL) SPLENDA® Granular, water and lemon juice over apple wedges; stir to combine. Microwave on high power 4 minutes. Drain apples. Pat dry between paper towels. Prepare Creamy Vanilla Frosting, page 173. Frost one cooled cake layer liberally and arrange apple wedges on frosting, reserving 3 pieces. Place remaining cake layer on top and frost, garnishing center with reserved apple. Cover and refrigerate. Remove cake 1 hour before serving.

Helpful Hint: Drain apple wedges and keep liquid. Refrigerate liquid to add to a lemonade drink for added flavor, if desired.

APPLE PECAN UPSIDE-DOWN CAKE

This delightful, attractive cake will never last more than a few hours!

2 apples, peeled and cored
$^1/_3$ cup water (75 mL)
2 tbsp SPLENDA® Granular (25 mL)
1 tbsp unsalted butter (15 mL)
$^1/_4$ tsp cinnamon (1 mL)
$^3/_4$ cup pecans, ground (175 mL)
$^1/_8$ tsp salt (0.5 mL)
$^1/_4$ cup unsalted butter, melted (50 mL)
6 extra-large eggs, separated
$^1/_4$ tsp lemon juice (1 mL)
$^3/_4$ cup SPLENDA® Granular (175 mL)

Yield: 16 servings
1 serving
76.8 calories
2.8 g protein
5.3 g fat
4.4 g carbs

Slice apples in thin wedges and place in small bowl with water, 2 tbsp (25 mL) SPLENDA® Granular, butter and cinnamon. Microwave on high power 4 minutes, stir and drain. Layer apples in overlapping fashion in well-greased nonstick tube pan. Set aside.

In large bowl, combine pecans and salt. Stir in butter lightly. In food processor or electric mixer, beat egg whites with lemon juice until thickening. Add $^3/_4$ cup (175 mL) SPLENDA® Granular and continue beating until stiff. While beating, add egg yolks one at a time until thick and creamy. Fold egg mixture into ground pecans using a quick scooping-type motion with wooden spoon, until pecans are evenly distributed throughout.

Pour over apples evenly and bake in 325°F (160°C.) oven, on middle rack, 30 minutes. Allow cake to cool 2 minutes in pan and immediately invert tube pan over serving platter. Serve warm, with Crème Fraiche, page 172, if desired.

GROUND COCONUT CAKE
No flour in this unusual cake!

6 large eggs, separated
$^1/_4$ tsp lemon juice (1 mL)
$1^1/_4$ cups coconut, ground (300 mL)
1 cup SPLENDA® Granular (250 mL)
1 tsp vanilla extract (5 mL)
Creamy Lemon Frosting, page 173

Yield: 16 servings
1 serving
134.4 calories
3.8 g protein
11.1 g fat
3.4 g carbs

In large bowl, beat egg whites and lemon juice until stiff. While beating, add egg yolks one at a time until thick and creamy. In medium bowl, combine coconut and SPLENDA® Granular. Make well in center. Pour in egg mixture and vanilla extract; fold in.

Pour into well-greased 10-inch (4 L) nonstick tube pan and bake in 350°F (180°C) oven 25 minutes. Invert on cake plate. When cooled, cut cake in half with long, sharp bread knife. Frost bottom and top layers with Creamy Lemon Frosting, page 173.

Helpful Hints: Grind coconut in food processor food mill, coffee grinder or blender.

For a different, rich frosting, try Chocolate Cream Cheese Frosting, page 171

PIES

STRAWBERRY CREAM PIE
Easy as pie!

Coconut Almond Crust:
$^2/_3$ cup blanched almonds, ground (150 mL)
$^1/_3$ cup SPLENDA® Granular (75 mL)
$^1/_4$ cup medium-flaked coconut, (50 mL)
  (unsweetened)
2 tbsp soy, OR spelt flour (25 mL)
3 tbsp butter, melted (45 mL)
1 egg yolk
Filling:
1 envelope unflavored gelatin (15 mL)
$^1/_2$ cup water (125 mL)
10 oz frozen unsweetened strawberries, (284 g)
  thawed, undrained
1 cup SPLENDA® Granular (250 mL)
$^1/_2$ cup whipping cream (125 mL)
1 tsp lemon juice (5 mL)

Yield: 10 servings
1 serving
161.5 calories
3.1 g protein
13.3 g fat
6.4 g carbs

Coconut Almond Crust: In medium bowl, combine ground almonds, SPLENDA® Granular, coconut and soy or spelt flour. Stir in melted butter and egg yolk using fork. Press into 9-inch (23 cm) springform pan. Bake in 350°F (180°C) oven 10 minutes. Set aside to cool.

Filling: In small saucepan, sprinkle gelatin over water. Over medium heat, dissolve gelatin. Pour into bowl. Add undrained strawberries and SPLENDA® Granular. Chill until syrupy. Beat whipping cream and lemon juice until stiff. Fold into syrupy gelatin mixture. Pour into pie shell. Chill. Garnish with strawberry fan in center, whipped cream around perimeter and chocolate drizzle, page 168, if desired.

Helpful Hint: To make strawberry fan, use one large strawberry and cut several vertical slits, without cutting right through. Gently spread open to form fan.

LEMON MOUSSE PIE

This pie has a stupendous filling!

Cookie Crust:
$^3/_4$ cup Whey Ultimate Bake (175 mL)
  Mix, page___
1 tbsp SPLENDA® Granular (15 mL)
$^1/_4$ tsp baking soda (1 mL)
$2^1/_2$ tbsp butter, melted (32 mL)
1 oz regular cream cheese, softened (30 g)

Lemon Filling:
2 egg yolks
$^3/_4$ cup water (175 mL)
$^2/_3$ cup SPLENDA® Granular (150 mL)
1 tbsp lemon rind (15 mL)
1 envelope unflavored gelatin (15 mL)
$^1/_3$ cup lemon juice (75 mL)
$^1/_2$ cup whipping cream (125 mL)
3 tbsp SPLENDA® Granular (45 mL)
$^1/_3$ cup sour cream (75 mL)
4 drops yellow food coloring (optional)

Yield: 10 servings
1 serving
148.2 calories
5.0 g protein
11.7 g fat
6.1 g carbs

Cookie Crust: In small bowl, using electric mixer, beat Whey Ultimate Bake Mix, page 108, SPLENDA® Granular, baking soda, butter and cream cheese, until coarse crumbs form. Turn out on "floured" surface (use either whey protein powder or soy protein isolate). Roll and/or pat into 8-inch (20 cm) circle. Using lifter, lift carefully into shallow 9-inch (23 cm) glass pie dish. Using small rolling pin, roll and pat dough in evenly and up sides. "Flour" rolling pin as necessary. Set aside. With fork, prick crust all over. Bake in 350°F (180°C) oven 10 to 15 minutes or until browned slightly.

Lemon Filling: In saucepan, whisk egg yolks. Add water, $^2/_3$ cup (150 mL) SPLENDA® Granular and lemon rind. Cook over low heat, stirring constantly about 10 minutes or until mixture thickens slightly. Remove from heat. Sprinkle gelatin over lemon juice to soften and stir into egg yolk mixture until gelatin dissolves. Place in refrigerator 15 minutes to cool. Meanwhile beat whipping cream and 3 tbsp (45 mL) SPLENDA® Granular until stiff; stir in sour cream. Whisk into cooled lemon mixture with wire whisk. Pour over crust and chill until set.

Variation: **Lime Mousse Pie:** Use lime juice, lime rind and green food coloring, if desired. (**5.9 g Carbs**)

APPLE CUSTARD TART

Did you think Apple Pie would ever be on your diet again?

Almond Crust:
$^2/_3$ cup slivered almonds, ground (150 mL)
$^1/_3$ cup SPLENDA® Granular (75 mL)
2 tbsp soy, OR spelt flour (25 mL)
3 tbsp butter, melted (45 mL)
1 egg yolk

Apple Custard Filling:
2 cooking apples
3 tbsp SPLENDA® Granular (45 mL)
2 eggs
$^1/_2$ cup whipping cream (125 mL)
$^1/_3$ cup SPLENDA® Granular (75 mL)
1 tbsp vanilla extract (15 mL)

Yield: 10 servings
1 serving
175.8 calories
4.3 g protein
14.1 g fat
7.4 g carbs

Almond Crust: In medium bowl, combine almonds, SPLENDA® Granular and soy or spelt flour. Stir in butter and egg yolk. Cover with plastic wrap. Press crust out evenly into 9-inch (23 cm) glass pie dish. Bake in 350°F (180°C) oven 10 minutes.

Apple Custard Filling: Peel, core and slice apples thinly into thin wedges. Layer apples in circle around perimeter of pie dish and in center on cooled crust. Sprinkle apples with 3 tbsp (45 mL) SPLENDA® Granular. Bake in 375°F (190°C) oven 20 minutes.

In small bowl, whisk eggs, cream, $^1/_3$ cup (75 mL) SPLENDA® Granular and vanilla extract together. Pour over apples. Bake 25 to 30 minutes longer. Serve warm or at room temperature with Delicious Pouring Custard, page 138 or Crème Fraiche, page 172, if desired.

Variations: Other Fruit Custard Pies: Use 2 large peaches (**5.3 g Carbs**), 2 cups (500 mL) sliced, canned peaches in juice, drained and sliced even thinner (**6.4 g Carbs**), $1^1/_2$ cups (375 mL) blueberries (**6.2 g Carbs**), 2 cups (500 mL) strawberries, sliced thinly or 2 cups (500 mL) raspberries. (**5.4 g Carbs**)

PUMPKIN CHEESE PIE

Thanksgiving would not be Thanksgiving for some folks without Pumpkin Pie.

Crust:
$^{1}/_{2}$ cup ground pecans (125 mL)
2 tbsp SPLENDA® Granular (25 mL)
1 tbsp soy, OR spelt flour (15 mL)
2 tbsp butter, melted (25 mL)
1 egg yolk

Cream Cheese Layer:
8 oz light cream cheese, softened (250 g)
$^{1}/_{3}$ cup SPLENDA® Granular (75 mL)
1 egg
1 tsp vanilla extract (5 mL)

Pumpkin Layer:
1 cup canned pumpkin (250 mL)
2 eggs
$^{3}/_{4}$ cup SPLENDA® Granular (175 mL)
1 tsp cinnamon (5 mL)
$^{1}/_{2}$ tsp ginger (2 mL)
$^{1}/_{4}$ tsp nutmeg, (optional) (1 mL)
$^{1}/_{2}$ cup half-and-half cream (125 mL)
$^{1}/_{2}$ cup whipping cream (125 mL)

Yield: 10 servings
1 serving
183.5 calories
5.4 g protein
14.9 g fat
7.0 g carbs

Crust: In medium bowl, combine pecans, SPLENDA® Granular and soy or spelt flour. Stir in butter and egg yolk. Spread in 9-inch (23 cm) pie plate. Cover with plastic wrap and press crust out evenly; remove plastic wrap. Bake in 350°F (180°C) oven 10 minutes.

Cream Cheese Layer: In food processor with sharp blade, blender or in bowl with electric mixer, process cream cheese, SPLENDA® Granular, egg and vanilla extract until smooth. Pour over crust evenly.

Pumpkin Layer: In medium bowl, combine pumpkin, eggs, SPLENDA® Granular, cinnamon, ginger and nutmeg. Beat well with wire whisk. Whisk in half-and-half cream and whipping cream. Pour over Cream Cheese Layer. Bake in 350°F (180°C) oven 40 minutes or until cake tester inserted in center comes out clean. Garnish with whipped cream and additional pecan halves, if desired.

MERINGUE FRUIT TART

A beautiful, crispy golden meringue basket to showcase your prettiest fruit combinations.

5 egg whites
1 tsp vanilla extract (5 mL)
$^1/_4$ tsp cream of tartar (1 mL)
$^1/_2$ cup SPLENDA® Granular (125 mL)
Crème Fraiche, page 172 (625 mL)
$1^1/_2$ cups canned fruit cocktail in juice, drained (375 mL)

Yield: 10 servings
1 serving
130.5 calories
2.9 g protein
10.5 g fat
6.7 g carbs

Let egg whites stand at room temperature about half an hour. In medium bowl, beat egg whites, vanilla extract and cream of tartar, until soft peaks form. Add SPLENDA® Granular, 1 tbsp (15 mL) at a time, while continuing to beat until stiff peaks form. Spray 9-inch (23 cm) pie dish liberally with nonstick cooking spray and spread meringue inside and up sides to top edge. Bake in 300°F (150°C) oven on bottom rack 45 minutes or until golden brown. Switch off oven and leave meringue inside oven one hour to dry further.

Fill meringue basket with Crème Fraiche, page 172. Place fruit on top. Serve immediately.

Helpful Hints: Slice pie with wet knife and lift slice of pie with cake lifter.

If not using crust right away, store in cupboard uncovered until ready to fill. This is a wonderful tart which children and adults alike just rave about!

FRUIT PIZZA

Jonathan asked to have this on his birthday! Use your own fruit variations.

Crust:
1²/₃ cups ground almonds (400 mL)
¹/₃ cup SPLENDA® Granular (75 mL)
2 tbsp soy, OR spelt flour (25 mL)
1 tbsp unsalted butter, melted (15 mL)
1 egg white
¹/₄ tsp almond extract (1 mL)

Filling:
8 oz regular cream cheese, softened (250 g)
¹/₂ cup sour cream (125 mL)
¹/₄ cup SPLENDA® Granular (50 mL)
1 tsp vanilla extract (5 mL)

Topping:
1 cup fresh strawberries (250 mL)
¹/₄ cup fresh raspberries (50 mL)
¹/₄ cup fresh blueberries (50 mL)
1 kiwi

Pineapple Glaze:
¹/₂ cup SPLENDA® Granular (125 mL)
¹/₂ tsp Thickening Agent, page 109 (2 mL)
¹/₂ cup unsweetened pineapple juice (125 mL)
2 tbsp lemon juice (25 mL)

Yield: 16 slices
1 slice
156.4 calories
4.7 g protein
12.3 g fat
6.3 g carbs

Crust: In medium bowl, combine almonds, SPLENDA® Granular and soy or spelt flour. Stir in butter. Beat egg white with fork until frothy; stir in almond extract. Stir egg white mixture into crust mixture. Place dough ball on 12-inch (30 cm) pizza pan. Use small rolling pin or small cylindrical object (such as baking powder container) to roll dough to fit inside edges of pan. Bake in 325°F (160°C) oven 20 to 25 minutes or until golden.

Filling: In food processor with sharp blade or in blender, process cream cheese until smooth. Add sour cream, SPLENDA® Granular and vanilla extract; process. Spread smoothly over crust.

Topping: Arrange strawberries, raspberries, blueberries and kiwi on cream cheese filling. Spread glaze over fruit, using pastry brush where necessary. Pineapple Glaze must cover entire fruit pizza.

Pineapple Glaze: In small saucepan, place SPLENDA® Granular and Thickening Agent, page 109. Gradually stir in pineapple juice and lemon juice. Bring to boil. Sieve. Thin glaze with some water, if too thick.

CHOCOLATE MOUSSE PIE
A rich, smooth chocolate pie.

Chocolate Coconut Crust:
$^1/_2$ cup ground almonds (125 mL)
$^1/_2$ cup SPLENDA$^®$ Granular (125 mL)
$^1/_3$ cup medium-flaked coconut, (75 mL)
   (unsweetened)
3 tbsp Grape-Nuts cereal, ground (45 mL)
2 tbsp cocoa (25 mL)
3 tbsp unsalted butter, melted (45 mL)
1 tbsp whipping cream (15 mL)
1 egg yolk

Filling:
8 oz light cream cheese, softened (250 g)
$^3/_4$ cup SPLENDA$^®$ Granular (175 mL)
$^1/_3$ cup cocoa (75 mL)
3 tbsp Confectioner's Sugar Substitute, page 173 (45 mL)
$1^1/_2$ tsp vanilla extract (7 mL)
1 cup whipping cream (250 mL)
1 cup water (250 mL)
1 envelope unflavored gelatin (15 mL)

Yield: 10 servings
1 serving
269.1 calories
6.1 g protein
23.7 g fat
7.5 g carbs

Crust: In medium bowl, combine almonds, SPLENDA$^®$ Granular, coconut, Grape-Nuts cereal and cocoa. Stir in butter, whipping cream and egg yolk. Spread in 9-inch (23 cm) pie plate. Cover with plastic wrap and press crust out evenly; remove plastic wrap. Bake in 350°F (180°C) oven 10 minutes. Set aside to cool.

Filling: In food processor with sharp blade, blender or in bowl with electric mixer, process cream cheese until smooth. Add SPLENDA$^®$ Granular, cocoa, Confectioner's Sugar Substitute, page 173 and vanilla extract; process. Add whipping cream; process. In small bowl, add water and stir in gelatin. Microwave 2 minutes and stir to dissolve gelatin. Add to mixture and process on low speed. Pour over cooled crust. Refrigerate until set. Garnish as desired with whipped cream or Crème Fraiche, page 172.

CONFECTIONS AND FROSTINGS

CHOCOLATE-DRIZZLED MARSHMALLOWS

Nicer than real marshmallows! My sons love these!

1 recipe Crème Fraiche, page 172
Syrup:
1 cup SPLENDA® Granular (250 mL)
3 envelopes unflavored gelatin (45 mL)
$^1/_2$ tsp xanthan gum (2 mL)
$^1/_4$ tsp guar gum (1 mL)
$^1/_8$ tsp salt (0.5 mL)
1 cup water (250 mL)
1 tsp vanilla extract (5 mL)
Chocolate Drizzle:
1 tbsp unsalted butter (15 mL)
1 tbsp whipping cream (15 mL)
$^1/_4$ tsp vanilla extract (1 mL)
$^1/_2$ cup SPLENDA® Granular (125 mL)
$^1/_2$ oz unsweetened baking chocolate, melted (15 g)

Yield: 36 squares
1 square
42.1 calories
0.8 g protein
3.6 g fat
1.7 g carbs

Prepare Crème Fraiche, page 172 and set aside.

Syrup: In medium saucepan, combine SPLENDA® Granular, gelatin, xanthan gum, guar gum and salt. Gradually whisk in water and bring to boiling point. Stir in vanilla extract. Allow to cool about 5 minutes. In food processor or blender, gradually beat syrup into Crème Fraiche, page 172 until well combined. Quickly pour into 9-inch (23 cm) square, glass baking dish.

Chocolate Drizzle: In small bowl, melt butter in microwave oven. Stir in cream, vanilla extract and SPLENDA® Granular until smooth.   Stir in chocolate. If necessary, microwave 10 seconds until molten. Use teaspoon to drizzle chocolate over marshmallows. Freeze $^1/_2$ hour and refrigerate. When set completely, these can either be refrigerated or stored covered at room temperature for a day or two.

Variation: Plain Marshmallows: Omit chocolate drizzle. (**1.4 g Carbs**)

MILK CHOCOLATE

This is my husband's favorite. I prefer the dark chocolate variation.

$1^3/_4$ cups skim milk powder, OR (425 mL)
  *whole milk powder
2 cups SPLENDA® Granular (500 mL)
$^1/_2$ cup unsalted butter, melted (125 mL)
$^1/_2$ cup whipping cream (125 mL)
1 tbsp water (15 mL)
1 tbsp vanilla extract (15 mL)
2 oz unsweetened baking chocolate, (60 g)
  melted
1 cup roasted unsalted whole almonds, OR cashews, (250 mL)
  coarsely chopped

Yield: 160 pieces
1 piece
16.9 calories
0.5 g protein
1.3 g fat
0.8 g carbs

In blender, blend skim milk powder, until it forms a very fine powder. *If using whole milk powder, blending it will not be necessary. In food processor with sharp blade, or in blender, add skim milk powder or whole milk powder, SPLENDA® Granular, butter, cream, water and vanilla extract; process until smooth. Add chocolate; process until smooth.

Stir in almonds or cashews and turn out into greased 9 x 13-inch (23 x 33 cm) glass baking dish. Cover with plastic wrap. Press down with palms of hands on plastic wrap to smooth out chocolate evenly. Freeze several hours. Let stand 5 minutes on countertop before serving, if desired. Keep remainder in freezer.

Variation: **Dark Chocolate:** Use $2^3/_4$ cups (675 mL) SPLENDA® Granular and 3 oz (90 g) unsweetened chocolate. Freeze until hard and then refrigerate.

To keep at room temperature, add 1 oz cocoa butter, melted. (***1.0 g Carbs***)

CHOCOLATE PEANUT BUTTER FUDGE
Tastes sinfully delicious!

2 oz unsweetened baking chocolate (60 g)
$^1/_2$ cup whipping cream (125 mL)
1 envelope gelatin (15 mL)
2 tbsp whipping cream (25 mL)
4 oz regular cream cheese, softened (125 g)
2 cups SPLENDA® Granular (500 mL)
$^1/_4$ cup soy protein isolate, OR (50 mL)
  natural whey protein powder
$^1/_4$ cup peanut butter, no sugar or salt added (50 mL)
$^1/_2$ tsp vanilla extract (2 mL)
$^3/_4$ cup unsalted raw peanuts, (175 mL)
  (optional)

Yield: 64 pieces
1 piece
39.0 calories
2.1 g protein
3.3 g fat
0.6 g carbs

In double boiler, over medium heat, melt chocolate in $^1/_2$ cup (125 mL) whipping cream. Remove from heat, add gelatin softened in 2 tbsp (25 mL) whipping cream, stirring until chocolate is dark, smooth and thickened.

In food processor with sharp blade or blender, process cream cheese. Add SPLENDA® Granular, soy protein isolate or natural whey protein powder, peanut butter and vanilla extract; process. Add chocolate; process until smooth. Stir in peanuts, if using. Turn out into 8-inch (2 L) square, glass baking dish. Press into pan firmly and freeze 30 minutes, then refrigerate. Cut into small squares.

Helpful Hint: The fudge is more solid with soy protein isolate, however, it is creamier and sweeter with natural whey protein powder. My personal preference is the latter.

DRIZZLING CHOCOLATE

This is a useful recipe for adding interest and flavor to a dessert.

1 oz unsweetened baking chocolate (30 g)
2 tbsp unsalted butter (25 mL)
2 tbsp whipping cream (25 mL)
$^1/_2$ tsp vanilla extract (2 mL)
1 cup SPLENDA® Granular (250 mL)

> *Yield:* 6 servings
> 1 tbsp (15 mL) per serving
> 83.7 calories
> 0.6 g protein
> 8.2 g fat
> *2.8 g carbs*

In small bowl, melt chocolate in microwave oven 2 minutes; stir until smooth. In another small bowl, melt butter in microwave oven, about 50 seconds. Add cream, vanilla extract and SPLENDA® Granular to melted butter; stir until smooth with wire whisk. Stir in melted chocolate.

If necessary, microwave about 5 to 10 seconds until molten. (Do not overheat or chocolate will seize). Using teaspoon, drizzle molten chocolate over dessert. Allow to harden in refrigerator or several hours at room temperature.

Variations: **Bittersweet Chocolate Sauce:** Use $^1/_2$ cup (125 mL) whipping cream. To warm sauce, microwave prepared Chocolate Sauce 25 seconds, or until molten. Stir with wire whisk.
Yield: 1 cup (250 mL), 1 tbsp (15 mL) per serving. (*1.9 g Carbs*)

Bittersweet Dipping Chocolate: Use only 1 tbsp (15 mL) whipping cream.
Yield: 1 batch. (*28.4 g Total Carbs*)

Chocolate Cream Cheese Frosting: Beat together 4 oz (125 g) softened light cream cheese, 1 cup (250 mL) Bittersweet Chocolate Sauce and $^1/_4$ cup (50 mL) Confectioner's Sugar Substitute, page 173 until smooth. *Yield:* 16 servings for Bundt Cake. (*2.8 g Carbs*); 12 servings for double layered cake. (*3.8 g Carbs*)

Helpful Hint: Bittersweet Dipping Chocolate hardens well and also makes a great hardening chocolate when poured over ice cream. Freeze 5 minutes and serve.

CRÈME FRAICHE

Lovely sweetened whipped topping for serving with desserts or for garnishing desserts. It holds up better than plain whipped cream.

1 cup whipping cream (250 mL)
$^1/_2$ cup SPLENDA® Granular (125 mL)
$^1/_4$ tsp Thickening Agent, page 109, (1 mL)
  (optional)
$^1/_2$ tsp vanilla extract (2 mL)
$^2/_3$ cup sour cream (150 mL)

Yield: $2^1/_2$ cups (625 mL)
$^1/_4$ cup (50 mL) per serving
106.3 calories
1.0 g protein
10.5 g fat
2.5 g carbs

In medium bowl, beat whipping cream with SPLENDA® Granular, Thickening Agent, page 109, if using, and vanilla extract until stiff. Stir in sour cream. It will keep at least one week or longer in refrigerator.

Helpful Hints: Thickening Agent, page 109, makes Crème Fraiche firmer and easier to garnish desserts using a pastry bag {use up to $^1/_2$ tsp (2 mL)}. This recipe may easily be doubled or halved. Half this recipe will suffice as a topping for a cheesecake. (***1.2 g Carbs***)

MAPLE SYRUP

This is a lower carb syrup for serving with pancakes, crepes or French toast.

1 cup SPLENDA® Granular (250 mL)
$^1/_8$ tsp salt (0.5 mL)
$1^1/_2$ cups water (375 mL)
2 tbsp butter (25 mL)
1 tsp Thickening Agent, page 109 (5 mL)
$1^1/_2$ tsp maple extract (7 mL)
$^1/_2$ tsp light-tasting olive oil (2 mL)

Yield: $1^1/_2$ cups (375 mL)
1 tbsp (15 mL) per serving
13.3 calories
0.0 g protein
1.0 g fat
1.0 g carbs

In medium saucepan, combine SPLENDA® Granular and salt. Stir in water with whisk and add butter. Sprinkle Thickening Agent, page 109 over warm syrup and bring to boil. Remove from heat and stir in maple extract and olive oil. Sieve. Serve warm or at room temperature. Refrigerate leftover syrup. To reuse: whisk a little water into thickened cold syrup and heat in microwave oven 30 seconds.

CREAMY FROSTINGS

This Substitute (whey option) makes an incredible coffee creamer. Handy for coffee in hotels or motels, when all they have in the rooms is creamer with sugar.

Confectioner's Sugar Substitute:
$2^1/_4$ cups SPLENDA® Granular (550 mL)
$1^1/_3$ cups whole milk powder (325 mL)
$^1/_2$ cup whey protein powder, (125 mL)
  (natural), OR soy protein isolate
Creamy Vanilla Frosting:
$^3/_4$ cup whipping cream (175 mL)
2 tbsp Confectioner's Sugar (25 mL)
  Substitute
2 tbsp SPLENDA® Granular (25 mL)
1 tsp vanilla extract (5 mL)
$^1/_4$ tsp Thickening Agent, page 109 (1 mL)
$^1/_4$ cup sour cream (50 mL)

Yield: 3 cups (750 mL)
2 tbsp (25 mL) per serving
47.2 calories
3.1 g protein
1.8 g fat
4.7 g carbs

In large bowl, combine SPLENDA® Granular, whole milk powder and natural whey protein powder or soy protein isolate. Blend in small batches in blender. Stir together in bowl to combine well. This mixture will keep well in airtight container at room temperature.

Creamy Vanilla Frosting: In food processor with sharp blade or blender, combine cream, Confectioner's Sugar Substitute, SPLENDA® Granular, vanilla extract and Thickening Agent, page 109. Process until stiff. Stir in sour cream.

Yield: $1^1/_2$ cups (375 mL) - to frost a 2-layer cake, 12 servings (**1.3 g Carbs**) or tube cake (sliced horizontally in half), 16 servings. (**1.0 g Carbs**)

Variations: Creamy Lemon Frosting: Omit vanilla extract. Also add 2 tbsp (25 mL) lemon juice and $^1/_2$ tsp (2 mL) lemon extract.
Yield: 12 servings. (**1.5 g Carbs**) **Yield:** 16 servings. (**1.1 g Carbs**)

Creamy Chocolate Frosting: Add 2 tbsp (25 mL) cocoa and also 1 extra tbsp (15 mL) SPLENDA® Granular.
Yield: 12 servings. (**1.6 g Carbs**) **Yield:** 16 servings. (**1.2 g Carbs**)

Creamy Maple Frosting: Omit vanilla extract. Add 2 tsp (10 mL) maple extract. **Yield:** 12 servings. (**1.4 g Carbs**) **Yield:** 16 servings. (**1.0 g Carb**)

Helpful Hints: For frosting to frost sides of cake as well, use 1 cup (250 mL) whipping cream, 3 tbsp (45 mL) Confectioner's Sugar Substitute, $^1/_4$ cup (50 mL) SPLENDA® Granular and remaining ingredients as for principal recipe.

MARZIPAN

Use this recipe to fashion "fruits" or "vegetables" for garnishing desserts or a confection tray. See Helpful Hints below for working out carbs for individual servings.

1 cup ground almonds (250 mL)
*1 cup Confectioner's Sugar Substitute, page 173 (250 mL)
$^1/_2$ cup SPLENDA® Granular (125 mL)
1 tbsp butter, melted (15 mL)
$^1/_2$ tsp almond extract (2 mL)
1-2 tbsp lemon juice (15-25 mL)

Yield: 1 batch
1 entire batch
1210.6 calories
49.0 g protein
87.7 g fat
56.0 g total carbs

In medium bowl, combine ground almonds, Confectioner's Sugar Substitute, page 173, SPLENDA® Granular, butter and almond extract. Add just enough lemon juice to make a firm dough. Color Marzipan with food coloring. To make an orange color for Marzipan "carrots", combine red and yellow food coloring and a drop of whipping cream. Use chopped chives for "carrot" top. Use cloves for top of "apples," "oranges" or "pears."

Variation: **Chocolate-coated Marzipan:** Using Marzipan recipe above and 2 tbsp (25 mL) lemon juice, spread Marzipan in 8-inch (20 cm) square glass baking dish (cover with plastic wrap to press dough out evenly). Sprinkle with $^1/_3$ cup (75 mL) roasted whole almonds (optional), pressing slightly into Marzipan surface, and cover evenly with Dipping Chocolate, page 175. Freeze half an hour and refrigerate. *Yield:* 36 squares. (*2.6 g Carbs*)

Chocolate-drizzled Marzipan: Use Chocolate Drizzle, page 168 to drizzle over prepared marzipan in 8-inch (20 cm) square glass baking dish.
Yield: 36 squares. (*2.2 g Carbs*)

Helpful Hint: If, for example, you make 28 fruits or vegetables, then divide 56 grams carbohydrate (for one batch of Marzipan) by 28 to arrive at 2 g carbohydrate per serving. *Use $^1/_3$ cup (75 mL) SPLENDA® Granular with whey option in Confectioner's Sugar Substitute, page 173.

CHOCOLATE AFTER DINNER MINT LOG

Arrange this log on a pretty oblong serving plate, with several slices around it.

8 oz regular cream cheese, softened (250 g)
3 tbsp butter, softened (45 mL)
$^3/_4$ tsp peppermint extract (3 mL)
$1^1/_2$ cups Confectioner's Sugar (375 mL)
  Substitute, page 173
green food coloring
Dipping Chocolate:
1 cup SPLENDA® Granular (250 mL)
$^1/_4$ cup skim milk powder (50 mL)
3 tbsp whipping cream (45 mL)
2 tbsp unsalted butter, melted (25 mL)
1 tbsp water (15 mL)
$^1/_2$ tsp vanilla extract (2 mL)
1 oz unsweetened baking chocolate (30 g)

Yield: 56 slices
1 slice
43.7 calories
2.5 g protein
2.9 g fat
2.0 g carbs

In food processor with sharp blade, blender or in bowl with electric mixer, process cream cheese, butter and peppermint extract until smooth. Add Confectioner's Sugar Substitute, page 173 and green food coloring to achieve a light green, pleasing color; process. In 9 x 13-inch (23 x 33 cm) glass baking dish, fashion 13-inch (33 cm) log. Freeze while preparing Dipping Chocolate.

Dipping Chocolate: In blender or food mill (food processor attachment), blend SPLENDA® Granular and skim milk powder until fine. In cereal bowl, combine blended mixture, whipping cream, butter, water and vanilla extract. Stir with wire whisk until smooth.

In another cereal bowl, microwave chocolate 2 minutes or until almost completely melted (do not overheat or chocolate will seize). Stir until chocolate is completely melted. Use soft spatula to scrape all chocolate out of bowl and stir into creamy mixture with wire whisk. If chocolate cools, warm at 5 to 10 second intervals, being careful not to overheat as chocolate will seize and become bitter (skip this step for Chocolate After Dinner Mint Log). Frost entire log with chocolate. Freeze half an hour, then refrigerate. Cut into thin slices to serve.
Yield: 1 batch. (***30 g Total Carbs***)

Variation: **Snowflake Log:** Use $^1/_4$ cup (50 mL) unsalted butter, $^1/_4$ cup (45 mL) cocoa in filling, omit peppermint extract, food coloring; sprinkle 2 tbsp (25 mL) finely desiccated, unsweetened coconut over chocolate frosting. (***2.1 g Carbs***)

Chocolate-Dipped Strawberries: This chocolate is great for dipping strawberries. Freeze dipped strawberries very briefly and refrigerate or serve.

CHOCOLATE WALNUT FUDGE

Can we ever have enough chocolate recipes?

2 oz unsweetened baking chocolate (60 g)
$^1/_4$ cup unsalted butter (50 mL)
$^1/_2$ cup whipping cream (125 mL)
$1^3/_4$ cups SPLENDA® Granular (425 mL)
1 envelope unflavored gelatin (15 mL)
2 tbsp whipping cream (25 mL)
4 oz regular cream cheese, softened (125 g)
2 tbsp whey protein powder, OR (25 mL)
  soy protein isolate
$^2/_3$ cup walnut pieces (150 mL)

> **Yield:** 64 pieces
> 1 piece
> 38.5 calories
> 1.3 g protein
> 3.4 g fat
> **1.0 g carbs**

In double boiler, over medium heat, melt chocolate and butter. Stir in whipping cream. Stir in SPLENDA® Granular. Remove from heat. In cereal bowl, microwave gelatin softened in 2 tbsp (25 mL) whipping cream, about 40 seconds. Stir into chocolate sauce.

In food processor or blender with sharp blade, process cream cheese until smooth. Add chocolate sauce and whey protein powder or soy protein isolate. Process, scraping sides occasionally. Stir in walnut pieces. Turn out into 8-inch (2 L) square, glass baking dish. Press into pan firmly and freeze 45 minutes, then refrigerate. Cut into small squares.

Variation: **Plain Fudge:** Omit walnuts. Freeze, if desired, for chocolate pieces that slowly melt in your mouth for greater satisfaction! (*0.9 g Carbs*)

RASPBERRY CREAM TRUFFLES

Delectably delicious treats! These fillings also make good cream cheese frostings for cakes.

4 oz regular cream cheese, softened (125 g)
7 tbsp Confectioner's Sugar Substitute,
  page 173 (105 mL)
2 tbsp unsalted butter, softened (25 mL)
2 tbsp sieved raspberry fruit
  spread (Splenda-sweetened) (25 mL)
$1^1/_2$ tsp cherry extract (7 mL)
*Dipping Chocolate, page 175

Yield: 40 truffles
1 truffle
37.7 calories
1.4 g protein
2.9 g fat
1.7 g carbs

In food processor with sharp blade or in blender, process cream cheese. Add Confectioner's Sugar Substitute, page 173, butter, raspberry fruit spread and cherry extract; process.

Freeze $^3/_4$ hour or until firm enough to handle. Using melon baller, scoop scant amounts of mixture. Roll in hands to form smooth balls. Place balls on wax paper on dinner plate. Freeze until firm. Using a spoon, dip balls in Dipping Chocolate, page 175 and place on wax paper on dinner plate. Place in freezer until chocolate coating is firmer, then refrigerate.

Variations: **Orange Cream Truffles:** Omit raspberry fruit spread and cherry extract. Use 6 tbsp (90 mL) Confectioner's Sugar Substitute, page 173, in addition to, 2 tsp (10 mL) orange juice concentrate, 1 tsp (5 mL) grated orange peel and $^1/_2$ tsp (2 mL) orange extract or Cointreau (orange liqueur). (***1.6 g Carbs***)

Chocolate Cream Truffles: Omit raspberry fruit spread and cherry extract. Use $^1/_4$ cup (50 mL) Confectioner's Sugar Substitute, page 173, 2 tbsp (25 mL) cocoa, 1 tbsp (15 mL) whipping cream and 2 tbsp (25 mL) SPLENDA® Granular. (***1.5 g Carbs***)

Chocolate Mint Cream Truffles: As above, except add $^1/_2$ tsp (2 mL) peppermint extract.

Helpful Hints: These treats may be kept in the freezer instead, depending on taste preference.

*It is awkward dipping the last few balls, therefore I suggest making 2 batches of Dipping Chocolate, page 175. Use remaining chocolate to dip fresh strawberries or frozen banana slices, garnish a cheesecake or simply refrigerate for use at a later date.

WHITE CHOCOLATE

This dipping chocolate makes a nice change.

1 cup skim milk powder (250 mL)
1 cup SPLENDA® Granular (250 mL)
3 tbsp whipping cream (45 mL)
2 tbsp water (25 mL)
$^1/_2$ tsp vanilla extract (2 mL)
2 oz cocoa butter, melted (60 g)
$^1/_2$ cup chopped, roasted almonds, (125 mL)
   or chopped hazelnuts or Macadamias

> *Yield:* 64 pieces
> 1 piece
> 21.5 calories
> 0.7 g protein
> 1.6 g fat
> *1.1 g carbs*

In blender, blend skim milk powder and SPLENDA® Granular until fine. In medium bowl, combine sweetened skim milk powder mixture, whipping cream, water and vanilla extract with wire whisk. In small bowl, microwave cocoa butter on high power 4 minutes. Gradually stir melted cocoa butter into prepared mixture. Stir almonds into chocolate and spread in 8-inch (20 cm) glass baking dish. Cover with plastic wrap and freeze.

Variation: **White Dipping Chocolate:** In blender, blend 1 cup (250 mL) SPLENDA® Granular and $^1/_4$ cup (50 mL) skim milk powder until fine. In cereal bowl, whisk sweetened skim milk powder mixture, 3 tbsp (45 mL) whipping cream, 1 tbsp (15 mL) water and $^1/_2$ tsp (2 mL) vanilla extract together until smooth. Gradually stir in $1^1/_2$ oz (45 g) melted cocoa butter (microwave 3 minutes to melt).

If dipping chocolate cools, microwave 5 seconds (and whisk again), however, no longer than that, otherwise cocoa butter might separate and dipping will not be successful. If that does happen, just stir nuts in and freeze on wax paper on dinner plate. Then refrigerate. *Yield:* 1 batch. (*35.4 g Total Carbs*)

Helpful Hints: The dipping chocolate is especially good using blanched, whole hazelnuts. Either dip or just stir them in, freeze until set and then refrigerate. Macadamia nuts would probably be good as well.

YOGURT WHIPPED TOPPING

This is easy to whip up and tastes delicious!

$3/4$ cup plain yogurt (175 mL)
$1/2$ cup SPLENDA® Granular (125 mL)
$1/4$ cup whipping cream (50 mL)
$1/2$ tsp vanilla extract (2 mL)
2 tsp unflavored gelatin (10 mL)
2 tbsp water (25 mL)
2 blocks ice

Yield: $1^1/2$ cups (375 mL)
$1/4$ cup (50 mL) per serving
65.6 calories
2.2 g protein
4.5 g fat
2.8 g carbs

In blender, combine yogurt, SPLENDA® Granular, whipping cream, and vanilla extract. In cereal bowl, soften gelatin in water. Microwave on high power 40 seconds. Add to blender ingredients and blend until smooth. Add ice and blend again on ice crusher setting. Store in closed plastic container in refrigerator. Just before serving, use wire whisk to whisk topping vigorously until smooth.

Helpful Hint: Add cocoa to taste and blend for a great pudding-like chocolate fix. To make a whipped topping which forms a softer set after being refrigerated, use $1^3/4$ tsp (8 mL) unflavored gelatin.

FUDGE TOFFEE

Amazing chewy candy! Add little extra melted butter, if mixture is too stiff.

2 cups SPLENDA® Granular (500 mL)
1 cup whole milk powder (250 mL)
1 cup whey protein powder, (250 mL)
 (natural)
$1/2$ cup unsalted butter, melted (125 mL)
$1/4$ cup whipping cream (50 mL)
2 tbsp water (25 mL)
2 oz unsweetened baking chocolate, (60 g)
 melted

Yield: 36 squares
1 square
66.4 calories
3.0 g protein
5.0 g fat
2.9 g carbs

In large bowl, combine SPLENDA® Granular, whole milk powder and whey protein powder. In small bowl, combine butter, cream and water. Stir into dry ingredients. Stir in chocolate until well combined. Press into 9-inch (23 cm) square glass baking dish. Freeze approximately half an hour and refrigerate.

COOKIES AND SQUARES

SHORTBREAD

These cookies are a real treat. Try both versions and decide which you prefer.

1 cup ground almonds (250 mL)
³/₄ cup SPLENDA® Granular (175 mL)
3 tbsp spelt flour (45 mL)
2 tbsp soy, OR spelt flour (25 mL)
7 tbsp butter, melted (105 mL)

Yield: 28 cookies
1 cookie
41.6 calories
1.2 g protein
3.3 g fat
2.1 g carbs

In medium bowl, combine ground almonds, SPLENDA® Granular, spelt flour and soy or spelt flour. Stir in melted butter. Form into ball, cover in plastic and freeze 5 to 10 minutes. Divide ball in two and form two 6-inch (15 cm) ropes about 1-inch (2.5 cm) in diameter. Slice each into 14 segments. Place each segment on ungreased cookie sheet.

Bake in 375°F (190°C) oven 10 minutes.

Variation: Use ground cashews instead of ground almonds. (*2.8 g Carbs*)

Helpful Hint: The ground cashew version is particularly rich-tasting. At room temperature the cashew shortbread cookies melt in your mouth and become crisper if refrigerated. However, the almond shortbread cookies do not need to be refrigerated. Store uncovered in cupboard.

COCONUT MACAROONS

Timeless cookies! These taste great and are a good source of fiber.

$^3/_4$ cup Crème Fraiche, page 172 (175 mL)
2 egg whites, fork beaten
$^1/_2$ tsp vanilla extract (2 mL)
$2^1/_2$ cups unsweetened medium flaked
  coconut (625 mL)
$^3/_4$ cup SPLENDA® Granular (175 mL)

Yield: 54 cookies
1 cookie
39.1 calories
0.5 g protein
3.4 g fat
0.7 g carbs

In medium bowl, combine Crème Fraiche, page 172 egg whites and vanilla. In another medium bowl, combine coconut and SPLENDA® Granular. Stir sweetened coconut into Crème Fraiche mixture until well combined. Drop heaping teaspoons onto greased cookie sheet and bake in 325°F (160°C) oven 20 minutes or until edges are browning slightly.

WALNUT THUMBPRINTS

An imitation of this all-time favorite cookie.

$^1/_4$ cup butter, softened (50 mL)
$^1/_4$ cup whipping cream (50 mL)
1 egg yolk
$1^1/_2$ cups Walnut Bake Mix, (375 mL)
  page 107
$^1/_2$ cup SPLENDA® Granular (125 mL)
$^1/_2$ tsp baking powder (2 mL)
$^1/_8$ tsp salt (0.5 mL)
7 tbsp walnut crumbs (105 mL)
3 tbsp Strawberry Jam, page 91 (45 mL)
  or commercial sugarless Jam

Yield: 36 cookies
1 cookie
51.7 calories
1.6 g protein
4.4 g fat
1.8 g carbs

In large bowl, beat butter, cream and egg yolk. In medium bowl, combine Walnut Bake Mix, page 107, SPLENDA® Granular, baking powder and salt. Add dry ingredients to creamed mixture and beat until combined.

Form dough into 1-inch (2.5 cm) smooth balls. Roll in walnut crumbs. Place on greased cookie sheet and press thumb or forefinger in middle of each cookie. Fill each cookie with $^1/_4$ tsp (1 mL) Strawberry Jam, page 91. Bake 15 minutes in 350°F (180°C) oven. Allow to cool on wire racks.

RASPBERRY CREAM MERINGUES

These are delightful and pretty! My sons, Daniel and Jonathan, prefer a double batch!

3 extra-large egg whites
$^1/_4$ tsp cream of tartar (1 mL)
1 tsp vanilla extract (5 mL)
$^1/_2$ cup SPLENDA® Granular (125 mL)
Filling:
*$^1/_2$ Crème Fraiche recipe, page 172
30 raspberries

Yield: 25 meringues
1 meringue
16.6 calories
0.6 g protein
0.9 g fat
1.2 g carbs

Spray cookie sheet with nonstick cooking spray. Line with wax or parchment paper. Set aside.

In medium bowl, beat egg whites until stiff with cream of tartar and vanilla extract. While beating, add SPLENDA® Granular 1 tbsp (15 mL) at a time. Spoon mixture into pastry bag fitted with small, fluted nozzle. On wax paper, form 30 small, flat buttons. Pipe around circular edge of buttons, making about 2 layers, and keeping well inside bottom to form an encasing, with center forming small hollow or "basket."

Bake in 300°F (150°C) oven 10 minutes. Reduce heat to 250°F (120°C) and bake 25 minutes. Move meringues to top oven shelf and bake another 15 minutes or until light, crisp and just beginning to color. Cool on cookie sheet on wire rack. Carefully, remove meringues from wax paper with hard, thin, flat spatula. Fill meringues just before serving.

Filling: Prepare Crème Fraiche, page 172. Place one large, juicy raspberry or two small ones in center of each meringue on bed of Crème Fraiche. Serve immediately.

Helpful Hints: *Make half Crème Fraiche recipe, page 172 or the whole batch, and refrigerate the remainder. It will last at least a week in the refrigerator.

LADY FINGERS

Useful for Trifle recipe, page 134. These are quite bland, therefore, if you plan to eat it as a cookie, try the variation below.

$^1/_3$ cup spelt flour (75 mL)
$^1/_3$ cup soy flour (75 mL)
$^1/_8$ tsp salt (0.5 mL)
4 eggs, separated
$^3/_4$ cup SPLENDA® Granular (175 mL)
$^1/_2$ tsp vanilla extract (2 mL)
1 tbsp Confectioner's Sugar Substitute,
  page 173, (15 mL), (optional)

Yield: 27 servings	
1 serving	
16.7 calories	
1.3 g protein	
0.6 g fat	
1.5 g carbs	

Over medium bowl, sift spelt flour, soy flour and salt. Beat egg whites in medium bowl until beginning to get thick; add $^1/_2$ cup (125 mL) SPLENDA® Granular and continue beating until thick. In another medium bowl, beat egg yolks, remaining SPLENDA® Granular and vanilla extract until thickened and smooth. Sift flour mixture again, this time over egg yolks. Spoon half egg whites over flour and carefully fold in. Add remaining egg whites, folding in gently. Spoon mixture into pastry bag fitted with plain nozzle or one with pattern around edge of large opening.

Cut a straw to 4-inches (10 cm) long. Grease and flour two cookie sheets; shake off excess. Pipe 4-inch (10 cm) long lines next to straw and space cookies about 1-inch (2.5 cm) apart. Sift over Confectioner's Sugar Substitute, page 173, if using. Invert cookie sheets quickly to get rid of excess Confectioner's Sugar Substitute. Let rest 10 minutes, then bake in 300°F (140°C) oven 20 minutes or until crusty on outside, but soft inside.

Variation: ***Chocolate-Drizzled Lady Fingers:*** Use Drizzling Chocolate, page 168 for drizzling chocolate on each Lady Finger. (***2.3 g Carbs***)

Helpful Hint: Store in covered plastic container.

ALMOND COOKIES

These fast and easy almond cookies have a soft texture.

$^1/_4$ cup butter (50 mL)
1 cup ground almonds (250 mL)
$^2/_3$ cup SPLENDA® Granular (150 mL)
2 egg yolks
2 tbsp spelt flour (25 mL)
2 tbsp whipping cream (25 mL)
1 tbsp soy, OR spelt flour (15 mL)
$^1/_4$ tsp baking soda (1 mL)
$^1/_4$ tsp almond extract (1 mL)

Yield: 32 cookies
1 cookie
43.3 calories
1.0 g protein
3.9 g fat
1.1 g carbs

In medium saucepan, over low heat, melt butter. Remove from heat. Stir in ground almonds, SPLENDA® Granular, egg yolks, spelt flour, whipping cream, soy or spelt flour, baking soda and almond extract. Form level teaspoonfuls of dough into smooth balls. Place one inch (2.5 cm) apart on cookie sheet. Press horizontally with tines of fork. Bake in 350°F (180°C) oven on middle shelf 7 minutes or until brown underneath.

Variation: Use ground walnuts, hazelnuts, or pecans, if desired. Omit almond extract and use vanilla extract. Ground cashews may be used, however the carbs will go up slightly.

Helpful Hints: Use a measuring teaspoon, because as cutlery set teaspoons go, they can vary in size quite a bit.

If fork sticks to dough, dip in whey protein powder or soy protein isolate before using.

NANAIMO CUSTARD SQUARES

Who would have thought we low-carbers can still indulge in these?

Crust:
$^1/_2$ cup ground almonds (125 mL)
$^1/_2$ cup SPLENDA® Granular (125 mL)
$^1/_3$ cup medium-flaked coconut, (75 mL)
  (unsweetened)
3 tbsp Grape-Nuts cereal, (45 mL)
  finely ground
2 tbsp cocoa (25 mL)
3 tbsp unsalted butter, melted (45 mL)
1 tbsp whipping cream (15 mL)
1 egg yolk

Custard Layer:
$1^1/_2$ cups half-and-half cream (375 mL)
$^2/_3$ cup SPLENDA® Granular (150 mL)
$^1/_2$ cup whipping cream (125 mL)
4 tsp unflavored gelatin (20 mL)
6 egg yolks
1 tbsp vanilla extract (15 mL)

Chocolate Layer:
Dipping Chocolate, page 175

Yield: 36 squares
1 square
80.3 calories
1.9 g protein
6.6 g fat
3.0 g carbs

Crust: In medium bowl, combine, almonds, SPLENDA® Granular, coconut, Grape-Nuts cereal and cocoa. Stir in butter, whipping cream and egg yolk. Spread in 9-inch (23 cm) pie plate. Cover with plastic wrap and press crust out evenly; remove plastic wrap. Bake in 350°F (180°C) oven 10 minutes. Set aside to cool.

Custard Layer: In double boiler, combine half-and-half cream, SPLENDA® Granular, whipping cream and gelatin. Heat to scalding. Stir some of hot cream mixture into egg yolks. Return to double boiler and continue stirring until custard begins to thicken. Sieve. Stir in vanilla extract. Pour over cooled crust. Cover surface with plastic wrap. Refrigerate until custard is firm.

Chocolate Layer: Prepare Dipping Chocolate, page 175. Spread over cooled custard.

Helpful Hint: One packet of gelatin does not equal 3 tsp (15 mL).

GERMAN CHOCOLATE CHEESECAKE SQUARES

These squares are great to take along to a function.

Crust:
1 cup ground almonds (250 mL)
1 cup SPLENDA® Granular (250 mL)
$^2/_3$ cup unsweetened medium-flaked coconut (150 mL)
6 tbsp Grape-Nuts cereal, (90 mL) finely ground
$^1/_4$ cup cocoa (50 mL)
6 tbsp unsalted butter, melted (90 mL)
2 tbsp whipping cream (25 mL)
2 egg yolks

Chocolate Cream Cheese Topping:
$^3/_4$ cup whipping cream (175 mL)
$^3/_4$ cup SPLENDA® Granular (175 mL)
2 tbsp unsalted butter (25 mL)
2 envelopes unflavored gelatin (25 mL)
$^1/_4$ cup water (50 mL)
$^1/_4$ cup cocoa (50 mL)
1 tsp vanilla extract (5 mL)
8 oz light cream cheese, softened (250 g)
$1^1/_4$ cups sour cream (300 mL)
$^1/_4$ cup SPLENDA® Granular (50 mL)
$^1/_2$ oz unsweetened chocolate, finely grated (15 g)

Yield: 54 squares
1 square
78.3 calories
1.7 g protein
7.0 g fat
2.2 g carbs

Crust: In medium bowl, combine almonds, SPLENDA® Granular, coconut, Grape-Nuts cereal and cocoa. Stir in butter, cream and egg yolks. Spray an 11 x 17-inch (28 x 43 cm) jelly roll pan with nonstick cooking spray. Spread mixture evenly in pan. Bake in 350°F (180°C) oven 10 minutes.

Chocolate Cream Cheese Topping: In medium saucepan, stir cream, $^3/_4$ cup (175 mL) SPLENDA® Granular and butter until butter melts. Lower heat and stir in gelatin softened in water, until dissolved. Stir in cocoa over very low heat until smooth. Remove from heat and stir in vanilla extract.

In food processor with sharp blade, blender or in bowl with electric mixer, process cream cheese until smooth. Add sour cream; process. Add chocolate mixture and $^1/_4$ cup (50 mL) SPLENDA® Granular; process until smooth. Pour over crust. Sprinkle with grated chocolate. Chill several hours or overnight.

HAZELNUT BROWNIES

Moist, dense, delicious brownies!

$1^1/_4$ cups SPLENDA® Granular (300 mL)
$^2/_3$ cup hazelnuts, ground (150 mL)
2 eggs
6 tbsp unsalted butter, melted (90 mL)
$^1/_4$ cup cocoa (50 mL)
$^1/_4$ cup whipping cream (50 mL)
3 tbsp soft, plump raisins, ground (45 mL)
1 tbsp spelt flour (15 mL)
$^1/_4$ tsp vanilla extract (1 mL)

Yield: 25 brownies
1 brownie
67.7 calories
1.2 g protein
6.2 g fat
2.0 g carbs

In medium bowl, combine SPLENDA® Granular, hazelnuts, eggs, butter, cocoa, whipping cream, raisins, spelt flour and vanilla extract. Stir until smooth and well combined. Scoop into greased 8-inch (20 cm) square, glass baking dish. Smooth surface evenly with back of spoon.

Bake in 350°F (180°C) oven 20 minutes.

PEANUT BUTTER MERINGUES

Light-tasting cookies.

4 egg whites
$^1/_4$ tsp lemon juice (1 mL)
$^1/_2$ cup SPLENDA® Granular (125 mL)
$^1/_2$ tsp vanilla extract (2 mL)
$^1/_2$ cup smooth peanut butter, (125 mL)
  (no sugar or salt added)

Yield: 36 cookies
1 cookie
13.8 calories
1.1 g protein
1.7 g fat
0.9 g carbs

In medium bowl, beat egg whites and lemon juice until thickening. Add SPLENDA® Granular and vanilla extract and beat until very stiff. Melt peanut butter in microwave oven about 40 seconds. Fold into egg whites. Drop by heaped teaspoonfuls onto greased cookie sheet. Bake in 325°F (160°C) oven 15 to 20 minutes or until slightly brown underneath.

CRAGGY-TOP COCONUT BROWNIES

These are best refrigerated and eaten the next day.

1¼ cups coconut, ground (300 mL)
1 cup SPLENDA® Granular (250 mL)
¼ cup ground hazelnuts (50 mL)
¼ cup cocoa (50 mL)
2 tbsp vital wheat gluten (25 mL)
1 egg
¼ cup unsalted butter, melted (50 mL)
2 tbsp sieved raspberry jam (25 mL)
  (sugarless)
1 tbsp water (15 mL)

Yield: 25 brownies
1 brownie
68.7 calories
1.4 g protein
5.9 g fat
1.7 g carbs

In medium bowl, combine coconut, SPLENDA® Granular, hazelnuts, cocoa and vital wheat gluten. In another bowl, combine egg, butter, raspberry fruit spread and water. Stir into dry ingredients. Spread in 8-inch (20 cm) glass baking dish. Bake in 350°F (180°C) oven 20 minutes.

PEANUT BUTTER OAT COOKIES

These are great for kids!

1 cup butter, melted (250 mL)
1 cup creamy peanut butter (250 mL)
  (no sugar or salt added)
¼ cup whipping cream (50 mL)
1 extra-large egg
1 tsp vanilla extract (5 mL)
1½ cups SPLENDA® Granular (375 mL)
1¼ cups oat flour (300 mL)
1 cup wheat bran (250 mL)
¾ cup minute oats (175 mL)
1 tsp baking soda (5 mL)
1 tsp baking powder (5 mL)

Yield: 94 cookies
1 cookie
41.9 calories
1.0 g protein
3.5 g fat
2.5 g carbs

In food processor or electric mixer, combine butter, peanut butter, whipping cream, egg and vanilla extract. Process. Add SPLENDA® Granular; process. In large bowl, combine oat flour, wheat bran, oats, baking soda and baking powder. Stir in butter mixture. Drop by teaspoonfuls onto ungreased cookie sheets. Bake in 350°F (180°C) oven 15 to 18 minutes or until golden brown underneath. Cool on wire rack.

NUT SQUARES WITH FRUIT SYRUP

These are different. If you can handle more carbs, add a little extra fruit spread.

$^1/_2$ cup walnuts, ground (125 mL)
$^1/_4$ cup ground almonds (50 mL)
2 tbsp SPLENDA® Granular (25 mL)
1 tbsp soy, OR spelt flour (15 mL)
2 tsp lemon peel (10 mL)
3 extra-large eggs, separated
$^1/_2$ tsp lemon juice (2 mL)

Fruit Syrup:
$^1/_4$ cup SPLENDA® Granular (50 mL)
2 tbsp water (25 mL)
2 tbsp unsweetened pineapple juice (25 mL)
1 tbsp lemon juice (15 mL)

Topping:
$^1/_4$ cup apricot fruit spread (50 mL)
1 tbsp SPLENDA® Granular (15 mL)
1 tbsp water (15 mL)

Garnish:
3 tbsp almond flakes or walnut pieces, (optional) (45 mL)

Yield: 25 squares
1 square
36.2 calories
1.7 g protein
2.1 g fat
2.7 g carbs

In small bowl, combine walnuts, almonds, SPLENDA® Granular, soy or spelt flour and lemon peel. In medium bowl, beat egg whites with lemon juice until stiff. While beating, add egg yolks one at a time until thick and creamy. Fold into dry ingredients. Pour into greased 8-inch (20 cm) square, glass baking dish. Bake in 350°F (180°C) oven 15 minutes. Poke few holes with cake tester. Allow to cool couple of minutes and pour syrup over cake.

Fruit Syrup: In small saucepan, combine SPLENDA® Granular, water, pineapple juice and lemon juice. Heat until SPLENDA® Granular dissolves completely.

Topping: In small saucepan, heat apricot fruit spread, SPLENDA® Granular and water. Sieve and spread over cake. Store at room temperature. Wait 4 to 6 hours before serving. Garnish with almond flakes or walnut pieces, if desired.

WALNUT RAISIN CAKE SQUARES

So nice to have with a cup of tea or coffee! The raisins are distributed evenly for sweetness and appearance.

$1^1/_2$ cups walnuts, ground (375 mL)
$1^1/_4$ cups SPLENDA® Granular (300 mL)
$1/_3$ cup Walnut Bake Mix, (75 mL)
  page 107, OR
  *Walnut Whey Bake Mix, page 106
4 eggs, separated
$1/_4$ tsp lemon juice (1 mL)
2 tsp vanilla extract (10 mL)
2 tbsp raisins, snipped (25 mL)
  (use scissors)

Yield: 36 squares
1 square
50.9 calories
1.7 g protein
4.0 g fat
2.3 g carbs

In large mixing bowl, combine ground walnuts, SPLENDA® Granular and Walnut Bake Mix, page 107 or Walnut Whey Bake Mix, page 106. In food processor or electric mixer, beat egg whites with lemon juice until stiff. Add egg yolks one at a time, while beating until thick and creamy, adding vanilla extract as well. To well in dry ingredients, add beaten eggs and fold in.

Evenly spread in 9-inch (23 cm) square glass baking dish. Sprinkle raisins over top and press into batter ever so slightly. Bake in 350°F (180°C) oven 25 to 30 minutes or until cake tester comes out clean. Allow to cool on wire rack. Cut into squares.

Helpful Hint: *If using Walnut Whey Bake Mix, page 106, use 3 large eggs, separated.

CHOCOLATE COCONUT SQUARES

A lovely treat with good fiber. Take some along on vacation!

$1^1/_2$ cups SPLENDA® Granular (375 mL)
$^1/_2$ cup skim milk powder (125 mL)
3 tbsp whipping cream (45 mL)
2 tbsp unsalted butter, melted (25 mL)
1 tbsp water (15 mL)
$^1/_2$ tsp vanilla extract (2 mL)
1 oz cocoa butter, melted (30 g)
1 oz baking chocolate, melted, (30 g)
  (unsweetened)
$1^1/_2$ cups unsweetened medium-flaked coconut (375 mL)

> **Yield:** 36 squares
> 1 square
> 55.4 calories
> 0.8 g protein
> 4.7 g fat
> *1.9 g carbs*

In blender, blend SPLENDA® Granular and skim milk powder until fine. In medium bowl, combine blended mixture, whipping cream, butter, water and vanilla extract. Use wire whisk to whisk smoothly. Stir in cocoa butter and then stir in chocolate.

Stir in coconut and press into 9-inch (23 cm) square glass baking dish. Freeze half an hour and refrigerate. These squares may be kept in closed plastic container in either the refrigerator or at room temperature.

ALMOND MACAROONS

Simple, tasty cookies.

2 cups ground almonds (500 mL)
$^3/_4$ cup SPLENDA® Granular (175 mL)
2 egg whites, fork beaten
$^1/_4$ tsp almond extract (1 mL)

> **Yield:** 30 cookies
> 1 cookie
> 63.5 calories
> 2.3 g protein
> 5.4 g fat
> *1.4 g carbs*

In medium bowl, combine ground almonds, SPLENDA® Granular, egg whites and almond extract. Drop by rounded teaspoonfuls, one inch (2.5 cm) apart on foil-lined baking sheet. Bake in 350°F (180°C) oven 15 minutes or until browning underneath. Remove foil with cookies to cake rack and when cool peel cookies off foil

INDEX

E

EGGNOG 16
EGGPLANT PARMIGIANA 79
EGGS 37
    BACON AND TOMATO FRITTATA 38
    BREAKFAST SQUARES 41
    CHEESE AND BACON SOUFFLE 39
    CREAM CHEESE SCRAMBLED EGGS 39
    DELUXE OMELET PIZZA 42
    DELUXE QUICHE LORRAINE 37
    FRENCH OMELET 38
    HARD-BOILED EGGS 40
    MUSHROOM QUICHE 37
    QUICHE LORRAINE 37
    QUICK STRAWBERRY OMELET 43
    SCRAMBLED EGG BAKE 41
    SCRAMBLED EGGS ARCHDUCHESS 39
    SHRIMP SCRAMBLE 39
    STRAWBERRY DESSERT OMELET 43
    STUFFED EGGS 40
    SWISS CHEESE & ONION QUICHE 37
    TUNA-CHEESE ROLL 42

F

FAUX MASHED POTATOES 84
FAUX POTATO SALAD 35
FISH AND SHELLFISH 72
    BAKED SOLE WITH LEMON SAUCE 77
    CHEESY POLLOCK PATTIES 76
    CHEESY SALMON LOAF 73
    COD FILLETS IN MUSHROOM SAUCE 76
    CREAMY POLLOCK IN CREPES 73
    CRUNCHY TUNA PIE 72
    FRIED SOLE OR COD WITH VEGGIES 74
    GARLIC BUTTER SHRIMP & POLLOCK 75
    SALMON BURGERS 73
    SALMON PIZZA 78
    SCALLOPS IN ALFREDO SAUCE 75
    SHRIMP SCRAMBLE 39
    TUNA BURGERS 73
    TUNA-CHEESE ROLL 42
FLAX BREAD MACHINE BREAD 115
FLAX SEED CRACKERS 126
FOCACCIA 113
FRENCH OMELET 38
FRENCH ONION SOUP 29
FRENCH TOAST 112
FRESH GARDEN SALAD 33
FRIED EGGPLANT 79
FRIED SOLE OR COD WITH VEGETABLES 74
FROSTED BANANA LOAF 129

FROZEN DESSERTS, POPSICLES,
JELLIES AND PUDDINGS 132
    BAKED CUSTARD 138

BLUEBERRY FROZEN YOGURT 141
CAPPUCCINO FROZEN YOGURT 141
CAPPUCCINO ICE CREAM 137
CHOCOLATE ICE CREAM 137
CHOCOLATE MINT ICE CREAM 137
CHOCOLATE MOUSSE 136
COCONUT BANANA CRM POPSICLES 135
CRANBERRY-RASPBERRY SHERBET 140
CREAMY DELIGHT ORANGE MOUSSE 136
CREAMY ORANGE POPSICLES 135
CREAMY STRAWBERRY POPSICLES 135
DIET POPSICLES 133
DRY DIET JELLY MIX 133
FROZEN RASPBERRY CREAM SQRS 143
FROZEN STRAWBERRY CREAM SQRS 143
FRUIT COCKTAIL FROZEN YOGURT 141
ICED MOCHA JELLY 133
INSTANT CHOCOLATE PUDDING 139
INSTANT STRAWBERRY ICE CREAM 135
KOOL-AID JELLY 133
LEMON FROZEN YOGURT 141
LEMON ICE CREAM 132
LEMON OR LIME JELLY 133
LEMON SHERBET 140
LEMON-LIME SHERBET 140
LIGHT VANILLA ICE CREAM 132
LIME SHERBET 140
MAPLE WALNUT FROZEN YOGURT 141
MAPLE WALNUT ICE CREAM 137
ORANGE SHERBET 140
PEACH SORBET 142
PEACH VANILLA FROZEN YOGURT 141
PEACH VANILLA ICE CREAM 137
PUDDING IN A CLOUD 139
RASPBERRY FROZEN YOGURT 141
RASPBERRY ICE CREAM 137
RASPBERRY SORBET 142
RASPBERRY TRIFLE 134
STRAWBERRY FROZEN YOGURT 141
STRAWBERRY ICE CREAM 137
STRAWBERRY OR CHERRY PUDDING 139
STRAWBERRY SORBET 142
STRAWBERRY-LEMON ICE CREAM 132
THREE-LAYER JELLY 136
VANILLA ICE CREAM 137
VANILLA PUDDING 139
FROZEN RASPBERRY CREAM SQRS 143
FROZEN STRAWBERRY CREAM SQRS 143
FRUIT COCKTAIL CHEESECAKE 148
FRUIT COCKTAIL FROZEN YOGURT 141
FRUIT PIZZA 166
FUDGE TOFFEE 179

G

GARDEN VEGETABLE SHRIMP SPREAD 23
GARLIC BREAD 112
GARLIC BUTTER SHRIMP AND POLLOCK 75

GARLIC MUSHROOMS 80
GERMAN CHOCOLATE CHEESECAKE SQRS 186
GERMAN SAUSAGE MINESTRONE SOUP 26
GLAZED LEMON LOAF 129
GRANOLA 109
GREEK DRESSING 30
GREEK SALAD 30
GREEN BEANS IN LEMON SAUCE 85
GROUND COCONUT CAKE 160
GUACAMOLE DIP 25

H

HAM ROLL-UPS 21
HAMBURGER BUNS 114
HAMBURGER PIZZA 55
HAMBURGERS 24
HAMBURGERS 47
HARD-BOILED EGGS 40
HAWAIIAN PIZZA 55
HAZELNUT BAKE MIX 107
HAZELNUT BROWNIES 187
HAZELNUT WHEY BAKE MIX 106
HEALTHY BUTTER 96
HERBAL VINAIGRETTE DRESSING 34
HERBED CHICKEN BAKE 71
HIGH-PROTEIN TORTILLAS 124
HOLLANDAISE SAUCE 92
HOT CHOCOLATE DRINK MIX 15

I

ICED LEMON TEA 18
ICED MOCHA JELLY 133
IMITATION CORN BREAD 118
INDONESIAN COCKTAIL MEATBALLS 24
INDONESIAN SAUCE 24
INSTANT CHOCOLATE PUDDING 139
INSTANT STRAWBERRY ICE CREAM 135

J

JELLIED CRANBERRY SAUCE 101

K

KOOL-AID JELLY 133

L

LADY FINGERS 183
LAMB GRAVY 94

LAMB MARINADE 45
LASAGNA 48
LEMON FROZEN YOGURT 141
LEMON ICE CREAM 132
LEMON ICE CUBES 18
LEMON MOUSSE PIE 162
LEMONADE 18
LEMON OR LIME JELLY 133
LEMON SAUCE 77
LEMON SHERBET 140
LEMON TEA SPARKLER 18
LEMON-LIME SHERBET 140
LEMONY CAKE 155
LIGHT VANILLA ICE CREAM 132
LIME GINGER COCKTAIL MOLD 36
LIME MOUSSE PIE 162
LIME SHERBET 140
LOAF PAN BREAD (BRAN) 110
LOAF PAN BREAD (FLAX) 115
LOW-CARB BREADCRUMBS 110
LOW-CARB PASTA 127

M

MAPLE SYRUP 172
MAPLE WALNUT CHEESECAKE 146
MAPLE WALNUT FROZEN YOGURT 141
MAPLE WALNUT ICE CREAM 137
MARINADE 90
MARSHMALLOWS 168
MARZIPAN 174
MAYONNAISE DRESSING 32
MEAT 44
    BACON-WRAPPED MEAT LOAF 47
    BAKED BARBECUE POT ROAST 49
    BARBECUED RASPBERRY SPARERIBS 57
    BOBOTIE 44
    BURRITOS 52
    CURRIED PORK LOIN CHOPS 54
    HAMBURGER PIZZA 55
    HAMBURGERS 24
    HAMBURGERS 47
    HAWAIIAN PIZZA 55
    LASAGNA 48
    MEATBALLS IN SPAGHETTI SAUCE 53
    MEATZA PIZZA PIE 56
    MEXICAN LASAGNA 51
    MOUSSAKA 50
    PEPPERONI PIZZA 55
    RACK OF LAMB 45
    SAUSAGE IN ZUCCHINI BOATS 58
    SPICY PORK CHOPS 49
    STUFFED ROLLED ROAST 46
    ZESTY SHORT RIBS 49
    ZUCCHINI PASTA & MEAT SAUCE 53
MEATBALLS IN SPAGHETTI SAUCE 53
MEATZA PIZZA PIE 56

SPICY BARBECUE SAUCE 90
SPICY CALIFORNIA-STYLE DRESSING 89
SPICY CHEDDAR BITES 21
SPICY CHICKEN AND VEGETABLES 63
SPICY PORK CHOPS 49
SPLENDA KETCHUP 89
STIR-FRIED CHICKEN AND VEGETABLES 59
STRAWBERRY CREAM SWISS ROLL 156
STRAWBERRY CUSTARD TART 163
STRAWBERRY DESSERT OMELET 43
STRAWBERRY FROZEN YOGURT 141
STRAWBERRY ICE CREAM 137
STRAWBERRY JAM 91
STRAWBERRY OR CHERRY PUDDING 139
STRAWBERRY MILK SHAKE 16
STRAWBERRY SORBET 142
STRAWBERRY-LEMON ICE CREAM 132
STRAWBERRY-RHUBARB JAM 91
STRAWBERRY TRUFFLE CHEESECAKE 145
STUFFED EGGS 40
STUFFED ROLLED ROAST 46
SUNFLOWER CHEESE CRACKERS 125
SUNFLOWER SEED CRACKERS 126
SWEET MUSTARD SAUCE 82
SWEET ONION PEPPER STIR-FRY 82
SWISS CHEESE AND ONION QUICHE 37

T

TANDOORI CHICKEN OR TURKEY 62
TARTAR SAUCE 89
TERIYAKI SAUCE 81
TERIYAKI VEGETABLES 81
THICKENING AGENT 109
THINNER CHEESE SAUCE 88
THOUSAND ISLAND DRESSING 100
THREE-LAYER JELLY 136
TOFU MAYONNAISE 92
TUNA BURGERS 73
TUNA-CHEESE ROLL 42

U

ULTIMATE BAKE MIX 108

V

VANILLA ICE CREAM 137
VANILLA PUDDING 139
VEGETABLES 79
   ASPARAGUS 83
   BOUNTIFUL BROCCOLI CASSEROLE 80
   CAULIFLOWER PUFF 86
   CHINESE VEGETABLE STIR-FRY 87
   EGGPLANT PARMIGIANA 79
   FAUX MASHED POTATOES 84
   FRIED EGGPLANT 79
   GARLIC MUSHROOMS 80
   GREEN BEANS IN LEMON SAUCE 85
   MEXICAN RATATOUILLE 85
   SEASONED FRIED TOMATOES 86
   SEASONED POTATO SKINS 83
   SWEET ONION PEPPER STIR-FRY 82
   TERIYAKI VEGETABLES 81
   VEGETABLES & SESAME CRM CHEESE 84
   ZUCCHINI SAUTE 82
VEGGIE TURKEY LOAF 69
VEGGIES WITH SESAME CREAM CHEESE 84

W

WALNUT BAKE MIX 107
WALNUT RAISIN CAKE SQUARES 190
WALNUT THUMBPRINTS 181
WALNUT WHEY BAKE MIX 106
WHEY BAKE MIX 106
WHEY PIZZA CRUSTS 105
WHEY TORTILLAS 123
WHITE CHOCOLATE 178
WHITE DIPPING CHOCOLATE 178
WHITE SAUCE 93

Y

YEAST-FREE FLAX BREAD 121
YOGURT WHIPPED TOPPING 179

Z

ZESTY SHORT RIBS 49
ZUCCHINI MARMALADE 97
ZUCCHINI PASTA & SPAGHETTI SAUCE 53
ZUCCHINI SAUTE 82

ORDERING INFORMATION

SPLENDID LOW-CARBING $24.00 US
MORE SPLENDID LOW-CARBING $16.00 US (September 2002)

SPLENDID DESSERTS $13.00 US
MORE SPLENDID DESSERTS $16.00 US

Please note: Recipes in "Splendid Desserts" and "More Splendid Desserts" can now be adapted to suit a low-carb lifestyle by using the "*Ultimate Bake Mix*," on page 108 of "Splendid Low-Carbing" or by requesting a copy of this recipe. Orders/Inquiries can be sent to the address below, or to **Desserts@Sweety.com**

Or order **Both** "SPLENDID DESSERTS" cookbooks $25.00 US
Or order **Both** "SPLENDID LOW-CARBING" cookbooks $37.00 US

Or **All 4** of the (above) "SPLENDID series" cookbooks $59.00 US

(*All prices above include S&H via airmail to the USA and Canada*)

These books can be ordered by MAIL simply by indicationg your,
Choices and sending a *check, money order or Bank draft* to:

Jennifer Eloff
P.O. Box 2305
Station "M"
Calgary, Alberta
T2P 2M6

Please do allow 4-6 weeks for delivery when ordering by mail !

Or you can save time and money *and get the books much sooner* by

ordering SECURELY online from Jennifer at **www.sweety.com**
since all internet orders are processed both *securely and speedily.*